Positive Behavior Management in Physical Activity Settings

SECOND EDITION

Barry W. Lavay, PhD
California State University, Long Beach

Ron French, EdD
Texas Woman's University, Denton

Hester L. Henderson, PhD
University of Utah, Salt Lake City

Human Kinetics

Library of Congress Cataloging-in-Publication Data

Lavay, Barry Wayne.
    Positive behavior management in physical activity settings / Barry W. Lavay, Ron French, Hester L. Henderson.--2nd ed.
        p. cm.
    Rev. ed. of: Positive behavior management strategies for physical educators. c1997.
    Includes bibliographical references and index.
    ISBN 0-7360-4911-8 (hard cover)
    1. Physical education and training--Study and teaching. 2. Classroom management. 3. Reinforcement (Psychology) I. French, Ronald W. II. Henderson, Hester. III. Lavay, Barry Wayne. Positive behavior management strategies for physical educators. IV. Title.
    GV363.L36 2006

                                    2005012482

ISBN-10: 0-7360-4911-8
ISBN-13: 978-0-7360-4911-5

The Web addresses cited in this text were current as of April 12, 2005, unless otherwise noted.

Acquisitions Editor: Bonnie Pettifor; **Developmental Editor:** Melissa Feld; **Assistant Editor:** Derek Campbell; **Copyeditor:** Alisha Jeddeloh; **Proofreader:** Joanna Hatzopoulos Portman; **Indexer:** Sharon Duffy; **Permission Manager:** Dalene Reeder; **Graphic Designer:** Fred Starbird; **Graphic Artists:** Denise Lowry and Yvonne Griffith; **Photo Manager:** Sarah Ritz; **Cover Designer:** Keith Blomberg; **Photographer (cover):** © Human Kinetics; **Photographer (interior):** Kelly Huff, unless otherwise noted; © Human Kinetics (pp. 3, 15, 21, 59, 99, 117, and 161, and the three Case Studies photos that appear at the ends of chapters 1-8), © Hester L. Henderson (pp. 73 and 93); photos for In the Trenches appear courtesy of the authors of those elements, unless otherwise noted; **Art Manager:** Kelly Hendren; **Illustrators:** Andrew Tietz (figures on pp. 19, 24, 38, and 178) and Al Wilborn; **Printer:** Versa Press

We thank Cerro Gordo Middle School in Cerro Gordo, Illinois, for assistance in providing the location for the photo shoot for this book.

Printed in the United States of America   10   9   8   7   6   5   4   3

Human Kinetics
Web site: www.HumanKinetics.com

United States: Human Kinetics
P.O. Box 5076
Champaign, IL 61825-5076
800-747-4457
e-mail: humank@hkusa.com

Canada: Human Kinetics
475 Devonshire Road, Unit 100
Windsor, ON N8Y 2L5
800-465-7301 (in Canada only)
e-mail: info@hkcanada.com

Europe: Human Kinetics
107 Bradford Road
Stanningley
Leeds LS28 6AT, United Kingdom
+44 (0)113 255 5665
e-mail: hk@hkeurope.com

Australia: Human Kinetics
57A Price Avenue
Lower Mitcham, South Australia 5062
08 8372 0999
e-mail: info@hkaustralia.com

New Zealand: Human Kinetics
Division of Sports Distributors NZ Ltd.
P.O. Box 300 226 Albany
North Shore City, Auckland
0064 9 448 1207
e-mail: info@humankinetics.co.nz

I would like to recognize my parents, Gabriel and Sylvia Lavay,
who instilled in me when I was young the importance and power of receiving an education.
I also dedicate this book to my family, Penny, Nicole, and Danielle,
who continue to be supportive of what I do and who, most importantly, make life special.

—B.L.

I would like to thank Lisa Silliman-French for her practical guidance
in editing several chapters of the book based on her teaching experience
in the public school setting. I would like to dedicate this book to her.

—R.F.

I would like to thank my parents, Hester and Tom Henderson,
who always supported any educational endeavor I ever pursued.
They instilled in me the value of learning at an early age,
which is still a driving force in my life.
I am grateful for the love they gave me, the lessons they taught me,
and the role models they are for me.
I would like to dedicate this book to them.

—H.H.

Contents

CHAPTER **8** **Biophysical Approach** **143**

CHAPTER **9** **Developing Your Own Behavior Management Plan** **161**

Preface

The first edition of this book, *Positive Behavior Management Strategies for Physical Educators,* contained information to promote responsible behavior and learning in school-aged children in a physical education environment. The primary audience was K through 12 physical education teachers. In this second edition, *Positive Behavior Management in Physical Activity Settings,* we have made additions and revisions to reflect current research and practices in the physical activity settings and beyond. Included are information on behavior management and examples that appeal to a wider audience of physical activity professionals, including K through 12 physical education teachers, adapted physical education specialists, school and youth sport coaches, recreation specialists, and future physical activity professionals.

This text provides the reader with a variety of ways to promote positive behavior and learning in *all* young people including those at risk and those with disabilities. Many professionals equate behavior management with corrective methods that can be harsh. Today behavior management is more positively focused and in most cases involves methods to develop self-responsibility and lead to self-empowerment in young people. These are the methods we have focused on in this edition.

This text incorporates theories, methods, and instructional practices from the disciplines of psychology, pedagogy, recreation, athletics, and coaching. A unique aspect of the text is the blending of theory with the application of realistic instruction, coaching, and recreation practices that have proven to be effective in physical activity settings such as schools, youth sport programs, and recreation sites. Whether you are a current or future teacher, coach, or recreation specialist who is working with different age groups, the second edition of this book provides guidance in motivating young people, managing behavior, and creating a physical activity environment that is conducive to performance and learning and is designed to empower rather than control behavior.

To facilitate your learning, numerous aids have been included such as checklists, worksheets, and case studies. In appendix A, you'll find reproducible worksheets to help you further assess your own style and the needs of individuals in your program. Appendix B contains a list of Web sites you can visit to help you with your program.

Physical activity professionals consistently cite lack of discipline and control as one of the major obstacles to effective instruction. For example, an inability to manage and motivate behavior is the reason most often given by beginning teachers for leaving the profession. In recent years, promoting positive behavior has become even more challenging with the increased number of young people who are at risk or have disabilities. A group that is unmanageable is unteachable.

Physical activity professionals face a number of unique challenges, such as providing instruction to large groups in limited or distracting settings. It would be unthinkable to place 50 or 60 students in English class while having them share a handful of textbooks. However, many physical educators are expected to teach to 50 or 60 students outdoors or in a small gymnasium or cafeteria with only a few pieces of equipment to share among the students. This same challenge can also occur in community-based sport and recreation programs. In such situations it is difficult to maximize learning without systematic, effective behavior management practices.

Physical activity preparation programs have a responsibility to graduate future physical education teachers, coaches, and recreation specialists with the training to meet the instructional needs of all young people, especially those who lack discipline and are unmotivated. Too often students graduate with knowledge and training based in scientific principles but lack the necessary knowledge and practices to promote responsible behavior and consequently are unable to promote performance and learning. They also often lack the behavior management skills that can help young people take responsibility for their own behaviors, be positive, and cooperate with one another. The second edition addresses these issues and helps you effectively meet the needs of all young people in various physical activity settings.

Acknowledgments

Many people supported and helped with our efforts to write *Positive Behavior Management in Physical Activity Settings*. We would like to acknowledge the outstanding staff at Human Kinetics and their continued commitment to quality physical activity. A special thanks to Bonnie Pettifor, acquisitions editor, who always believed in and supported our project and helped make the second edition a reality. A heartfelt thanks to Melissa Feld, our developmental editor, who was a pleasure to work with. She provided the editorial assistance and organizational skills necessary to allow us to develop a new edition of the book. She had a very relaxed but efficient way of assisting us to get the book to completion. Special thanks go to Sandy Negley, MS, MTRS, CTRS, of the University of Utah, who critically reviewed the manuscript and gave us her thoughtful comments and suggestions, especially related to the field of recreation.

Writing a book can be a tedious process. We are grateful that we have been able, over all these years and two book editions, to keep our friendship and humor. We also wish to recognize all the present and future physical activity professionals who make a difference in the lives of the individuals they work with and who realize the importance of behavior management in helping the youth of today become self-sufficient, responsible citizens.

Barry would like to acknowledge the College of Health and Human Services and the department of kinesiology at California State University, Long Beach, for their support of his scholarly endeavors.

Ron would like to acknowledge Lisa Silliman-French, his wife, for the numerous ideas of actual practices and experiences in physical activity environments that are sprinkled throughout the book.

Hester would like to acknowledge Barry for his leadership from inception to completion of both editions of this book. He kept us on track and was always there to give advice when needed in a timely manner. She would also like to acknowledge Ron for his diligent work not just on his chapters but in sharing information with us for our chapters and for using his sense of humor to get us through the process.

Finally, we would like to acknowledge all the physical activity professionals who have shared with us numerous behavioral methods and those participants in structured physical activity environments who have challenged us to be creative in our development and implementation of techniques to help facilitate their performance and learning.

I

Developing a Positive and Proactive Management Plan

In part I, we introduce the reader to the need to develop structured, systematic approaches to promote responsible behavior in young people. The approaches are both positive and proactive. Our goal is to prevent, reduce, or stop inappropriate behaviors that interfere not only with performance of physical and motor skills but also with socially acceptable and responsible interactions. It has been suggested that at least 80% of inappropriate behavior will not occur if the physical activity professional is positive and proactive! Chapter 1 discusses the challenge of individual differences among young people. A behavior management model is presented with ideas of resources that can help you in your challenge. In chapter 2, we explore how to create a positive physical activity environment by examining your current behavior management approach, getting to know participants as individuals, and avoiding negative approaches. In chapter 3, we examine ways you can use proactive behavior management methods in planning and implementing your classes, practices, and programs to prevent problems before they start. Specifically, we look at ways to develop and implement rules and routines to make each class, practice, or program run more smoothly.

The Challenge Facing Physical Activity Professionals

Appropriate behavior does not automatically happen but must be learned and practiced.

Many people believe that today's children and young adults are not disciplined, are irresponsible, and do not demonstrate the moral values to develop into self-sufficient, contributing members of society. More and more it seems that young people are entering structured settings, including physical education classes, sport teams, and recreation environments, unable to cope with the demands of a learning environment. This problem has many sources and numerous solutions have been proposed. This text focuses on possible solutions to the problem in the physical activity setting.

WHY A CHALLENGE EXISTS

The majority of young people focus on performing and learning and rarely break the rules. However, some individuals break the rules on a regular basis and need clear expectations and consequences.

Behavior of children is not a new issue. For instance, Socrates (469 b.c.) stated that the youth of his time loved luxury and had bad manners and contempt for authority. They showed disrespect for elders and loved to chatter instead of exercise. Children were tyrants, not the servants of their households. They would not rise when elders entered the room, contradicted their parents, chattered before company, gobbled their food, and terrorized their teachers.

Over the past 30 years, an increasing number of young people around the world have been exhibiting disruptive behaviors (Fox News Channel, 2004; Zeira, Astor, and Benbenishty, 2004). Factors involved in this escalation include parents, social advances, technology, schools, and sport. Increasingly, media coverage of sport figures has focused on socially inappropriate behaviors such as assault, rape, drunken driving, and manslaughter. Because it is often difficult to find appropriate role models, in many cases physical activity professionals may be the only emotional- and social-change agent in an individual's life. This makes it even more difficult to develop moral and ethical values in their students or participants.

Lack of education in promoting responsible behavior is another cause of increased disruptive behaviors. Many physical activity professionals use methods that others used in the past, never considering why they were used. Others use a spur-of-the-moment method that seems to fit the "crime" at the time, using a hope model to promote responsible behavior (that is, design and implement a behavioral program and "hope" it works). Authorities suggest that a systematic approach based on sound principles of behavior management is necessary for creating behavioral change in young people (Charles, 2002).

School Environment

Today, 1 out of every 20 preschoolers in the United States will commit a serious crime before adulthood (Cain, 2004). Violent behavior has become a reality with guns and knives added to the use of fists and name-calling, particularly in the upper grades. Who would have thought that a teacher would be afraid of a student? Unfortunately, in too many schools, this is the case.

Consider the following incidents:

- Ten-year-old girl bites teacher's arm
- Woman arrested after middle school scuffle with vice principal
- School administration calls police to control unruly boy
- Fifteen-year-old girl stabbed to death at high school
- Teacher hit in face by student

Surprisingly, these incidents all occurred in a single middle-class, suburban school district.

Teachers increasingly must deal with fights, bullying, rapes on campus, and even the deaths of students or teachers. Fear of bullies hinders a student's ability to concentrate, resulting in poor performance and learning. Teachers need special skills to deal with explosive situations. At the same time, many lack the legal, social, and practical support they need to promote responsible behavior.

In 1999, students 12 to 18 years old were victims of approximately 2.5 million school crimes, including 186,000 serious crimes such as rape, sexual assault, robbery, and aggravated assault. In addition, 30 to 40% of high school students have witnessed at least one fight in the last month (U.S. Department of Education, 2002).

In 2000, students aged 12 to 18 were victims of 1.9 million total crimes of violence or theft, 128,000 of which were serious violent crimes. Between July of 1988 and June of 1999 there were 47 school-associated violent deaths (National Center for Education Statistics, 2003). In addition, girls are turning to violence to solve problems more often than boys (Hall, 2004). Violence is perhaps the most pressing societal issue for children today.

Bullying-intervention programs have been established in schools throughout the United States. These programs are designed to reduce bullying and its effects. For the last 3 decades the annual Gallup poll of people's attitudes toward public schools, published each September in *Phi Delta Kappa,* has identified lack of discipline and uncooperative students as the biggest problems educators face. Most experts agree that lack of behavior management skills in teachers is the most significant barrier to effective teaching (Harrison, Blakemore, Buck, and Pellecttu, 1996; Rink, 2002; Siedentop and Tannehill, 2000). This problem is intensified in settings with a large number of children who have diverse emotional, social, cognitive, and motor abilities. The difficulties faced by the physical educator and coach are clearly illustrated in *Too Dangerous to Teach,* a book written by a physical educator teaching in New York City (Kleinman, 2003).

Collier and Hebert (2004) and Hill and Brodin (2004) believe that we need to focus more on classroom organization and behavior management skills in the preservice training of physical activity professionals. The need for in-depth preparation in promoting responsible behavior is illustrated in the *Guidelines for Advanced Physical Education Program Reports* (NASPE and AAHPERD, 2001). For example, teachers need the appropriate knowledge and skills to "access students' understanding of the consequences of inappropriate language and behavior related to issues of equity, fairness, and diversity" (p. 15). In adapted physical education, the standards related to student management in the Adapted Physical Education National Standards (APENS) are even more in depth (Kelly, 1995). Teachers must know how to prevent and redirect most disruptive behaviors. State standards for physical educators also often include this kind of standard. For instance, in California, one standard is devoted to creating and monitoring effective environments for student learning (San Diego County Office of Education, 2003).

Teacher evaluation systems also reveal what is considered important in teaching. For instance, one teacher evaluation system in Texas contains eight domains. One domain exclusively focuses on behavior management and at least three other domains have a behavior management component. In addition, recent textbooks on teaching methods are including more information on managing student behavior (Graham, Holt/Hale, and Parker,

2004; Himberg, Hutchinson, and Roussell, 2003; Pangrazi, 2004; Pangrazi and Darst, 1997; Wuest and Lombardo, 1994).

In-service training workshops for teachers often address behavior, as do Web sites that provide information for teachers. Many of these Web sites are listed in appendix B.

School and Community Sport and Recreation

Many parents and coaches believe sport and physical activity are beneficial to psychological health. They believe that sport participation encourages children to be active and fit, provides a support system with adult role models who exemplify good behavior and moral integrity, and influences students to stay in school and be more dedicated to their academic studies.

Young people who participated in traditional extracurricular activities or community-based sport programs and had positive attitudes toward sport were less likely to engage in delinquent acts and substance abuse, while young people who participated in unstructured, individual physical activities were more likely than their peers to engage in delinquency and substance abuse. Social policies and programs that emphasize these opportunities and instill a healthy lifestyle produce the best results. Ommundsen (2002) concluded that sport is indeed important for modifying disruptive behavior. For many young people, school or recreation sport programs are the only sanity in a chaotic environment. These programs are often an alternative to violence at home and in the street.

Coaches must design programs with a twofold focus of developing player self-responsibility and sustaining a high level of motivation. This will increase the confidence and performance of players. More specifically, the National Association of Sport and Physical Education (NASPE) (2001) has provided guidelines for developing self-responsibility and self-motivation, which are (a) react positively to mistakes and provide a consequence; (b) use goal-setting strategies and arousal techniques; and (c) use a variety of positive instructional approaches.

Unfortunately, players are not the only problem; coaches are becoming more violent too. Recently a coach reportedly spanked a player for poor grades, another bit the head off of a live sparrow to demonstrate toughness to his team, and another made a player run laps for punishment, causing the player to die of kidney failure.

In the United States, young people are dropping out of sport at an alarming rate. A major contributing factor is the "win at all cost" mentality of many parents and coaches. This mentality creates a pressure-filled environment that ultimately turns young people away from sports. A number of organizations have set a goal of changing the climate of coaching and making sport fun again. One such organization is the Positive Coaching Alliance. This nonprofit organization, based at Stanford University, was created to transform the culture of youth sport so that it gives all young athletes the opportunity for positive character-building experiences. The Positive Coaching Alliance has three goals:

1. Replace the "win at all cost" model of coaching with the "double-goal coach" who wants to win but has a second, more important goal of using sports to teach life lessons.
2. Teach youth sport organization leaders how to create a culture in which honoring the game is the norm.
3. Spark and fuel a "social epidemic" of positive coaching that will sweep the country.

The alliance conducts training workshops for coaches, parents, and leaders, giving them practical tools for creating a positive sport environment for young people. They also develop partnerships with youth sport organizations with the same goal in mind. For more information on this organization, see their Web site at www.positivecoach.org.

At youth sport events another group contributes to the problem of poor sportsmanship: the spectators. Spectators are composed mostly of the players' parents. Fights between spectators and other spectators, coaches, referees, umpires, and so on are plentiful. For instance, at a sporting event for 10-year-olds, a father became so angry at the umpire's call, he pointed a gun at the umpire. Recently, one parent killed another parent at their children's ice hockey game. Several organizations now require spectators at games to be silent. Other organizations have been developed to teach appropriate behaviors to coaches and parents. One such group originated from the Department of Parks, Recreation, and Tourism at the University of Utah. See In the Trenches for a description of their program to develop good sportsmanship.

In addition, the National Recreation and Park Association has developed standards for individuals earning a 4-year degree in recreation (2004). Selected competencies related to the ability to promote responsible behavior include the following:

- Create, promote, and maintain a positive group atmosphere.
- Use motivation methods, team leadership, and self-managed team concepts when providing individual group programs.
- Motivate and manage the performance of volunteers as well as part-time and seasonal staff.

IN THE TRENCHES

Play Hard, Play Fair, Play Fun Sportsmanship Program
Gary D. Ellis, Professor and Chair, University of Utah, Salt Lake, Department of Parks, Recreation, and Tourism

The Play Hard, Play Fair, Play Fun Sportsmanship Program was developed by the Department of Parks, Recreation, and Tourism at the University of Utah and implemented through a partnership with Salt Lake County Parks and Recreation's Cooperview Community Center. This program was designed to increase good sportsmanship in a youth basketball program while also increasing players' intentions to participate in the program the following year. More generally, the program sought to reduce violence, aggression, and poor sportsmanship among participants and spectators in youth sport while also addressing the alarming problem of sedentary lifestyles and obesity among young people.

The program introduced mechanisms deducted from prosocial behavior theory and theory about human experiences. One prominent example of these mechanisms was increased personalization. People tend to behave in more prosocial ways toward people they know and people they believe are like them. The program used a variety of methods to achieve greater personalization. Pregame introductions of coaches, referees, and players were given. Postgame social events were held after every game. At postgame events, the home team was responsible for food snacks while the visiting team brought juice. Each team voted for a player on the other team for the sportsmanship award for the day. Those players received a prize (T-shirt, small rubber basketball, poster) and got their photograph posted on the Web site that was created for the league. The Web site also contained information about the teams, a schedule of games, and action photographs.

In support of good sportsmanship they also created a common symbol (the Utah Jazz bear) with the league slogan, "Play hard, play fair, play fun," on stickers and signs. They also created an enormous Good Sportsmanship petition that players, parents, and coaches signed. The petition was prominently displayed at the games to remind everyone of the commitment they made to good sportsmanship and youth development.

The program also used social reinforcement methods associated with prosocial behavior theory. One of these was a blue flag system. When any player, coach, parent, or spectator exhibited poor sportsmanship, a staff member would raise the blue flag to remind everyone that they signed a pledge for good sportsmanship.

To decrease the occurrence of lopsided wins, which are humiliating for the losing team and discourage further participation, the program attempted to balance skill and experience levels across teams in the league before it started. A game was declared over and teams were reconstituted when one team was 16 points ahead. Last year was the first year of the program and they received very positive feedback about the program from all involved. They plan to run the program again next year.

BEHAVIOR MANAGEMENT MUST BE TAUGHT

Learning cannot take place in an atmosphere of chaos. The ideal learning environment must be safe, structured, consistent, and motivating. No method for promoting responsible behavior will work if effective teaching or coaching instruction is absent. We cannot stress this point strongly enough. The greatest physical activity professionals in the world cannot provide instruction unless positive behavior is maintained in participants.

Many physical activity professionals do not know how to design, implement, or evaluate a program for reducing behavior problems. The best lesson and coaching plans can become a waste of time when participants behave inappropriately. Young people must learn proper social skills through a school and community curriculum that involves nonviolent and responsible means of resolving conflicts.

BEHAVIOR MANAGEMENT MISUNDERSTOOD

Methods for promoting responsible behavior are grossly misunderstood, and because of this, practitioners must receive more training in it (Cook, Tankersley, Cook, and Landrum, 2000). Many physical activity professionals have told us that in their preparation programs, little time if any was devoted to promoting responsible behavior. Others were told that the ability to manage behavior comes with experience and that they had to develop their own formula to control their classes.

Experience is important, but we can and must learn how to use methods that redirect disruptive behavior and motivate individuals to perform and learn. It is our responsibility to develop the skills to handle disruptive behavior.

As physical activity professionals we face unique conditions that affect our ability to promote responsible behavior. For example, many classroom teachers and school administrators regard physical education as unimportant. This attitude is often communicated to the students who, as a result, fail to take physical education seriously. In addition, some young people in school- and community-based sport activities are so unmotivated that their performance suffers significantly.

If we are to overcome these challenges, we must first look at ourselves. We must have expectations that go beyond participants complying with the rules. We must recognize that in an effective physical activity program, participants are engaged in the content, interact productively in cooperative pairs or groups, and work independently to achieve individual goals. To create an environment conducive to learning, we must first have the knowledge and skills necessary to promote responsible behavior and motivate success, which leads to less hostility and frustration, less violent behavior, greater achievement, and the development of life skills, including social skills and personal responsibility.

RESPECTING CULTURAL AND RELIGIOUS DIFFERENCES

Physical activity professionals need to be aware of and respect cultural and religious differences. The behavior of individuals from other cultural backgrounds could be perceived as disrespectful, noncompliant, or disinterested when in actuality the behavior is appropriate in the student's culture. Sometimes certain rules violate the beliefs and practices of some cultures (Bartlett, Weisenstein, and Etscheidt, 2002). For example, in some cultures girls are not allowed to wear shorts, so they could be breaking a rule when they are required to dress in shorts. In addition, Muslim girls may need to wear a hijab over their hair and long pants over their shorts, Sikh boys may need to wear turbans, and Jewish boys may need to wear yarmulkes. Other students may have cultural or religious rules related to physical contact and modesty in coeducational settings, particularly in activities such as swimming and dance (Kahan, 2003).

In some cultures individuals are taught to fight so that they will not be victimized in their neighborhood; others are often under great cultural pressure to not achieve at school and to misbehave to hide their ability. Further, individuals from different cultural and religious backgrounds act differently toward authoritative approaches. Many Asian, African, and Hispanic individuals lower their eyes as a sign of submission, which Caucasian physical activity professionals may interpret as defiance.

The key to understanding cultural and religious differences is to make compromises as long as safety and hygiene are not sacrificed. Physical activity professionals must guard against stereotyping specific cultures and religious groups. We need to

respect the unique customs, values, and languages of smaller groups existing within the larger culture. Many school districts and sport programs offer sensitivity training workshops to assist in developing these skills. Johnson (1986) stated that although the approaches for promoting responsible behavior follow our knowledge of general human growth and development, no one particular approach is the best approach. Further, different cultural and ethnic backgrounds provide different ways of coping with and satisfying basic needs. Because of this, not all individuals look at each reward or consequence with equal satisfaction. Isolating one individual to a chair outside the gym by the door is food for one and poison for another.

The need to be aware of other cultures and religions and respond appropriately has been identified by national organizations that have developed professional standards. For instance, one standard of NASPE and the American Alliance for Health, Physical Education, Recreation and Dance (AAHPERD) (2001) is related to promoting appropriate behavior in a diverse society by respecting and valuing all individuals.

ASKING FOR HELP

Partnerships are a key to promoting positive behavior. Many people perceive asking others for help as a sign of weakness. However, this is not the case. The focus must be on the individual's behavior, not your ego. The most effective physical activity professional is one who partners with other professionals to discuss and develop effective approaches to engaging participants in the process.

For example, in schools there is a trend toward designing schoolwide programs rather than teacher-specific programs, including sport programs. These schoolwide programs emphasize positive behaviors and reinforcement as a way to prevent problems. At the same time they concentrate on removing students who contribute to discipline infractions (Hartzell and Petrie, 1992). Schoolwide programs generally contain policies such as those presented in figure 1.1.

Schoolwide programs enforce behavioral principles uniformly. Students are grounded in values and are expected to know what types of good behavior can lead to a lifetime of good citizenship. Students exhibit fewer problem behaviors and are sent to the principal less often, and the overall learning environment improves. This approach could also easily be adapted to a communitywide sport and recreation program.

1. Require visible commitment by all faculty and staff.
2. Develop an overall statement of positive expectations for behavior that applies in different school environments (i.e., raising hands, taking turns, practicing positive behaviors).
3. Require each professional to establish a set of relevant, clear, and broad-based rules.
4. Make a list of unnacceptable behaviors and determine which behaviors should be referred to the administrator.
5. Develop an administrative referral form.
6. Determine what actions will be taken if a rule is broken.
7. Establish procedures for implementing consequences when referrals are made.
8. Write the schoolwide behavior management plan.
9. Develop a procedure for repeated referrrals.

Figure 1.1 Guidelines for schoolwide behavior management programs.

IS ONE BEHAVIORAL APPROACH ENOUGH?

Your approach to promoting positive behavior must be systematic, flexible, and ever changing based on the needs of each individual as well as the specific goals and objectives of the program. Any effective approach must also incorporate the sequential steps of planning, observing and analyzing, implementing, and evaluating the approach. These four steps include not only the physical but also the social environment. Factors that may affect the physical and social environment include equipment, the activity itself, interaction among participants, and extrinsic and intrinsic motivation to learn and perform.

In addition, the program must be ecological in nature. That is, an individual is continuously interacting with his or her environment. This may be a positive or negative experience. In addition, the program must reflect and be guided by the community and its beliefs, attitudes, and philosophy. Any physical activity program should be considered a small but integral component of the community and greater society.

There are numerous methods to maintain, increase, stabilize, and reduce behaviors. Most of these methods fall under one of three major approaches: behavioral, humanistic, and biophysical. The behavioral approach includes methods that involve manipulation of the environment, such as reorganizing the physical or social environment or using positive reinforcement. In contrast, the humanistic approach involves asking "Why?" or determining the underlying psychosocial causes of an individual's behavior. Humanistic interven-

tion includes psychological methods such as self-responsibility training. The biophysical approach focuses on what is within an individual (physiologically or anatomically) that is causing the behavior to occur, such as attention-deficit/hyperactivity disorder (ADHD). Intervention could involve relaxation training, biofeedback, diet modification, or even medication.

Before you continue on in this book and learn what type of behavior approach you value most, take the behavior survey in figure 1.2. It is unlikely that you will score 100% under one approach; most of us have a dominant approach but use other approaches in some cases. This is to be expected; one approach will not work all the time. A model based on this overlap of approaches is an eclectic approach (see figure 1.3 on p. 12).

Interaction among the approaches as well as among the methods within an approach constricts or expands depending on the type and severity of the inappropriate behavior. No matter what the plan is, it must emphasize respect and responsibility while addressing behavioral problems (Curwin and Mendler, 1988; Walker, Shea, and Bauer, 2004).

Identifying behavioral problems is often based on the tolerance level of the physical activity professional. Some can tolerate more disruptions than others. For example, you could walk into one physical education class where the students are quietly standing in their spot, all making eye contact with the teacher who is explaining the day's lesson. You then might walk into another class and observe most of the students standing around the teacher listening but a few whispering in the back of the group. It doesn't seem to bother the teacher that

BEHAVIOR SURVEY

Following are 10 scenarios. To better understand the type of approach you value and will incorporate into your physical activity setting, select what you feel is the best response in each of the scenarios.

Please respond to all 10. Remember, there is no single right answer.

Directions: Read each scenario and circle the letter of the suggestion that you feel is the single best response.

1. Niki is not achieving as well as her physical education teacher has expected. A possible cause of her behavior might be that
   a. interpersonal conflicts with the physical educator are interfering with Niki's work
   b. Niki's appropriate behavior is not consistently reinforced
   c. Niki needs to have her eyes checked

2. As the players line up to exit the gymnasium, Dean cuts in front of John. The two boys begin shoving each other. It is important first to
   a. recommend a physical exam to understand the cause of Dean's irritability
   b. find ways to meet Dean's need to belong
   c. establish a token economy reward system for Dean

3. When Jessica asks the recreation leader for assistance and demands an immediate response, an appropriate action would be to
   a. respond to Jessica only when she asks for help appropriately
   b. convince Jessica's parents and physician to put Jessica on medication to see if this will improve her impulse control
   c. determine effective ways to help Jessica interact with authority figures

4. Luke is involved in several fights with other players about the score in various sports. The other players say he is a bully. An appropriate action would be to
   a. accept that Luke has an intense temperament and not get upset when he fights
   b. teach Luke to recognize what thoughts trigger his inappropriate behavior
   c. consider a referral for family therapy because Luke's angry outbursts are probably related to his family situation

5. Louis is continually late for practice. A likely cause would be that
   a. Louis does not feel he is a skilled athlete
   b. Louis' teacher in his previous class keeps him after class because of disruptive behavior
   c. Louis has to stop at the nurse's office to receive medication to manage his behavior but does not want his coach to know

6. Charlisa will not participate in the volleyball unit. A likely cause would be that
   a. Charlisa feels the points she can earn from participation are not enough of an incentive to participate
   b. Charlisa feels she does not have the basic skills to participate in the volleyball unit
   c. Charlisa has a balance problem caused by the new medication she's taking

7. Christine directs numerous emotional outbursts toward teammates during softball practice. An appropriate intervention would be to
   a. use a biofeedback method to help Christine relax
   b. implement a team contingency plan
   c. talk with Christine about why she demonstrates this type of behavior

8. Young Hoo's increased weight is becoming a hindrance in physical activities. An appropriate action would be to
   a. send Young Hoo to the school psychologist to determine if there is a psychological basis for this weight change
   b. invite the school district's nutritionist to speak in class
   c. develop an individualized contract that includes earning points for losing weight, which contributes to his class grade

9. Alfred continually brings candy to the recreation program. A probable reason for this is that
   a. Alfred believes that if he shares candy, others will like him better
   b. Alfred trades candy to others to receive their vote to be the team captain
   c. the program is just before dinner so Alfred is tired and the candy gives him a sugar high

Figure 1.2 Physical activity professional behavior approach.

(continued)

10. Mandy swears often during competitive activities. A probable reason for this is that
    a. Mandy has a mild form of Tourette's syndrome that has not been diagnosed
    b. swearing gets Mandy attention from other athletes
    c. swearing is a behavior Mandy has learned at home

Scoring: Go back and review your answers, circling your responses.

	Behavioral	Humanistic	Biophysical*
Question 1	B	A	C
Question 2	C	B	A
Question 3	A	C	B
Question 4	A	B	C
Question 5	B	A	C
Question 6	A	B	C
Question 7	B	C	A
Question 8	C	A	B
Question 9	B	A	C
Question 10	C	B	A

Total number of questions circled in each column

Percentage response (Number of responses × 10)   %   %   % = 100

While this survey is not scientifically designed, by counting the number of responses in each approach and then noting the percentages, you can get an idea of what approach or approaches you lean toward when determining cause and intervention. Most of the time one approach is not selected every time, but one is dominant.

*Examples are nutritional treatment, relaxation training, and medication.

Figure 1.2   *(continued)*

some students are not listening. He does not consider it to be a behavior problem because his tolerance level is higher for disruptions than the teacher in the first classroom. In contrast, no teacher has tolerance for severe behavior problems such as verbal and physical abuse, rape, or stealing.

WHAT'S TO COME?

This book is divided into two parts. Part I, which includes chapters 1, 2, and 3, is an introduction to the general strategies, principles, and procedures you'll need in order to develop a positive and proactive management plan. In part II, chapters 4, 5, and 6 examine behavioral approaches to management, while chapter 7 discusses the humanistic approach and chapter 8 discusses biophysical approaches. Chapter 9 applies all the concepts and methods covered in the previous chapters to show you how to develop a program that works for you.

To help you review, assimilate, and apply the information you will learn, we have included a list of questions, titled What Do You Think?, at the end of chapters 1 through 8. To apply the methods and demonstrate how they apply to real-life situations, we have developed three case studies for your consideration. You'll meet Hector, an overactive 3rd grader; Ashante, an instructor at a community health fitness center; and Molly, an overly aggressive player on a community soccer team. At the end of each

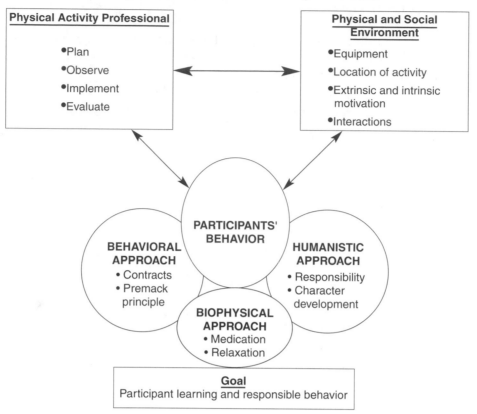

Figure 1.3 The ecological and eclectic behavior management model (BMEE) blends the behavioral, humanistic, and biophysical approaches.

chapter, we'll ask you to revisit these case studies and apply the methods covered in each chapter. Read the three case studies carefully and keep them in mind as you progress through each chapter. Ask yourself if there are strategies you might use to handle these case studies other than the methods provided in the text.

Reproducible worksheets are also provided in appendix A. You can share these with students, players, participants, parents, and others to help you assess how best to approach the particular individuals you serve. Appendix B provides a list of Web sites that will help you gain more information about promoting responsible behavior.

As you absorb the information in this book, keep in mind that no one method will always be appropriate. This variability is due to the variety of teaching, coaching, and leadership styles; the uniqueness of any given situation; and the differences in schools and other environmental settings. Thus, we encourage you to develop a solid base of knowledge and a wide variety of skills and knowledge to call on in times of need.

WHAT DO YOU THINK?

1. Analyze the behavior methods you use. Which ones are positive?

2. List the top five individuals you feel can help you implement an effective behavior plan. Justify your choices.

3. Discuss the importance of ethical standards when it comes to behavior management in the physical activity setting. Are national standards important or a hindrance in reforming your role?

4. Based on your past physical activity experiences, identify the importance of understanding the role of culture and ethnicity in effectively performing your role.

5. Discuss your main approach to promoting responsible behavior. Was it reflected in the behavioral survey you completed in figure 1.2? Based on the results of the survey do you think you should make any changes? If so, what?

CASE STUDIES

CASE 1
Hector, a Disruptive 3rd Grader

Hector is a 3rd grader who has a learning disability and attention-deficit/hyperactivity disorder. He is considered overactive. He is unable to stand or sit in his assigned spot in the gym for any length of time, and he runs when he should walk. In addition, Hector has difficulty following a series of directions, becomes easily upset and irritated, and has poor gross motor coordination. His behavior has become so distracting that the physical educator has asked the special education classroom teacher to not bring him to physical education class because he constantly causes chaos.

CASE 2
Ashante, an Instructor in Charge of Weight-Room Cleanup

Ashante is one of the instructors in the weight room at the local community recreation center. She attends college during the day and works at the center from 6 p.m. to closing every day. When she starts her shift, the weight room is a total disaster and she must clean it up because it is an unsafe environment. By closing, it is in the same shape and she must stay late to put away the weights that are lying all over the room. Ashante believes she is involved in more strength

training than the clients because of the work it takes to clean up the mess, which has become a major frustration.

CASE 3
Molly, an Overly Aggressive Soccer Player

Molly is an 8th-grade student who plays on a community soccer team. She often starts arguments and fights during practices and games. The coach is frustrated. Molly is the best player on the team, but is her contribution worth the trouble? Other players want her removed or punished in some way, such as not letting her play as much. On the other hand, the fans like the winning season, which is due in great part to Molly's skillful performance in games.

2

Creating a Positive Atmosphere

*P*reparation is a key to success in any endeavor, and sport and physical activity instruction is no exception.

Himberg, Hutchinson, and Roussell, 2003, p. 186

Right after practice, Mr. O'Brien, the middle school physical education teacher and basketball coach, and Ms. Truly, the assistant vice principal, were walking to their cars. Shoulders drooping, Mr. O'Brien said, "I've had an awful day. During first period, I caught Billy and Shane fighting in the locker room and had to send them to the principal's office. It was the third time this month I've had to break up fights in the locker room!"

He continued in exasperation, "That's not all. During 3rd period I began a new unit on volleyball. Only a few of the students seemed interested, and I had to keep quieting the class because they were whispering while I was giving instructions. It went downhill from there. None of them had basic volleyball skills, at least not the skills that they were supposed to practice at the learning stations. I also learned today that five students with intellectual disabilities from Mr. Taylor's adapted physical education class were added to my 5th period. I wasn't told that they were coming and had no idea what an effect they would have on my class. To top it all off, at basketball practice three of the players were late again and two weren't dressed properly. So I had to interrupt practice to deal with them. They really show a lack of responsibility. Bad days are becoming a chronic problem! Teaching and coaching aren't fun anymore. I feel so burned out."

Managing young people who act inappropriately is neither fun nor satisfying. Siedentop and Tannehill (2000) discuss three myths about behavior. First, with good management, problems will not occur. Second, young people will come to physical education, sport, and recreation programs with the necessary behaviors. Third, all young people automatically enjoy physical activity and are enthusiastic about learning.

Because these assumptions are false, as physical activity professionals we must set the stage for learning by creating a positive, exciting environment. Most individuals want to listen, participate, and learn from leaders who are competent and prepared, so we must be knowledgeable about the subject, be able to perform the skills, and perhaps most important, be able to promote responsible behavior. This means going beyond behavior and offering a creative learning environment to meet the complex needs of individuals.

In chapter 3, we'll provide you with specific strategies for preparing the physical activity setting so that it promotes performance, learning, and responsible behavior. Since your first task is to create a warm, nurturing environment that encourages performance and learning, in this chapter we will discuss the principles of creating a positive environment. Without such an environment, the best plan in the world would be far less effective than it could be.

EXAMINE YOURSELF

Excellent physical activity professionals have numerous attributes, including passion; a vibrant, animated approach; enthusiasm; optimism; respect for students and players as human beings; clear rules and expectations; approachability; and a safe and supportive environment (Williams, Alley, and Henson, 1999).

Socrates' observation that "the unexamined life is not worth living" is as true now as when he originally said it 24 centuries ago. You might apply it to your own situation by rephrasing it like this: "If you don't examine yourself as a physical activity professional, then you might as well give up now!" (See figure 2.1.) Let's look closely at four questions you should ask yourself and at the self-evaluation checklists at the end of the chapter (see page 32).

Am I Tuned In?

Tuned-in physical activity professionals know what is going on in the physical activity environment at all times. They act immediately, redirecting disruptive behavior before it has a chance to spread. For instance, William was up to bat for his third time during practice; he had already struck out twice. Ms. Speckhardt, the physical education teacher, could see the frustration in William's eyes, and his teammates were starting to groan. Ms. Speckhardt knew a problem was coming, so she incorporated a new rule that after three strikes, the batter could use a batting tee. This removed the peer pressure and allowed William to succeed.

Am I Enthusiastic?

Enthusiasm is contagious! To be an effective physical activity professional you must be enthusiastic about your work. To influence individuals, you must show them that they are more important than the subject matter, game, or activity. Your enthu-

Figure 2.1 Teacher reflecting about the most effective way to group teams.

siasm will spread, promoting a positive, nurturing climate. Take, for example, Mr. Angelo, a retired military officer who taught physical education at a local junior high school. He believed that enthusiasm or any other emotion was a sign of weakness, so he taught in a businesslike manner, giving the students no hint that he might be enjoying the class himself. Because Mr. Angelo was firm, there was little disruptive behavior: The students followed his instructions quietly and without question. But many of the students who were not already athletic were not improving and often made excuses in order to miss class. These problems were largely the result of Mr. Angelo's unenthusiastic attitude, clearly illustrated when he missed school for 2 weeks to meet his army reserve commitment and Mrs. Motta, a substitute physical education teacher with a buoyant personality, took over the class. While still using the basic command style of teaching, she incorporated music when she led the warm-ups and many times jogged with the students and participated in the games and activities. Not surprisingly, the number of absences decreased and students who had never improved began to show progress in both skill and fitness levels.

Am I Flexible?

Be willing to adapt each behavioral method. For instance, if you have designed and initiated a behavioral contract with a player on your team, you may need to renegotiate the contract if it proves insufficient. Write contracts in such a way that you can modify them if unforeseen circumstances arise. For example, Coach Zurel and Josh, an 11th grader, developed a behavioral contract to address Josh's frequent tardiness to practice. According to the contract (figure 2.2), Josh could earn 1 point per practice for being on time. Coach Zurel promised to start Josh in the next game if he was on time each practice and earned 4 or 5 points. For the first week, Josh was a few minutes late three times. The contract did not seem to be working, so Coach Zurel called Josh into his office to renegotiate it. They decided that Josh could still earn points by being on time, but every day that he was late he would spend 15 minutes after practice working on the skills that he missed by being late. After modifying the contract, Josh was still occasionally tardy, but overall his punctuality improved significantly. See chapter 5 for more information on contracts.

Am I Personable?

Coach Roberts makes it a point at the end of practice to shake the hands of her players, commenting to each one as she does so. Generally the comments are positive, but if need be, this approach gives her a chance to address the player's behavior or how the player practiced. While this takes Coach Roberts 1 or 2 minutes of practice time, she believes that interacting with her players on an individual basis saves time in the long run.

Even if you follow this suggestion, when you have a large group you may still have difficulty recognizing everyone. To minimize this problem, before activity starts identify a small group of individuals you will focus on during class that day.

SPORT BEHAVIORAL CONTRACT

January 15, 2006

I will be on time to practice. I will earn 1 point each practice each day. If I earn 4 out of 5 points during the week, I will start in the Saturday game. Any day I am late,

I will stay after practice for 15 minutes and continue to work on skills covered in practice.

_____
Josh Smith
Athlete

_____
Mr. Zurel
Head coach

Figure 2.2   A sample sport behavioral contract.

Spend no more than 45 seconds with each participant before moving to the next. The following day identify another set of participants who will receive your attention, and continue this process until you have learned everyone's name.

One final word about names: Always use an individual's name respectfully. If you use it with sarcasm, such as calling a child "French Fry" when his last name is French, he will most likely tune you out.

Do these strategies sound like a lot of work? Keep in mind that your efforts will pay off because participants will know you care. This will help you develop a stimulating learning climate in which they want to behave and learn.

USE POSITIVE STRATEGIES

Effective physical activity professionals use numerous strategies. The strategies presented in this section include catching students behaving well, expecting students to follow directions, keeping your cool and addressing problems quickly, focusing on the behavior, being consistent, incorporating social interaction, varying tasks, developing group spirit, creating a positive environment, playing music, relaxing students with physical activity, using a continuum of interactive styles, determining who owns the problem, and choosing your words carefully.

Learning Names

In a physical activity setting individuals are constantly moving and sometimes looking away from you. You must get their attention quickly so that they are safe and engaged in the process (Williams, 1995). Naturally, it is easier to get their attention if you know their names, but this is quite a challenge with large groups. The key is to acknowledge individuals when they enter the setting. Following are proven strategies for learning names for different age groups (Cusimano, Darst, and van der Mars, 1993; Petray-Rowcliffe, Williams, Lavay, and Hakim-Butt, 2002; Williams, 1995):

1. Greet each person by name during the warm-up and dismiss each person by name at the end of the class or practice, commenting about the individual's participation for the day.

2. Regularly include names when giving feedback, when reinforcing appropriate behavior, and when reprimanding inappropriate behavior.

3. Use name tags with younger participants during the first few weeks of class.

4. List the names that you can remember. These participants may be receiving a disproportionate amount of your attention.

5. List the names you couldn't remember on an index card to use as a quick reference.

6. Label names of participants on a photograph of each class and place it on the bulletin board to use as a reference.

Catch Them Being Good

Too often we fall into the trap of calling attention to participants who are off task or acting out, inadvertently reinforcing the inappropriate behavior we wish to stop. Unfortunately, individuals quickly learn that when they act out, they receive attention. Accentuate the positive by catching each individual being good. This is particularly important when someone demonstrates a new positive behavior. Simply complimenting the positive behavior goes a long way toward reinforcing it.

Recognize successes. Advertise their success by recognizing improvement, records, feats, and other accomplishments through the school and community newspaper, over the public-address system, on bulletin boards, or through public recognition. For instance, Ms. Garcia began a new aquatics program at her recreation center. In the program there was a boy named George who was often disruptive. George would continually say, "No, I can't do it," when learning how to swim. Then he would distract other children instead of trying the activity. A reporter from a local newspaper wanted to write a story about the program, and Ms. Garcia told George that in the next 2 weeks if he participated in all the swimming activities, she would make sure that his picture was put in the paper with the story about the aquatics program. His behavior immediately improved. Newspaper attention is especially motivating when you include participants' pictures (see figure 2.3).

This is only one of the many ways physical activity professionals have accented the positive. The In the Trenches example by John Hichwa, a physical educator, shows how he motivated his students to participate in his class. Many more creative ways to promote motivation exist, and we'll look at those methods in greater detail in chapter 3. You need to continually evaluate the approaches you use to create a positive atmosphere. Refer to checklist 2.1, page 32, for a basic self-evaluation inventory that you can use.

Figure 2.3 Including participants' pictures in the newspaper can be especially motivating.

A Physical Educator's Experience

John Hichwa, Physical Educator in Redding, Connecticut, Author of _Right Fielders Are People Too_

I'm often asked how I motivate students to participate enthusiastically in my classes and how I make physical education relevant for everyone. I believe it starts by developing a nonthreatening environment in which physical skills are taught in connection with conflict resolution, communication, and problem-solving skills.

An inexperienced teacher's main focus is usually the subject matter, but in time it becomes more centered on the students and their individual needs. The planning, curriculum, methodology, and style of teaching are a lifelong quest for meeting the physical, cognitive, and affective needs of each student. This teaching journey is often challenging, but the rewards of effective teaching become motivation to continue. We have a legacy to leave no child behind, and with experience and vision that can be done.

Excellence in teaching does not come automatically, and it takes perseverance, patience, and a passion for improving the lives of young people. I would like to share with you an experience I had several years ago on the first day of school with an incoming 6th-grade class. My colleague and I had the students on the bleachers, and we began to talk about what we would be doing during the fall semester and what themes we would be covering. We explained how we would begin by playing a series of keep-away games using different throwing objects. We would review the basic skills and strategies and then we would play the game. We talked about our upcoming fitness-testing program and how playing the keep-away games would improve their cardiovascular endurance before they were tested on the mile run.

We also covered our dress requirements and informed the students about the criteria they would be using to grade themselves.

The bell rang and as the students filed out of the gymnasium, a boy named Josh stopped and said, "Mr.

Hichwa, that was a very interesting talk but I need to tell you that I don't do gym. You see, I was cut from my 3rd-grade soccer team, no one ever asks me to play in their recess games, and no one wants me on their team in gym class. I'm just not a very good athlete!"

His comments left me speechless. I had little time to think, but I said, "Josh, I hear you and I want you to know that I will do everything possible to help you any way I can in my class. For the next two or three classes, why don't you just observe and see what happens and then we can talk further."

Josh thought that made sense and agreed. In the third class, Josh came with his sneakers, shorts, and T-shirt and said that he was going to give it a try. I was relieved and once again assured Josh that I was there to help. It wasn't long before Josh discovered he was a good runner, and he used that talent to his advantage by showing his peers that he could be successful at something. In the remaining middle school years, Josh was enthusiastic, worked hard, and slowly gained enough confidence to play in the many small-sided games that we offered. He especially excelled in and was excited about the outdoor experiential education program that was part of his physical education classes. In high school, Josh had enough confidence to try out for the cross-country team. He successfully participated on the team all 4 years of high school. I often wondered what would have happened to Josh if I told him he had no choice, that all students must participate in physical education.

Then there was Rob. He was a little upset with us because we did not have an activity planned for that first day of school. He had his duffle bag, his change of clothes, and his sneakers, and he was ready to go. I knew Rob had just returned from a trip to Virginia where he was the center halfback on the all-Connecticut select soccer team. Rob's needs were different. He needed to learn how to be understanding and accepting of the Joshes in the class. I gave him some leadership responsibilities that challenged him to help motivate others. Rob matured nicely, was the star of his high school soccer team, and went on to play soccer at the college level. Even more important, he learned to be patient and considerate of those who were less physically gifted than he was.

Expect Them to Follow Directions

Give directions once. If you believe individuals were involved in an activity and simply did not hear the instruction, it is okay to repeat the instructions a second time. However, the more you give an instruction, the less likely participants are to follow it. It is best to give the instruction in a positive, assertive voice, then remain silent, maintain eye contact, and wait for individuals to comply. After 2 or 3 seconds, you should employ a consequence for not complying. For example, Mr. Jacino, a recreation specialist, had 10 players on his softball team and none of them put the equipment away immediately after his request. So he spoke with another recreation specialist about the problem. The other specialist said she used to have the same problem until she initiated a policy that stated, "The players who line up within 15 seconds after a request will receive an additional point toward earning a star that will be worn on their uniform." The next day Mr. Jacino tried this approach and to his surprise, the players lined up.

Figure 2.4 When communicating with a student, use direct eye contact.

Keep Your Cool and Address Problems Quickly

If you expect individuals to behave well, you must set a good example by being in control of yourself. When someone breaks a rule, you need to act, not react, so refrain from making on-the-spot judgments. Instead, make sure you know what happened before accusing an individual of a violation, and remember that disruptive behavior seldom starts with bad intentions. However, don't allow behavior problems to continue, because they often cause a ripple effect, spreading through the activity and escalating into a major problem. Once misbehavior occurs, even the best corrective methods may disrupt instruction and cause friction between you and the whole group, so do not add to the problem by losing self-control.

Remain calm, take the individual aside, and straightforwardly explain the rule and the consequence for not following it, all the while keeping an eye on the rest of the class. (See chapter 3 for additional information about consequences.) When communicating, use direct eye contact, which conveys a positive, assertive message (see figure 2.4). For example, you might say, "Nicole, I know you are capable of getting in your squad line on time because I have seen you do this many times before." Have her repeat the rule and how she will follow it in the future. This procedure reduces public confrontations between you and the individual.

Focus on the Behavior

Phrase your reprimands carefully. Describe the behavior rather than labeling or attacking the individual. For example, instead of saying, "Cindy, you are unmotivated," specify the behavior that concerns you. You might say, "Cindy, you are not participating during exercises."

Develop a "we" attitude. Young people need to know that they are working in concert with you to solve the behavior problem. When you use the question, "What can we do to solve this problem?", you focus on the behavior rather than the individual. This approach makes individuals feel that you care and want to help. Because focusing on the behavior instead of attacking the participant can be difficult, we'll examine it in more detail in chapter 4.

The inappropriate behavior must be the focus of your statements. If you put the individual down rather than addressing the behavior, you may create problems with self-esteem. People who feel good about themselves are more likely to act appropriately.

Here are some examples of dos and don'ts for focusing on the behavior rather than the individual:

Dos

- "I need you to stop talking when I am speaking."
- "You will be expelled for fighting."
- "It will help if you watch the ball going into your hands every time."

Don'ts

- "You will never make it in this sport."
- "You have lost my respect."
- "Can't you act like your brother?"

Be Consistent

Participants must know what to expect from you and what you expect of them. Thus, your treatment of all individuals must be predictable and fair. Focus on the topic, avoid ambiguity, use eye contact, choose the best words, use appropriate facial expressions and body language, and inject brief, intermittent summaries. Mrs. McCall, who was in her first year of teaching, knew that she must post rules and explain them in detail. But since she had befriended many of the students in her classes who were also members of her daughter's recreation-level soccer team, the other students felt that she allowed favorites to break rules. This caused them to lose respect for her, which led them to talk back to her.

Designing and implementing clear, consistent rules will be discussed in chapter 3.

Yes Should Remain Yes

Turning no to yes and yes to no is a sure way to cause behavior problems. For instance, say you

ask the players on your softball team to take a warm-up lap and one stubbornly says he does not want to warm up because he ran a lap during physical education class less than an hour ago. So you tell him, "Okay, you don't have to take a warm-up lap today." Running another lap as a warm-up would still be beneficial to the player. Making exceptions when the activity will be beneficial, knowing the player is not injured or physically exhausted, will provide others with a role model to follow. You will have other players in the future who will ask for the same exception using various reasons.

Or, say you tell a student she will be squad leader at the end of the week. She is excited and cannot wait for Friday. But when Friday comes, you change the lesson or practice plan and tell the class that they will be running an obstacle course. You tell the individual that she will be captain on Monday. In other words, you go from yes to no. Inconsistency creates behavior problems.

Check for Compliance

Telling individuals to do a task but not checking to see that they have done it can create problems. For example, following are three common tasks that a physical activity professional might ask individuals to do:

- "Please put away all the balls and bats in the equipment room."
- "Since it's the end of the season, I need you to clean out your lockers and turn in your locks."
- "Please perform all activities at each station, recording your performances as you go."

Assigning these tasks is only the first step. The second step is to follow up to make sure individuals have complied with your request. In the first instance, you need only make a short trip to the equipment room right after practice. In the second instance, you can simply have the participants stand by their opened lockers for you to check them. In the third instance, you can spot-check to see if the students are performing the activity at each station and recording their performances. Praise those who are doing the activity correctly so that others will be more likely to comply. If this is not effective, you can provide other incentives, which we'll discuss in chapter 3.

Ensure Consistency Among Staff

Professionals in a physical activity setting must work as a unit, setting the same basic rules and expectations for behavior. This structure and consistency prevents individuals from becoming confused because they can predict what will be expected of them. Teachers, coaches, and leaders must support each other because inconsistency undermines everyone's approach to promoting responsible behavior, allowing participants to play one adult against another to get their own way. When possible, have a system of behavior management that everyone can agree on. More on this topic is provided in chapter 9.

Promote Social Interaction

Be creative in finding new ways to motivate social interaction. Mr. Badashar noticed that during his 8th-grade physical education class many of the students walked during the jogging warm-up, so he decided to interact with the students when they completed each lap. He stood by the starting line, and as each student passed, he gave a positive comment and a high five (see figure 2.5). If the students had not jogged the lap, he would not physically interact with them. Simply because he incorporated this positive social interaction, all of the students began jogging their laps.

Assign Varied Tasks

Participants are motivated when you introduce new drills and activities, but then their enthusiasm decreases, leading to off-task, inappropriate behavior. How do you keep interest high? Vary the tasks! You don't always have to introduce new tasks when interest wanes, however; you can modify a task or interrupt it to emphasize a learning cue or give feedback. For example, if players are practicing basketball drills and boredom begins to set in, introduce another drill that has the same objective, briefly illustrate a new skill to be added to the original drill, or discuss a few tips to improve their skill performance.

Develop Group Spirit

There are many ways to develop group spirit. One method is the use of emblems or mottos. Emblems could be the school mascot, and mottos could be "Team United," "We Give 110%" or "We Do It As a Team." Colored shirts or armbands related to individual group performance and learning can also be used. At the high school or university level look at football players who have stars on their helmets,

Figure 2.5 One positive strategy is to give participants a high five after they complete each lap.

Figure 2.6 Stars on a helmet can be motivational and foster team spirit.

each one representing an exemplary performance (see figure 2.6).

You can incorporate these same group-spirit methods in community recreation programs. Many times community teams use high school teams' names and encourage community spirit about their recreation programs. Chapter 7 provides additional strategies for promoting group spirit.

Create a Positive Environment

Use bright displays (see figure 2.7), positive signs, and bulletin boards with organized information to help create a positive environment. You can post rules and directions for the students as well as pictures or collages of participants, sport heroes, special events, awards, and recognition. More information on this topic can be found in chapter 5.

Play Music

You can often increase interest and motivation by introducing music. You can add music to warm-up exercises, fitness routines, and regular practice sessions; as a relaxation technique; or to reward students for successfully completing a task (Sariscsany, 1991). Be sure to select music they like. You can even have them bring tapes or CDs in for you to play, though you should always preview their music for appropriateness! Refer to chapter 8 for more on this topic.

Figure 2.7 Bulletin boards with bright displays can help to create a positive physical activity environment and provide participants with such information as rules and routines to follow.

Use Physical Activity As Relaxation

You can use physical activity to relax individuals. For instance, vigorous exercise, such as 10 minutes of jogging, may promote fitness, reduce stress, and improve self-concept (Allen, 1980; Blue, 1979; Doyne, Chambless, and Bentley, 1983). Jogging can give students a time-out, removing them from external pressures or distractions. More about this method is provided in chapter 6.

Use a Continuum of Styles

At the beginning of the school year, athletic season, or community recreation session you may need to use a more controlling style of instruction. Carefully weighing maturity levels, you should lead the individuals toward making their own decisions more often. For example, at the beginning of the school year, Mr. Yu always uses a command style of teaching. He decides on the rules, the activity, the equipment, the location, and the consequences of all activities. As the school year progresses, he systematically allows students to take more responsibility, such as leading exercises, taking roll, and otherwise assisting him. If the students accept these responsibilities, he incorporates task cards, circuits, and obstacle courses into his classes. If this approach is successful, he allows students to help select appropriate activities to meet curriculum goals.

Focus on positive approaches to create the best possible learning atmosphere. Refer to checklist 2.2 often to see how you're doing, making sure negative approaches do not creep into your style.

Determine Who Owns the Problem

In resolving a conflict, analyze the situation to determine who owns the problem. If you are frustrated because an individual is disrupting the activity session, it's your problem. If the individual is frustrated because she does not have any friends, it's her problem. If each of you is making the other frustrated, then both of you own the problem. For participant-owned problems, you can try to understand and

clarify their problem through active listening (Gordon, 1994). This method involves listening carefully to individuals and trying to understand their point of view, then reflecting this information back to them (see figure 2.8). You could say, "What I hear you saying is that when your best friend gets around the older boys, he is mean to you, and that makes you sad. Am I correct in saying this or is something else going on?" More information on effective communication methods is offered in chapter 7.

Physical activity professionals can use "I" messages, explaining the effect the behavior has on your feelings and needs. For example, you can say, "I feel frustrated when you come to practice late because then I need to spend time explaining to you what we're doing after I've already explained it to the rest of the team. This wastes time." Or when Jose puts Brian down because Brian took the soccer ball away from him in a game, you might say, "I am not happy with your put-downs. We just talked about being a good sport yesterday. Perhaps we need to talk again about possible solutions to this problem." Using "I" messages creates a cooperative problem-solving attitude, minimizing blame and anger.

Once you identify the problem, work with the individual to generate possible solutions. At this stage, avoid evaluating ideas; let creative ideas flow freely. Then evaluate the possible solutions to determine which one is best in the situation.

© Human Kinetics

Figure 2.8 Listen carefully to understand the other person's point of view.

Choose Your Words Carefully

Think about what you are going to say or do and make sure there's a good chance it will maintain or increase positive performance and learning. If not, don't say or do it. A helpful saying to remember is, "Act, don't react, and count to 5."

Use words like *will* and *can* instead of the guilt-producing word *should*. For example, if Lu Ying, a dance instructor at the local recreation center, says that she was late for class because she wanted to talk to Keesha about the dance tomorrow night, you might say, "Lu Ying, what can you do next time so that you can talk to Keesha but not be late to my dance lesson?" Model appropriate behavior and keep your cool.

When it comes to athletes, positive statements are usually best administered immediately before, during, or after sport-specific actions. These statements could be individualized to make them more motivating. The following strategies may help you maximize the benefits of using positive statements with athletes (Donahue, 2001).

1. Talk with athletes about the importance of using positive statements and not using negative statements.
2. Have athletes brainstorm a list of statements they want to hear before, during, and after practice or competition.
3. Disclose at least one positive behavior or characteristic you appreciate about all teammates, then have them respond.
4. Establish a team rule prohibiting negative statements.
5. Ask each athlete and coach what they learned or liked about their performance.

Fronske and Birch (1995) make a number of suggestions for enhancing communication skills. For example, avoid the following tactics:

• **Giving advice.** This occurs when one person tells another how to deal with a problem. For example, say Maheshie comes to you with a problem, stating, "No one wants to be on my team." You may be inclined to give advice, such as, "Why don't you try to make friends with Sue?" When this happens, you take responsibility for the problem away from Maheshie. To help her take responsibility, you might say, "Maheshie, you seem concerned about no one wanting to be on your team. What can you do to change that?" When Maheshie offers a solution you should reinforce her initiative, suggest any appropriate modifications, and help her set a goal for making friends. Giving her advice only takes away her responsibility.

• **Passing judgment.** This occurs when you evaluate what someone says, whether favorably or unfavorably. This includes rewording, criticizing, blaming, and labeling. You may want to respond to Maheshie by saying, "You're popular, lots of kids like you." But this undermines her confidence in her ability to solve her own problems, possibly causing her to rely on external judgments. Instead, it is better to listen carefully to what she is saying and ask open-ended questions, such as, "What could you do to make others want to be on your team?" This approach empowers her to solve the problem.

• **Trying to persuade.** This happens when you try to convince someone that a particular position or action is correct, taking away the individual's responsibility for finding a solution. It's tempting to think that our experience and wisdom will lead to the best choice. But allowing individuals to make their own decision is more likely to result in long-term cooperation. For example, if a player has a poor batting average, ask, "What can you do to increase your batting performance?" This is in contrast to telling the player to go to the batting cage every Saturday and Sunday to practice until his average is 250 or above.

• **Playing psychoanalyst.** Refrain from suggesting that you know the cause of the individual's problem. Never assume anything and be sure to clarify what you think the individual is saying, or you will take power away from the individual.

• **Using diversionary tactics.** Don't divert the individual's attention from the behavior problem. For example, you shouldn't tell Maheshie, "Just join in the game today and we can discuss your problem some other time." This does not solve anything, except that it's more convenient for you for that day. You're better off dealing with problems as they occur.

You must be aware of these common roadblocks to communication so you can avoid them. Physical activity professionals must make positive statements that are age-appropriate, clear, concise, and consistent. To avoid negative approaches to communication, see checklist 2.3 on page 32.

SUPPORT RESOURCES

To create a positive atmosphere, you must use every available resource to ensure that inappropriate behavior will not affect learning or performance. In most cases, you will be able to deal with behavior problems yourself without going outside the physical activity environment. However, there are times when a collaborative team approach is necessary. Refer to checklist 2.4 for things to consider when collaborating (page 32).

Most administrators are supportive, and all have a duty to maintain a safe and orderly atmosphere in which professionals can provide instruction and individuals can perform and learn. Enlist the help of administrators and the help of others such as school psychologists and counselors. Also consult veteran teachers, coaches, or recreation specialists as well as parents who have experienced similar problems and have developed an effective program to reduce or eliminate the disruptive behaviors. Other physical activity professionals also may have developed a management program for the individual that you can modify to your situation.

Many school districts now employ adapted physical education specialists who can help you design a program to promote responsible behavior. When a student with a disability receives classroom instruction in a special education setting, the adapted physical educator often becomes an integral part of the program. One example is the special educator who uses a point system in her classroom that allows a student to earn rewards. To participate, you might send a note to the special educator after each class that specifies the number of points the student earned. You may want to develop a form (see figure 2.9) to simplify and standardize the process. In many community recreation environments you may work with a therapeutic recreation therapist to design and implement a similar program.

Parents have falsely accused physical activity professionals of prejudice, neglect, unprovoked hostility, unfair consequences, and other offenses. Some parents are overprotective and overemotional when it comes to their child. On the other hand, some parents are embarrassed by their child's behavior. Other parents may not show up for a meeting but are persistent and positive. Whatever the situation, exceptional care must be taken with the focus on the child to learn to be a functional member of society. This adds more responsibility for the physical activity professional.

Do not make the mistake of thinking you are only dealing with a group of students. Behind them stands a group of concerned parents who need to be informed of your expectations. It is essential that you effectively communicate with parents. Usually parents are eager to see their children

succeed in school and the community and will be supportive. Send a letter home to all parents at the beginning of the school year or season outlining program policies and rules (see figure 2.10). You might include your teaching, coaching, or recreation philosophy or expectations for class or team participation. Use language that parents can understand, avoiding complicated language. Be friendly and tactful. Encourage parents to contact you whenever they have concerns. After all, parents know their children best and can be helpful resources for you and valuable support for the overall program.

One method for communicating with parents about their child's behavior is the telephone. When the telephone call is necessary because other approaches to the individual's behavior have failed, consider these specific guidelines (Watson and Lounsbery, 2000):

1. Detach personal emotion.
2. Do not begin a conversation with a long list of what the child is not doing.
3. Compliment the child in the conversation.
4. Present facts.
5. Stay calm and be professional.
6. Relate to an "I" or "we" perspective, not a "their" perspective in blaming or judging.
7. Follow up with parents by communicating the results of any plan that was collaboratively developed.

The key is to use this strategy again when positive behaviors are demonstrated. This telephone call could shock some parents but will ultimately serve as fantastic public relations. These same guidelines can be used when communicating with parents through e-mail. This method and a letter home combined are appropriate for use in community recreation programs.

While many methods can be used in school where there is a built-in structure to promote behavior, in the community recreation program such structure does not exist. Individuals are participating because their parents have paid for them to be there, so methods may need to be creative. Again, a parent letter and a telephone call provide some structure and understanding of expectations.

Other ways to effectively communicate your expectations to parents include holding conferences, striking up conversations at PTA meetings (be sure to protect the family's privacy), and giving behavior progress reports. In addition, a

COLLABORATION BEHAVIORAL CONTRACT

Student name _____   Date _____

Goal: To attend to and respond to the instructor's requests.

• Walking into locker room	/2
• Dressing	/5
• Lining up for class	/2
• Warm-up activity	/5
• Instruction	/10
• Cool-down activity	/5
• Closure	/2
• Walking to locker room	/2
• Showering and dressing	/5
• Waiting for dismissal bell	/2
Total daily points	**/40**

Comments (e.g., mastery needed, contact parents, modify behavior plan) _____

_____

_____

_____

_____

_____

_____

_____

_____

_____

_____

_____

_____

_____

_____

_____

*Behavior and points briefly discussed with student immediately after dismissal bell.

_____   _____
Physical educator   Special educator

Figure 2.9   Sample collaboration form.

Dear Parents or Guardians:

Our community recreation soccer season is about to begin, and I would like to provide a short list of our expectations for and beliefs about our team that my coaching staff follows and that we would like you to respect and also follow.

1. Sports can be a terrific medium to develop honorable sportsmanship, courage, and a healthy self-concept if coaches and parents are supportive role models.

2. Players should be rewarded by coaches and parents for reaching their full capabilities in a win-or-lose environment. A "win at all cost" philosophy is inappropriate and is counterproductive in the development of young people. The focus should be on positive, reasonable expectations and keeping a sense of humor.

3. Coaches and parents must remain calm and respect the calls of the game officials. We cannot overreact. Our behavior is seen by our athletes as well as the fans who consider us role models.

4. Coaches and parents should focus on the individual player's performance and not compare the player to others on the team, brothers or sisters, or players on other teams.

5. Coaches and parents must live through themselves, not through their players or children.

6. Coaches must know their players physically, emotionally, and socially to facilitate their development within the medium of our community recreation program.

7. Parents must be careful not to overcoach. This may place undue pressure on children by putting them in the middle between you and our coaching staff. This can cause major frustration and reduce the enjoyment and other benefits that can be gained from the player's experience.

8. Parents or other fans who use inappropriate language; taunt players, coaches, and officials; or constantly give instructions from the sidelines will be given a warning, and if the behavior continues, they will be removed from the premises.

9. As the head coach, I believe we must form a partnership in the development of your child. I would be glad to discuss any of these expectations and beliefs with you individually. Just call and set up an appointment.

Coach Martin

Figure 2.10   A coach's letter to parents.

few parents may be willing to work with you to allow their children to earn privileges at home for better behavior at school. Again, don't limit your communication efforts to a single individual; consider sending a few positive notes every week. A certificate recognizing good behavior can go a long way toward engaging both student cooperation and parental support. Numerous computer programs easily design certificates. Carefully rotate whom you select so that everyone receives positive recognition when they earn it. For more examples of certificates see chapter 5 and figure 5.3 on page 78.

Problems may be an indirect result of parental unemployment, divorce, alcohol and drug abuse, domestic violence, child abuse, and other factors, including high rates of crime, unsafe neighborhoods, lack of community cohesion, few after-school activities, and weak bonding to the school process. Parents may be unable to help their children with problems because they may be preoccupied with matters that they feel are more pressing. Resolving these complex problems may require collaboration among the community, school personnel, and parents.

WHEN BEHAVIOR IS EXTREME

Although parents are among our best potential allies in the effort to create a positive atmosphere, this is not always the case. Increasingly parents who are asked to come in and discuss the behavior of their children verbally abuse, threaten, or even physically attack the teacher, coach, or school administrator. It seems parents are becoming less willing to discuss problems in a calm and rational manner, preferring to settle issues with violence. Violent parents often have violent children, and you must be prepared to handle them as well. To deal with this problem, some schools and recreation facilities have security guards to patrol halls, playgrounds, and parking lots, and programs have also been developed with the help of police to deal with violent parents and children. One park and recreation program developed and posted three adult rules for sports: make it fun, set a good example, and cheer for everyone (Barnett, 1998).

SUMMARY

The foundation of effective physical education, sport, and recreation is the ability to promote responsible behavior. This ability increases individual performance and learning, which is, after all, your main responsibility. To create this foundation, incorporate several methods into your instructional approach. All these approaches must be practiced and learned. Don't hesitate to tap into the talents of those who can help you develop and implement a behavior plan. You are not alone. You can incorporate the support of parents, community members and agencies, other teachers and coaches, recreation specialists, and administrators.

WHAT DO YOU THINK?

1. Analyze the methods you use to engage participants. Which ones are positive?
2. You have been asked to provide a 1-hour inservice session to new recreation coaches. Most of the coaches have a child of their own on the team. List the five most important topics you need to discuss at the inservice, ranked in order from most to least important.
3. Develop a note to send home with individuals related to appropriate behavior.
4. Make a telephone call to parents to discuss their child's behavior.
5. Briefly discuss Socrates' translated statement, "If you don't examine yourself as a physical activity professional, you might as well give up."

CASE STUDIES

For each of the three case studies in chapter 1 on page 13, select methods described in this chapter and discuss in detail how you would implement each of the methods to manage the behavior. After you have developed your own methods, read the following suggestions, which are only some of the many creative ways you might apply the information covered in this chapter.

CASE 1

Hector, a Disruptive 3rd Grader

▶ Give clear directions that are constant and systematic, provide additional verbal or visual cues, or assign a peer tutor to help Hector follow the directions.

▶ Place tasks in a rubric form related to the major skills performed in class.

▶ Develop a partnership with Hector's parents and create individualized homework assignments that they can work on as a team at home.

▶ Use a reward system, such as a certificate, for achieving a specific performance level.

▶ Use local recreation programs to develop skills that he needs to function better in his physical education class.

▶ Find physical education students at the local college or university who would be willing to help Hector for a small fee.

▸ Let Hector take a self-time-out such as a walk around the gymnasium or the track when he becomes frustrated as a method to reduce tension, as long as he can be observed.

▸ Work with the special education teacher and the adapted physical educator to implement other ideas, such as evaluating Hector for placement in an adapted physical education program or providing consultative services to the general physical educator on a regular basis.

CASE 2
Ashante, an Instructor in Charge of Weight-Room Cleanup

▸ Speak to the instructor in charge of the weight room to develop a plan to solve the problem.

▸ Post rules that members are expected to follow.

▸ Enlist the assistance of support resources such as other instructors and the recreation center director to implement a program to keep the weight-room equipment in the appropriate spots.

▸ If one or two clients continually leave the equipment out, speak to those individuals about the importance of following the rules because of safety reasons.

▸ If it seems to be a group problem, use music as an incentive, playing it only when the weight room is neat.

CASE 3
Molly, an Overly Aggressive Soccer Player

▸ Send a letter to the parents about the purpose of the community soccer league, the coach's philosophy, and policies related to players, parents, and fans.

▸ Develop newsletters that provide information on good sportsmanship and focus on those team members who have demonstrated qualities of sportsmanship.

▸ Have a team meeting and offer individual meetings to any parents who have specific concerns.

▸ Develop team spirit by choosing a team captain before each game based on which player showed the best sportsmanship in the previous game and practices leading up to the next game.

▸ Have a meeting with Molly and her parents where Molly is responsible for discussing player and team expectations about arguing and fighting and what those actions do to team spirit.

▸ If you determine that Molly is not an asset to the team, remove her for one game; if the behavior persists, remove her for the entire season (if that is an option in the league's policies).

Checklist 2.1 Personal Inventory

Rate yourself in regard to the following statements.

	Consistently	Inconsistently	Never
I am tuned in to individuals' needs and interests.	☐	☐	☐
I am enthusiastic when I teach.	☐	☐	☐
I am flexible in my approach to promoting responsible behavior.	☐	☐	☐
I am personable, putting individuals at ease.	☐	☐	☐
I strive to know my participants individually.	☐	☐	☐

Checklist 2.2 Creating a Healthy Learning Atmosphere

Rate yourself in regard to the following statements.

	Consistently	Inconsistently	Never
I catch individuals being good.	☐	☐	☐
I expect individuals to follow my directions.	☐	☐	☐
I keep my cool and address problems quickly.	☐	☐	☐
I focus on the behavior, not on the individual.	☐	☐	☐
My behavior toward and treatment of individuals is consistent.	☐	☐	☐
I do what I say I'm going to do.			
I check for compliance.	☐	☐	☐
I respond the same way to the same behavior.	☐	☐	☐
I encourage consistency among all physical education staff members.	☐	☐	☐
I use positive tools such as varying tasks, playing music, and using physical activity to help individuals relax.	☐	☐	☐
I use a continuum of appropriate styles.	☐	☐	☐

Checklist 2.3 Negative Communication Approaches

Rate yourself in regard to the following statements.

	Consistently	Inconsistently	Never
I refrain from making comparisons between individuals.	☐	☐	☐
I avoid making idle threats.	☐	☐	☐
I avoid sarcasm.	☐	☐	☐
I refrain from humiliating individuals.	☐	☐	☐
I avoid overstating the behavior problem.	☐	☐	☐

Checklist 2.4 Effective Counseling

Rate yourself in regard to the following statements.

	Consistently	Inconsistently	Never
I seek to determine who owns the problem.	☐	☐	☐
I choose my words carefully.	☐	☐	☐
I offer guidance rather than advice.	☐	☐	☐
I ask open-ended questions to help individuals with their own problems.	☐	☐	☐
I allow individuals to make their own decisions as to how to meet my long-term expectations.	☐	☐	☐
I clarify what I think individuals are saying instead of playing psychoanalyst and making assumptions.	☐	☐	☐
I deal with disruptive behaviors as they occur instead of using diversionary tactics.	☐	☐	☐

3

Designing a Proactive Management Plan

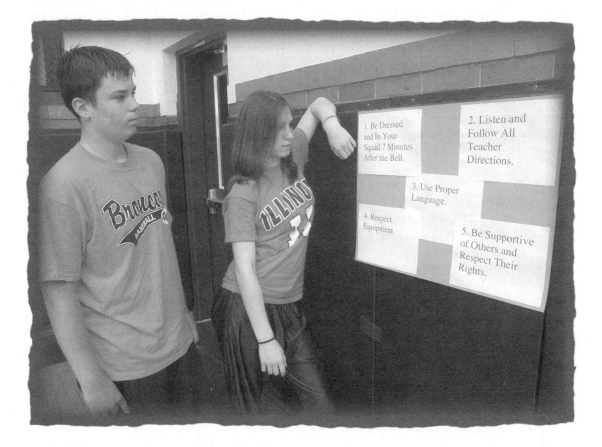

*P*hysical activity professionals who fail to plan
plan to fail!

Ms. Danielle was about to start her second year of teaching physical education at Kennedy High School. What a difference a year had made! When she began teaching, she had assumed all students would enter her program motivated to learn. Because she had started the school year with no real management plan to promote learning, she got off on the wrong foot with her students. She spent the majority of the year struggling to gain control over the class. But during the summer she had taken a behavior management workshop at a local university. Based on what she learned in the workshop, she designed a proactive management plan with clear rules and routines that included strategies for students to enter and leave the locker room, to enter the gym and meet in designated teams, to perform the warm-up routine in assigned groups while developing their own routines, and to transition smoothly from activity to activity. She also planned to develop rules and routines that allowed students to take more responsibility for their behavior, such as having rotating team leaders who help take attendance, distribute and collect equipment, and officiate games. During the orientation session, or the first 2 weeks of school, Ms. Danielle had decided to post the rules and routines on the gym bulletin board, discuss them with the students, and have the students practice them. In addition, throughout the school year she would review all management procedures with her students periodically when needed. A proactive management plan would be even more critical this year than last, as the number of students in most of her classes had increased. But this year, she was ready!

Many times physical activity professionals may be tempted to blame young people for disruptive behavior and respond with corrective methods. Inappropriate behavior, however, is often the result of boredom. When individuals are waiting in line to participate, do not have enough equipment to practice skills, or have already mastered the skills they are expected to practice, they understandably lose interest. Fortunately, you can plan activities to prevent the majority of inappropriate behavior.

WHY A PROACTIVE APPROACH?

Being proactive means taking the time to consider the strategies you need to establish to help participants understand what is expected of them. Effective instruction is based on sound management. Because you are more likely to encounter disruptive behavior during management time than instruction or activity time, it is important to develop a proactive management plan. An effective management plan will decrease behavior problems, increase learning time, and promote both the group's and your enjoyment of the physical activity program. But effective management does not just happen! You cannot manage a group by simply hoping that behavior problems will not arise. You must proactively plan learning experiences. Indeed, planning and organizing are the keys to preventing behavior problems. One method for preventing behavior problems is to design a proactive management plan that helps prevent inappropriate behavior from starting or escalating (Rink, 2002; Siedentop and Tannehill, 2000).

Physical activity environments are complex, dynamic settings. For example, instruction is often conducted in large open spaces such as gyms and playing fields with the activities, movement patterns, and equipment constantly changing. A connection between the environment and the content is important. Initially you may need to structure the environment by closely directing the activity, but ultimately the goal is for individuals to act responsibly with less direction or monitoring. Without establishing minimal levels of control in your instructional setting, it will be difficult for participants to move to greater self-responsibility (Rink, 2002).

Effective physical activity professionals are good managers who anticipate problems before they arise and go into the setting with a behavior plan, ready to react with consistency to any behavioral issues. Proactive management works best if you carefully consider and integrate your own teaching, coaching, or leadership style; unique individual and group needs; and the instructional environment. You must organize, deliver, and monitor your program with these factors in mind (Charles, 2002). In this chapter, we'll show you how to do this by providing proactive management strategies you can incorporate into a plan that will meet the unique needs of your group and the many situations that may arise in physical activity.

EVALUATING BEHAVIORS

The first step in developing a proactive management plan is to identify the behaviors you want your group to exhibit and not exhibit. You can start by asking yourself questions:

What behaviors will bring order to the program?

What behaviors may present problems?

What behaviors will enhance performance?

Use these questions to help clarify your thinking and guide your development of a proactive management plan.

To help you become more aware of how your behavior management plan may cause behavior problems and ineffective learning, use checklist 3.1 (see page 53) to identify strong and weak areas in your instruction. Determine whether you are consistent in your approach. You may find that you need to make your teaching, coaching, or recreation environment safer, more supportive, and more engaging; or you may recognize that you are inconsistent in explaining to the group your expectations and consequences. By identifying the problem areas provided in the checklist, you can begin to design a proactive management plan that works for you. The key is to identify potential problems and then develop a plan. The checklist will help you get started, and examples are provided later in this chapter (see Managerial Tasks starting on page 44) that will help you determine how much time you are spending on management.

Once you have identified potential problem areas, you can begin to formulate a solution bank consisting of a list of strategies about how you may handle potential problems. This allows you to use self-reflection and develop a simple list of if–then statements. For example, "If two players begin to argue during soccer practice, then I will separate them and ask them to work out their differences before they continue practicing." Another example is, "If participants have difficulty moving from one activity to the next, then I will provide more clearly defined signals." This way you can go into a situation prepared. If you are unprepared, your only solution is to "shoot from the hip and hope for the best" (Hellison, 2003, p. 83). Based on the if–then method, examine the list of preinstructional and instructional factors in checklist 3.2 on page 55.

PROACTIVE MANAGEMENT PLAN

The proactive management plan has three phases: preinstruction, instruction, and evaluation (see figure 3.1). During the preinstruction phase, you develop and mentally rehearse the management plan. During actual instruction you create a positive instructional atmosphere that promotes learning. At the same time, you implement your management plan, having your group practice it in the same way that they practice new motor skills. Finally, you evaluate the plan to determine its overall effectiveness. Proactive management is an ongoing process, so once you establish the management plan, you must maintain it and periodically review it (Rink, 2002). In the upcoming sections, we'll discuss each of the phases of proactive management plans.

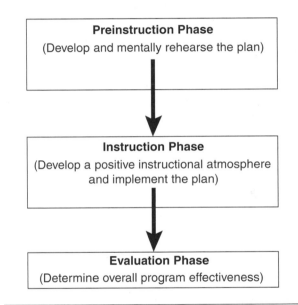

Figure 3.1 Three phases of a proactive management plan.

Preinstruction

The preinstruction phase occurs before the program begins. For example, you can design consistent drills and routines for individuals to follow when they first arrive at the physical activity setting. By leaving nothing to chance, you can avoid potential problems. Let's look at how to plan for different situations.

Safety

Safety must be your first and foremost consideration. Always arrange the environment so that participation is safe and all participants are in your line of sight. For example, establish boundaries to distinguish where it is appropriate and not appropriate for individuals to go. To better understand each individual and to prevent management and safety problems, identify those who have medical needs such as asthma, diabetes, or seizures. Be aware of individuals with special needs (i.e., takes medication, has difficulty getting along with others). Use this information not to label individuals, but to raise your awareness of any potential needs or emergencies. This will help you anticipate what might happen, allowing you to avoid injuries. It is also important to prepare the group in advance so that everyone knows what to do in case an injury occurs. For example, if an athlete on your team has asthma, explain to the team what asthma is and what procedures to follow if the athlete has an asthma episode during practice. To learn more about how you can help an individual with medical needs, contact the individual's parents and have them provide you with necessary medical information. Keep this information on file. Also speak with these participants individually. They may have a suggestion you didn't think of.

Although getting to know the special needs of individuals requires extra time, we guarantee it's worth the effort. More discussion regarding special needs will be presented in chapter 8. In schools, physical educators can check with the school nurse, ask other teachers who work with the student, or read the students' file. Remember, however, that this information is confidential. Coaches and recreation specialists can ask parents for this information.

Developmentally Appropriate Activities

Plan activities that are appropriate based on the individuals' chronological and developmental ages, then increase the degree of difficulty so as to challenge but not frustrate them. This will help cut down on potential behavior problems. Provide activities the individuals can relate to and find interesting. You might even ask them what types of physical activity they enjoy.

Check with your school district, coaching organization, or recreation program regarding national standards, curriculum guides, and coaching manuals. For example, the National Association for Sport and Physical Education (NASPE) (2004) has developed K through 12 national physical education standards for teachers to follow. These standards specify knowledge and skills by grade

level. The U.S. Department of Health and Human Services (1997) has developed national guidelines for coaches, and community sport organizers can follow those guidelines that include developmentally appropriate activities. The National Recreation and Park Association (NRPA) and the American Association for Leisure and Recreation Council on Accreditation (AALR) (2004) have developed standards and evaluative criteria for baccalaureate programs in recreation, park resources, and leisure services to assure sound practices among recreation specialists.

Facilities and Equipment

Consider the facilities, equipment, and space you will need for each activity. Be aware that certain activities require more resources than others. There is less opportunity for disruptive behavior when all facilities and equipment are accessible and everyone is on task and active. If you primarily instruct outdoors, have a backup plan for inclement weather.

The condition or appearance of the facilities and equipment can affect the group's behavior. Hazardous, disorganized, and unclean facilities do not reinforce good work habits. Periodically check facilities for potential hazards, such as holes in the playing field. Make sure that your facilities are neat and well lit and include interesting displays. For example, at a community-based recreation center a bulletin board can attractively display the components of health-related physical fitness and a chart showing the minutes participants exercised each week.

Equipment may break during use, resulting in falls, cuts, or other injuries. Be sure to check all equipment periodically and fix or replace anything that is worn or broken. Your efforts will help create a safe and positive atmosphere.

To expedite setup and instruction as well as cut down on confusion and potential behavior problems, clearly identify and carefully store equipment for easy access. The storage area is also a good place to keep first aid equipment. During orientation discuss appropriate procedures for accessing, setting up, and storing equipment, and periodically review and practice these procedures (see figure 3.2).

Instruction

Once you've laid the groundwork with preplanning so that the program will run more smoothly, it's time for actual instruction. The instructional phase

Figure 3.2 Proper storage of equipment is an important part of program planning.

includes all the tasks that occur once individuals enter the physical activity setting; it's when you put your plan into action.

Orientation

The first step of the instructional phase is an orientation that includes a discussion on rules and routines. In an effective orientation individuals learn what you expect of them. Also consider writing a letter discussing your program's expectations that needs to be signed by the parents and returned. In your letter, go over rules and routines of the program such as those discussed throughout the remainder of this chapter. For more information refer to the letter in figure 2.10 on page 29.

A good orientation lays the groundwork for your management plan and sets the stage for instruction with clearly defined rules and routines that will help you make your expectations understood. Early orientation to the rules and routines is a worthy investment of time because it will save instructional time later. Orientation starts during the first day and is repeated when needed, especially during the first 2 to 3 weeks. This sets the tone and expectations for the rest of the time you will spend with the group. The rules and routines need to be internalized by all participants, and this will take time (Boyce, 2003). Younger children may need more orientation time than older children.

Rules

Rules identify appropriate and inappropriate behaviors and situations where certain behaviors are acceptable or unacceptable. In other words, rules identify a range of behaviors you want the individuals to consistently exhibit, behaviors that are the building blocks of your program. Certain rules are situational and may have a range of meanings. For example, cooperation can mean putting equipment away, but it can also mean cooperating with a classmate during a game. Other rules can be specific such as asking permission before entering the recreational fitness facility.

You will usually need to instruct individuals on what each rule means in specific situations. When you neglect to clearly communicate rules, the individuals don't learn the rules until their actions are unacceptable (Charles, 2002). Instead, create a more effective instructional climate by stating your rules clearly the first day during orientation and by reviewing and practicing the rules as needed. Consider stating the rules in a way that the individuals can relate to, such as in a song.

Designing Rules

Rules need to encourage individuals to be responsible for their own behavior rather than simply control behavior. When designing rules, consider

BEST PRACTICES FOR DESIGNING RULES

- Involve individuals in the development of the rules when possible.
- Decide on clearly stated acceptable and unacceptable behaviors.
- Keep the rules simple and to the point with concrete examples.
- Make no more than five or six rules, as too many will cause confusion.
- State all rules in a positive, concrete, functional, and age-appropriate manner.

- Develop general rules that are flexible, covering different situations.
- Include clear consequences that are connected to each rule.
- Only develop rules that you can enforce and are reasonable.
- Develop specific rules for specific situations.
- Be sure individuals understand the rules and consequences.

Figure 3.3   When designing rules, choose the ones that work best for you, your group, and your setting.

your organization's policies in addition to identifying the specific behaviors you want individuals to exhibit. After thoughtful consideration, design rules that can be clearly understood. Ask yourself what is important to your program's success and what behaviors you want the group to demonstrate. For example, behaviors that may form the foundation of your rules include following safety guidelines, listening to instruction, showing respect for equipment, doing your best, and cooperating with others. These behaviors need to be developed into rules that work best for you, your group, and your setting. Figure 3.3 provides the best practices for designing rules.

Design rules for the entire group to follow; do not single out one particular individual. Never establish consequences that you cannot carry out. Provide the group with concrete reasons why each rule is necessary. For example, you might say, "You must listen when I am giving instructions so that you will know what to do," or "It is important to take care of equipment so that it will last for all of us to use." When possible involve participants in developing the rules. Individuals who feel ownership of the rules are more likely to follow them. In addition, it is always a good idea to send a list of the rules home to have the parents read, sign, and return. This makes parents part of your management team right from the start.

Large-format printers can be used to allow physical activity professionals to create large poster displays of the rules. These types of printers can be purchased or you can go to a commercial store. Many large-format printers are compatible with

software that can create and print different fonts and clip art (LaMaster, 2003). For durability be sure to laminate the poster (figure 3.4).

Figures 3.5, 3.6, and 3.7 are examples of rules that are appropriate in different physical activity settings. All rules are stated positively, telling the individuals what they can do rather than what they

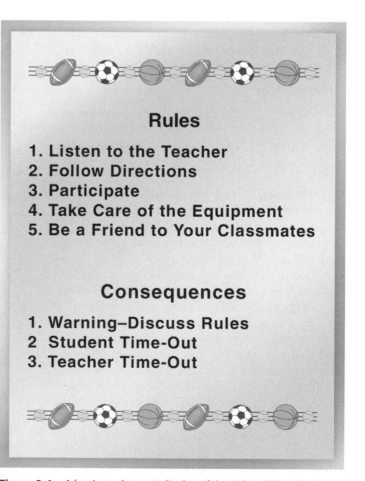

Figure 3.4   A laminated poster display of the rules will last longer.

can't. Rules that start with "Don't" are negative and convey a restrictive message. The Creating a Positive Climate for Learning section of PE Central (www.PECentral.com) provides additional sample rules.

Implementing Rules

It is one thing to develop rules but quite another to implement them. Discussing and posting the rules are no guarantee they will be followed. For many individuals each rule is a new behavior that must be practiced, similar to learning a motor skill (Rink, 2002). Reinforce those individuals who follow the rules by providing frequent praise and feedback. One way to check for understanding is to have the individual state the rules to you or ask questions about them. Another method is to role-play or demonstrate examples of appropriate and inappropriate responses to each rule. For example, place a basketball on the floor between your feet and say, "While I am speaking, any equipment you have should be right here on the floor between your feet." Then pick up the ball and bounce it while you explain, "It's hard to hear my instructions over this noise. That is why it is necessary to keep the ball on the floor while I'm giving instructions." Finish by placing the ball back between your feet and remarking, "Now, isn't it easier to hear what I am saying?"

For rules to be effective, you must consistently apply them to all individuals and follow through immediately with consequences for not following rules. Following are helpful hints for implementing rules:

- Post rules in an area where everyone can see them, such as the locker room or bulletin board. If you do not have a facility you can use a portable dry-erase board or equipment cart.
- Provide pictures of rules for nonreaders.
- Enforce the rules by providing consequences the first time, every time.
- Practice and review rules periodically.
- Reinforce individuals who follow the rules.
- Inform parents and others of the rules.
- Be consistent, calm, and nonjudgmental when implementing consequences.

Consequences

For rules to be effective, consequences must be connected to them. You should present consequences at the same time as the rules. If possible, have the group agree on the rules and con-

sequences. Most individuals are willing to accept consequences for inappropriate behavior if they feel they are being treated fairly (Pangrazi, 2004). If individuals cannot count on consistency, they will consider it a game to see if they can get away with breaking the rules. Remember, consequences are designed not be punitive but to ensure that rules are followed (Schempp, 2003).

Developing a continuum of consequences will provide flexibility. For example, for the first offense, warn the individuals and discuss your expectations with them as well as the consequences if they continue to act inappropriately. Have the individuals explain the rule and the correct behavior. After the second offense, give the individuals a time-out in a designated thinking or cool-off place for 1 minute while they watch the group. For the third offense, take the individuals aside from the group and have a discussion. During the discussion avoid confrontation, remembering to make eye contact, stay calm, and not be judgmental. More information on communicating effectively and the use of consequences is provided in chapter 6.

Routines

Routines are predetermined operational procedures that guide behaviors. Any task or situation that is repeated frequently needs to be made into a routine. Developing clear routines means fewer decisions to make and fewer repeated explanations of common tasks or situations (Schempp, 2003). Effective managers develop routines such as those listed in figure 3.8. Other routines are discussed in the managerial tasks section on page 44 and in checklist 3.2 on page 55.

As with rules, post routines and explain them clearly, providing examples and plenty of practice. Have the group follow these routines until they become automatic. Be sure to explain who, what, where, when, and how to each participant (Sanders, 1989). For example, "Each player (who) must line up for kicking drills (what) in the squad line (where) when practice starts (when) and use the instep kick (how)."

When participants follow established routines, you can devote more time to what is important: improving performance and increasing learning. Provide positive, specific feedback to those who correctly follow routines. This creates a ripple effect, influencing others to follow the routines as well. With praise and practice, you'll find that you only need to tell the individuals which routine to follow before proceeding. Eventually the group

Rules Chart

Actively listen.

Be safe with equipment and around others.

Cooperate and support the rights of others.

Do your best.

Figure 3.5 ABCD rules chart.

Modified from PE Central and Kent Kuelper, Spring Hill Elementary School, Anchorage School District, Anchorage, AK.

RESPECT Rules

Recognition gained properly by raising your hand, listening to the teacher, and following instructions.

Equipment used on the teacher's signal. The equipment is for you; treat it carefully.

Stay on task to have a safe and positive class.

Practice skills as best you can to become skillful movers.

Encourage each other to do your best and support each other with positive statements.

Considerate of others' feeling through good sportsmanship.

Together we learn and become our best.

Figure 3.6 RESPECT rules.

Reprinted, by permission, from T. Moone, 1997, "Teaching students with respect," *Teaching Elementary Physical Education* 8(5): 16-18.

Team Sport Rules

- Be on time and dressed for practice.

- Contact the coach if you will miss or be late to practice or games.

- Be safe with others and equipment.

- Help with all equipment setup and cleanup.

- Give your best effort and play fair.

- Respect and encourage your teammates and players on other teams.

Figure 3.7 Team rules.

Common Physical Activity Routines

1. Check off your name on the attendance sheet when first arriving to practice.

5. Move from one area to the next area on the signal and within the 10-second countdown.

2. Before starting the warm-up activities, read the day's instructions on the board and take your journal from the crate.

6. Put equipment on the floor between your feet during instructions.

3. Walk directly to your squad or team area.

7. Signal a group before entering their space to retrieve a ball.

4. Rotate clockwise (to the right) when changing practice stations.

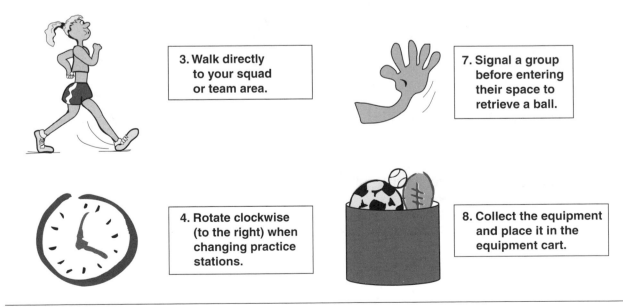

8. Collect the equipment and place it in the equipment cart.

Figure 3.8   Sample routines.

needs to be responsible for following certain routines automatically, for example, quickly moving to their squads when entering the gym or playing field without being reminded. Allow individuals to help with routines by making them responsible for certain assignments, such as being a squad or team leader (see figure 3.9), spotter, official, or equipment monitor. Remember to rotate helpers every few weeks.

Managerial Tasks

This section will look at common managerial tasks in the sequence in which they usually occur (see checklist 3.2). A managerial task is defined as the operational procedures to follow to complete the organizational and behavioral aspects of all the common tasks conducted in the physical activity setting. No matter how much structure and direction you provide, when your directions are unclear, behavior problems may develop. The key is to structure activities so that they proceed smoothly, maintaining momentum from one activity to the next. In general, the greater the amount of movement choice, the greater the need for managerial tasks. Often it is not just one managerial task but the combination of different tasks that causes confusion (Siedentop and Tannehill, 2000).

The following managerial tasks are sequenced in the order they will most likely occur and are designed to allow more time for what is important: instruction. The amount of time, structure, and assistance will vary from individual to individual and group to group. For example, a high school elective physical education class or a sport team may include individuals who are more motivated and are therefore able to handle less structure. But don't confuse less structure with less appropriate behavior; instead, expect all individuals to behave responsibly when you give less direction (Rink, 2002).

Locker-Room Procedures and Dressing for Activity

When necessary, establish appropriate locker-room procedures for showering, use of lockers and locks, and handling excuses for not dressing. For example, in one middle school physical education program, the majority of the first week is used for orientation, during which the teacher explains the benefits of physical education and clearly defines all class rules and routines including locker-room procedures. Students sign an agreement (to be kept by the instructor) that they understand the rules and are tested on all rules and routines to make sure they understand them (Summerford, 1996).

Squad- or Team-Leader Responsibilities

1. Face everyone in your squad so that they can all see you.

2. Provide hand signals to keep your squad organized.

3. Provide clear directions using a voice all can hear and understand.

4. Use correct form when demonstrating all activities.

Figure 3.9 Squad- or team-leader responsibilities.

Your goal is for each individual to be as physically active and involved in the program as possible. Individuals who are not dressed and participating are not only missing physical activity benefits, they may be causing behavior problems as well. In the Trenches provides the rationale for dressing for physical education at Hartsville High School in South Carolina.

Entering and Exiting

Establish a routine for entering and exiting the instructional area, one that establishes control and lets the individuals know where and when to enter and exit. Insist that all individuals enter and exit the setting in an orderly fashion. For example, one elementary school has a blue line that students follow from the classrooms to the gymnasium door

IN THE TRENCHES

Dressing for Physical Education
Murray Mitchell, Associate Professor, University of South Carolina, and Pat Hewitt, Hartsville Teacher and 2001-2002 NASPE Teacher of the Year

Students who don't dress for class are more than just a nuisance. These students often hang out near the activity space while the rest of the class carries on with assigned tasks. The consequence for nonparticipation is sometimes a loss of points resulting in a reduction of the final grade. Some resourceful teachers identify parallel challenges for students who haven't dressed, such as writing about the history of the activity, answering questions about some aspect of the activity, officiating, helping move equipment around, and so on. For the most part, however, students who do not dress for participation are not involved in the main purpose of the lesson, and this is a problem. Success in society involves learning the importance of fulfilling responsibilities.

Nonparticipants are a distraction to the teacher, other students, and the smooth operation of the activity. Nonparticipants are also at risk for injury to themselves or others and are thus a legal liability due to the reduced level of supervision that occurs when a teacher's attention must be split between actively engaged students and students who are sitting out. Another concern occurs when students can pass classes without demonstrating any learning, which threatens the continued presence of physical education programs in schools.

Coping strategies for teachers include documenting the degree of nondressing, gaining administrative and parent support by informing the principal and guidance staff of the benefits of physical education, implementing a policy to deal with students who don't dress to participate, and notifying parents and students at the beginning of the program that not dressing is direct disobedience to a teacher that will result in immediate removal from the class and possible failure in the course. Teachers must make every effort to reach out to students and understand their resistance to dressing for class. For example, they might give the students the opportunity to use clean "rental" clothing (shoes, shorts, shirt). Once students are present, teachers are responsible for designing and delivering defensible programs with goals for which students are accountable. Any necessary accommodations are implemented. See figure 3.10 for Hartsville's list of physical education rules.

HARTSVILLE HIGH SCHOOL PHYSICAL EDUCATION RULES

1. All students are expected to dress and participate every day of physical education class. Students who do not bring workout clothes may rent shirts, shoes, and shorts for a nominal fee ($.50) from their teacher. Students who choose not to dress for class will be removed from class immediately and cited for direct disobedience to a teacher.

2. Each student will be graded as follows: cognitive 30%, skills 30%, fitness 30%, affective 10%. Each time a student does not dress or participate completely with the class, he or she will lose 7% from the 9-week average.

3. Each student is to be dressed and seated in the assigned area by the time the gym clock counts down to 0. Failure to do so will count as a tardy. Each tardy will result in a loss of 2% from the 9-week average.

4. Students are reminded not to bring any valuables to the gym. If they do so, it is at their own risk.

5. Students with a doctor's excuse must dress for class unless physically disabled (short-term disabilities). To receive credit, students will be given a different assignment.

6. Dressing consists of PE shirt, red shorts, and shoes (tennis, basketball, running, or aerobic). When the weather is cold, students may wear red, black, or gray sweats.

7. Students should respect other students, teachers, and staff at all times.

8. Students will take the Fitnessgram, a fitness test given three times per year (August, October, and December). Students must meet minimum age and gender requirements.

9. Students are responsible for these rules, school rules, and general command.

   First offense.................Warning
   Second offense..............Lunch detention
   Third offense................Phone call to parents
   Fourth offense or more....Referral to the office

Direct disobedience will result in immediate removal from class and referral to the office for in-school suspension. A parent–teacher conference will be required in order for students to be allowed to return to class.

Parent signature _____   Date_____

Student signature _____   Date_____

Figure 3.10   Hartsville High School physical education rules.

Reprinted with permission from the August 2002 *Journal of Physical Education, Recreation & Dance,* a publication of the American Alliance for Health, Physical Education, Recreation and Dance, 1900 Association Dr., Reston, VA 20191.

and a red line that they follow to exit and go back to their classroom.

The routine for entering the setting can set the tone for the rest of the session. For example, upon entrance assign individuals to a designated area determined by squad or warm-up number. Post information and directions regarding the day's activity or practice on the bulletin board or dry-erase board. Start the session on time and expect all individuals to promptly begin participating in the activity.

At the end of the session gather everyone together for closure and a summary of what they learned. Check for understanding among the group. Relaxation activities may also be an effective way to end the session (see chapter 8). In addition, as they leave, participants can discuss their behavior and performance with you.

Attendance

Don't waste precious instructional time taking attendance. Instead, take attendance while individuals are warming up or are involved in the initial activity. Individuals can also sign in or check in once they enter the area. Or, you can have individuals report to squad leaders who are responsible for taking attendance. Another option is to use a tag board where students turn over their tags when they come into the area so that you can look at the open spots to see who is absent. To keep accurate records and save time, you can use a number system in which, for example, an individual who is number 24 on the roll-call floor or wall area is also number 24 in the attendance book. Finally, you can use a handheld computer for taking attendance. For more information on using handheld computers for taking attendance, go to www.pesoftware.com.

Initial Activity

Avoid lengthy discussions about what the individuals will be doing. Instead get them involved right away in the first activity. For example, have individuals enter the area and immediately begin a warm-up jog, go to exercise stations, or perform an activity they enjoy. This will help promote interest and establish a positive tone for the rest of the activities that follow (Graham, 2001). Individuals who are waiting for the activity to begin can become bored, which can lead to behavior problems. Directions and instructions should be given in small doses, no longer than 30 to 45 seconds, where you focus on one or two key points at time. You can alternate short instructional episodes with activity (Pangrazi, 2004). Give only the necessary directions to get started and give more information as needed while individuals are performing the activities. For example, when players enter the practice field, provide them with a familiar activity that requires little instruction, such as a warm-up routine or a previously learned drill. Choose an activity that the group feels fairly comfortable performing and can do with little instruction. Established routines are effective initial activities. For example, in Mr. Carman's middle school classes, students know without being reminded that they must enter the gym and get in their assigned squads for attendance and that while attendance is being taken by the squad leader, each group must work together to perform all the warm-up exercises at five different fitness stations. Each week Mr. Carman posts new fitness activities or routines for the stations based on student input and his own objectives.

Signals

Using a signal is one of the most effective methods you can use to start, stop, or get everyone's undivided attention (Pangrazi, 2004). With a signal there is no need to yell and repeat directions. Whatever signal you choose, individuals must be able to easily hear or see it. This is especially important when they perform activities while turned away from your voice. Signals must be used consistently and with reinforcement for paying attention or a consequence for not paying attention. In general, only give the signal once and do not give individuals more than 5 seconds to respond before applying a consequence.

Signals are especially important for individuals who have difficulty stopping an activity to listen to instructions or transitioning from one activity to the next. Without clear signals, the group may become confused. Signals also need to be age-appropriate. Teach younger children to move into a "frozen" position when you give the signal. For example, you might tell them, "When I say 'Surf, freeze, and stand like a surfer,' be ready to listen to instructions." Have groups practice reducing the time it takes to freeze when you give the signal. You can also have students raise a hand if they are listening to your instructions, or you can make a game out of it by stating, "Let's see how quickly we can freeze. Our best time so far has been 4 seconds." You can even have individuals suggest signals or vote on their own signal.

Other examples of signals that effectively capture a group's attention are a whistle, tambourine, raised hand above the head, scarf tossed into the air, or music. The signal may depend on the location. For example, in a larger outdoor space you could use a whistle or drum, while indoors a voice command may be effective. For older individuals, the signal might be a hand clap and raising your hand. The number of claps can correspond to the number of the squad you wish to signal. For example, one clap could mean squad 1 moves to the next activity and two claps could mean squad 2 moves.

Transitions

One of the more challenging aspects of managing a group is when a change in activity, space, or equipment occurs. A clear transition with a signal helps reduce management time and allows the activity to run more smoothly. Try to think of ways you can reduce the number of transitions or avoid them altogether. However, younger children who may have difficulty performing one task for a long period of time may require more activities and thus more transitions.

Effective transition signals and directions are clear and concrete. Keep transitions simple, give one instruction at a time, and be brief and to the point. You can use equipment such as cones, poly spots, flags, arrows, and task cards to make transitions concrete with clear boundaries and traffic patterns. Have an area such as a circle in the middle of the setting where individuals know to go for the next transition. Only bring the group into the circle to change the activity when needed.

An example of a clear transition within an activity is for a task card at station 1 to read, "Perform volleys with your racket against the wall for 2 minutes while the music plays. When the music stops, put down your equipment and power walk to station 2." An example of a clear transition statement from one activity to the next is, "Perform the aerobic warm-up routine we practiced this past week. When you hear the tambourine, you have 5 minutes to jog outside and be on the soccer field in your teams, ready to play."

Certain individuals may require a warning signal a few minutes before the actual transition signal. For example, you may need to gain the attention of an individual with autism or a learning disability who has difficulty processing the information that a transition is coming. To avoid singling out the individual, you and the individual can work together to develop a discrete hand signal. For example, one finger in the air means a transition will occur in 1 minute.

For transitions with large groups, have them travel in teams or squads. To transition quickly from one activity to the next, recognize and reinforce only those individuals and squads who move quickly to the next activity rather than calling attention to those who are moving slowly. Select the most responsive individual or squad to model the behavior. This method is called catching them being good, or positive pinpointing, and is discussed in detail in chapter 5.

Equipment Distribution and Collection

Establish procedures for equipment distribution, use, exchange, and collection. For example, never leave basketballs in a bag in the middle of the gym floor for individuals to fight over; instead, carefully distribute the balls around the gym, giving everyone an equal opportunity to secure a ball. To better secure the balls so that they don't roll away, you can place a ball for each participant in a hula hoop. Spread the hoops around the perimeter of the instructional area. This provides access points to the equipment for quick and efficient distribution (figure 3.11). Another strategy is to assign squad leaders who are responsible for securing, distributing, and collecting equipment for each member of their squad.

When individuals first receive equipment, they need to know what to do with it. They may be too

© Human Kinetics

Figure 3.11   Providing several access points with adequate spacing for equipment will help alleviate potential behavior problems.

excited to hold the equipment and listen to your instructions at the same time, so don't ask for too much when you introduce new equipment, especially with young children. Give them time to practice with the equipment or assign a specific task to complete, and then have them put the equipment on the floor beside them while you give instructions. To regain their attention, provide an incentive. For example, say, "The first three who are on their poly spots with their equipment on the floor at their side will get to demonstrate the next skill."

Organizing Partners, Groups, or Teams

Not only does having individuals choose partners, groups, or teams waste time, it also can be embarrassing for some, which does not make for a positive atmosphere. Establish a rule that it is not okay to say no to another person who picks you as a partner (Graham, 2001). This is also a great time to have a group discussion on appreciating individual differences.

Develop and practice routines so that everyone can quickly and efficiently organize into partners, groups, or teams. For example, divide younger children into groups by birth month, favorite color, or clothes (short sleeves or long sleeves, collar or no collar). The Creating a Positive Learning Climate section of PE Central (www.PEcentral.com) provides many more ideas for choosing teams.

Group size and opportunity for learning are closely related. Decide if the activity is best taught individually, in partners, in small groups (up to six), or in large groups (more than seven). Give the criteria for grouping individuals a great deal of thought, taking into consideration ability, size, gender, ethnicity, and interest. Work to keep everyone active and don't place individuals in larger groups than necessary so they don't have to share equipment or wait for a turn (Rink, 2002).

The challenge with large groups is to put them in smaller teams of six or seven. Have each team develop a team name, handshake, and cheer. This can foster group spirit from the year's first class, practice, or meeting. Using teams or squads can also provide opportunities for leadership such as taking attendance, leading warm-ups, and distributing equipment (Glover and Anderson, 2003).

For example, at the beginning of each month's unit, teachers at Manzano High School create new squads by rotating the names on the class rosters. They rotate two names into a different squad, making sure each squad includes fairly equal numbers of males and females. At the same time, they choose a new squad leader and then post all updated information on the gym bulletin board. Occasionally for special events such as tournaments or for variety, the squad members change based on a meeting between squad leaders and the teacher. Team selection is confidential with discussion ending once squad leaders leave the meeting.

Formations

Waiting in line is a waste of time. Further, individuals who are actively involved and not standing in long lines are less likely to be disruptive. Keep formations short (no more than five individuals). Turn frequent formations such as stations, lines, triangles, squares, or circles into routines, which maximizes active time and thereby increases on-task behavior. Formations start with making sure individuals know what you want them to do. Be clear in your directions and state, "Form your squads in practice squares with players 10 feet apart and each square 15 feet from the next. Go!" (Siedentop and Tannehill, 2000).

Inadequate spacing among individuals can cause behavior problems. One way to manage the environment is to properly space equipment and individuals, especially when equipment is potentially hazardous, such as jump ropes and bats. This planning helps maintain a safe environment and keeps everyone on task.

If you use circle or line formations for certain drills or activities, mark with poly spots, cones, or flags where you want individuals or groups to stand and move. This will help reduce confusion and increase time on task. For example, when the first player in line leaves to begin a drill and is 5 feet away or reaches a designated cone, the next player may begin. In a recreational setting with a passing drill using a circle formation, participant 1 passes the ball to participant 2, who passes the ball to participant 3. Once participant 3 has caught the ball, participant 1 passes another ball to participant 2. With six participants per circle, two balls used simultaneously will keep all participants continuously practicing.

Another way to maximize practice time is to give all individuals their own equipment. This may not always be possible with large groups and a limited budget. But lack of equipment should not be an excuse for participants being off task. For example, during a basketball program Mr. Knewitz, the youth leader at the community center, divided his 42 participants into groups of 3 in triangle formations. In each group, one participant practiced dribbling a basketball, another practiced defensive sliding, and the third skipped rope. Every 3 minutes each member rotated to the next activity until they completed all three activities, taking a total of 9 minutes. This approach gave each participant a specific task, created variety, and stretched a limited equipment supply, all of which worked together to keep everyone on task.

Anticipating Potential Situations

With-it-ness, instructional proximity, hustle and prompts, and overlapping are all effective ways to proactively manage problems that may occur.

With-It-Ness

With-it-ness is defined as being so closely attuned to the individuals' actions that you can anticipate and prevent problems before they occur or become serious (Kounin, 1970). Keeping the entire group in your field of vision and being aware of what is happening is not only necessary for managing behavior, but it is necessary for safety as well. One effective procedure to use is "back to the wall," where you stand at the boundaries, such as at the walls of the gym or edge of the playing field, so you can better scan the area and see what is going on with the entire group. When you are in the middle you lose sight of 50% of the group (Graham, 2001).

Instructional Proximity

Certain facial expressions, eye contact, postures, or signals can let individuals know they are off task without you saying a word. They quickly, quietly, and effectively send the message to stop (Markos and Boyce, 1999). The physical activity professional can circulate among the group and casually move toward individuals who are being disruptive to help get them back on task. Proximity control can eliminate the ripple effect through which misbehavior spreads to other individuals. Another effective strategy is to use an individual's name and ask if they need assistance.

Hustles and Prompts

It takes skill and insight to keep an activity or practice session going while recognizing potential events that will disrupt the flow. Use verbal and nonverbal hustles or prompts to remind participants to remain on task or to quicken the pace. A verbal hustle or prompt with a time limit can convey a feeling of high learning expectations. For example, you might say, "Each time you rotate to a new skill station, you have 30 seconds to run a lap around the gym and be at your next assigned station!" This statement conveys high expectations and enthusiasm and is contagious, helping energize participants. Provide feedback and recognize those individuals and groups who hustle to meet the time requirement. An example of a nonverbal hustle or prompt is clapping your hands or blowing a whistle.

Overlapping

It is important to be able to remain focused on the activity and deal with unforeseen situations at the same time. Overlapping is the ability to attend to more than one task at a time (Charles, 2002). Examples of potential disruptions include participants arriving late to class or practice, having to change activity locations, or an individual acting out or getting hurt. Work to recognize and react quickly to disruptions and inappropriate behaviors before they escalate. Expect the unexpected and plan for it! From the start, train the group to demonstrate responsible behavior and continue with the activity on their own while you handle a disruption or problem.

Developing Personal Responsibility

Standard 5 of NASPE (2004) states that individuals need to exhibit responsible behavior that respects self and others in physical activity settings. To meet this standard, in lower elementary grades individuals must recognize rules, procedures, and safety. In the upper elementary levels, individuals learn to work independently, with partners, and in small groups. In middle school, adolescents become involved in creating rules and procedures that guide specific situations. High school students initiate responsible behavior, function independently and responsibly, and positively influence the behavior of others.

One strategy is to establish a partnership with your group and get them involved in the behavior management plan so that there is a feeling of ownership among all individuals in building the program (Siedentop and Tannehill, 2000). For example, as mentioned earlier, enlist students' help in establishing rules, routines, and other managerial tasks. Have the group design a chart that includes examples of what constitutes respect and responsibility. Respectful behaviors may include being willing to share equipment, taking turns, calling each other by name, and listening when someone is speaking. Examples of responsible behaviors may include taking good care of equipment, coming to practice on time, and answering for your own behavior (Hichwa, 1998).

Plan a hierarchy of responsible behaviors, moving from simple to more complex behaviors. For example, once individuals have mastered such skills as standing appropriately in squad formation, place them in situations that demand more responsibility, such as helping others by distributing equipment or being a peer tutor. An individual or a group earning the privilege of more responsibility will help motivate and reinforce appropriate behavior. With time and practice, individuals learn to interact and work independently in groups. For example, you can ask more mature individuals how they would prefer to work and learn tasks. The primary goal is to move toward self-management where they complete tasks individually or in groups. Throughout the book and specifically in chapter 7, we'll look closely at methods for developing personal and social responsibility and self-directed, responsible, and caring behaviors.

Evaluation

Once you have designed and implemented your proactive management plan, you need to evaluate its effectiveness. View your management plan as an ongoing process of evaluation and refinement, continually tailoring it to fit your situation. Use checklist 3.2 on page 55 to help you determine how much time you are spending on managerial tasks and episodes. Ask yourself, "Is more time spent on activity so that more learning can occur and less time spent on management tasks?" To find the answer to this question, you can videotape one of your sessions (make sure you have permission to videotape). Choose a group for which you feel you are spending too much time on management. Next watch the video with a stopwatch. Each time the group is involved in a management task, start the watch. When the management task is over, stop the watch. Do this throughout the entire session. Add up all the time you spent on management and calculate the percentage of management time in relation to the total session time. For more sophisticated ways to calculate how you are spending your time in a session, see works by Petray-Rowcliffe, Williams, Lavay, and Hakim-Butt (2002) and Siedentop and Tannehill (2000). In addition, Boyce (2003) explains how to use different instruments to evaluate specific behavior management issues such as how quickly you attend to inappropriate behavior and the amount of time spent in transitions.

SUMMARY

Effective physical activity professionals are good managers who anticipate problems before they occur and go into the setting with a plan. But individual needs vary and unforeseen circumstances occur, so temper consistency with flexibility, making your leadership both a science and an art. For example, in physical education you might use a more student-directed style for a mature or motivated class of students and provide them with more responsibility than you would for students who are more immature. In fact, you may have to use different management styles with different individuals in a group. Use checklist 3.1 to help you assess your overall approach.

A key to your program's success is an orientation period with implementation of class rules, routines, and consequences. When designing your rules and routines, keep in mind the general considerations we have discussed, but tailor them to meet the needs of your situation. When possible, involve the individuals in the design of the behavior management plan. Refer often to checklist 3.2 to make sure you stay on track.

Once your plan is in place, take time to mentally rehearse, verbally explain, and physically practice your plan with your group. The initial time and energy investment will pay off when individuals become engaged in appropriate instructional endeavors, thereby fostering learning. One final point: View your management plan as an ongoing process of evaluation and refinement, continually tailoring it to better fit your situation.

Perhaps the best proactive management method is to keep individuals on task and excited about the program. But even this will not guarantee that there will be no behavior problems. In chapters 4 through 8 we'll explore strategies and methods for managing more challenging behavior.

WHAT DO YOU THINK?

1. Think about your own teaching, coaching, or recreation leadership and list ways you prevent behavioral disruptions. Now list ways you may be contributing to class disruptions, whether directly or indirectly. Are you preventing or reinforcing inappropriate behavior by bringing attention to the undesirable behavior?

2. Mentally rehearse or outline on paper the preventive management routines discussed in this chapter, relating them to your situation. Use checklist 3.2 as a guide. For example, develop routines for entering and exiting the setting, starting the initial activity, establishing signals,

transitioning from one activity to the next, distributing and collecting equipment, organizing students into groups, using hustles and prompts, and handling disruptions. Develop any other routines unique to your situation and the needs of the individuals.

3. Think about effective physical activity professionals with whom you have worked. List some of their characteristics as an effective manager. What strategies did they use to help instruction flow well?

4. Organize a 2-week orientation session. What would you include in your session?

5. Define the terms *rules* and *routines.* How are the terms different? List important considerations when developing class rules and routines. Design an age-appropriate rules or routines chart for your group.

6. Ask yourself how quickly your participants handle transitions from one activity to the next. How well do you handle disruptive behavior? Videotape and evaluate a session to determine the answer.

CASE STUDIES

For each of the three case studies in chapter 1 on page 13, select methods described in this chapter and discuss in detail how you would implement each of the methods to manage the behavior. After you have developed your own methods, read the following suggestions, which are only some of the many creative ways you might apply the information covered in this chapter.

CASE 1
Hector, a Disruptive 3rd Grader

▸ Review the rules, routines, and consequences with Hector to make sure he understands them.

▸ Use clear signals (start and stop; transitions).

▸ Structure the setting (i.e., poly spot for Hector to stand on during warm-ups).

▸ Use proximity control by standing near Hector.

▸ Give Hector one direction at a time and have Hector repeat each direction.

▸ Assign a classmate as a buddy to assist Hector, especially with following directions.

▸ Establish a signal for Hector to give the teacher when he is becoming frustrated.

CASE 2
Ashante, an Instructor in Charge of Weight-Room Cleanup

▸ During the orientation session involve members in a discussion of weight-room safety and cleanup.

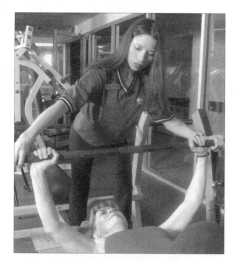

- ▸ Have the group help establish the rules, routines, and consequences for keeping the weight room safe and clean.
- ▸ Post the weight-room rules, routines, and consequences where all can see and review them periodically or when necessary. Quiz individuals on the rules.
- ▸ Post catchy slogans for weight-room safety and cleanup, such as "Be safe with the weights," throughout the facility.
- ▸ Assign and rotate squad leaders to oversee weight-room cleanup.

CASE 3
Molly, an Overly Aggressive Soccer Player

- ▸ Have the coach and players define good sportsmanship together and then establish team rules for it.
- ▸ Have players bring home the rules to discuss them with their parents and have their parents sign the rules for the players to return.
- ▸ Review and be sure Molly understands the league's policy for fighting and poor sports-

manship as well as team rules, routines, and consequences for behaviors.

- ▸ Develop a signal that Molly can give the coach when she is starting to get frustrated and feels like she is going to argue or fight with a teammate or opponent.
- ▸ Use proximity control when Molly begins to get frustrated.

Checklist 3.1   Evaluating Instructional Practices

Consider the following statements in regard to your participants. Then for each statement check the column that most accurately describes your current approach.

	Consistently	Inconsistently	Never
I explain to individuals why certain behaviors or expectations are necessary.	☐	☐	☐
I don't view inappropriate behavior as personally threatening.	☐	☐	☐
I interact positively with individuals.	☐	☐	☐
I learn and use each individual's name.	☐	☐	☐
I get the group's attention quickly and effectively.	☐	☐	☐
I reinforce individuals who act appropriately (i.e., catch them being good).	☐	☐	☐
I respect each individual's opinions and avoid sarcasm.	☐	☐	☐
I communicate realistic expectations to the group.	☐	☐	☐
I learn all I can about each individual.	☐	☐	☐
I provide developmentally appropriate activities for the group.	☐	☐	☐
I provide clear directions and check for understanding.	☐	☐	☐
I identify and monitor individuals who have medical problems and special needs.	☐	☐	☐
I encourage individuals to be responsible for their own behavior.	☐	☐	☐

(continued)

Consider the following statements in regard to your professionalism, then for each statement check the column that most accurately describes your current status or approach.

	Consistently	Inconsistently	Never
I am knowledgeable of subject content.	☐	☐	☐
I present information in a clear sequence that is easy for individuals to follow.	☐	☐	☐
I clearly communicate expectations and consequences.	☐	☐	☐
I am consistent in my expectations.	☐	☐	☐
I model appropriate behavior.	☐	☐	☐
I emphasize meeting instructional objectives.	☐	☐	☐
I am tuned in and closely monitor the group.	☐	☐	☐
I am enthusiastic with my group.	☐	☐	☐
I earn the individuals' trust and respect.	☐	☐	☐

Consider the following statements in regard to your learning environment, then for each statement check the column that most accurately describes your current approach.

	Consistently	Inconsistently	Never
I provide a warm, supportive learning climate.	☐	☐	☐
I design activities so that all individuals are actively involved.	☐	☐	☐
I design activities so that all individuals feel safe.	☐	☐	☐
I periodically check facilities and equipment for safety.	☐	☐	☐
I design activities to promote positive self-image.	☐	☐	☐
I design facilities to maximize learning.	☐	☐	☐
I have a backup plan for unforeseen circumstances or when facilities are not available.	☐	☐	☐
I match activities to individual needs.	☐	☐	☐
I orient individuals to management procedures, such as rules, routines, and transitions.	☐	☐	☐
I respond to inappropriate behavior quickly.	☐	☐	☐
I give directions quickly and keep the flow of activity moving.	☐	☐	☐
I design leadership activities that promote self-responsibility.	☐	☐	☐

Checklist 3.2   Proactive Planning

Mark when you have set and implemented your policy for each of the following aspects of your management plan.

Preinstruction Phase

___ Safety procedures

___ Developmentally appropriate activities

___ Facilities and equipment

Instruction Phase

___ Comprehensive orientation session

___ Rules with consequences

___ Routines and procedures

___ Locker-room procedures

___ Excuses from instruction

___ Entering and exiting the facility

___ Attendance

___ Instructional boundaries

___ Establishing the initial and closing activity

___ Signals

___ Transitions

___ Distribution and collection of equipment

___ Organization of partners, groups, and teams

___ Organization of formations

___ With-it-ness and instructional proximity

___ Hustles and prompts (i.e., I give directions quickly and keep the activity going)

___ Handling disruptions and unforeseen circumstances

___ Promoting self-responsible behaviors

Evaluation Phase

___ Total session time

___ Total time spent in management (add up all time spent in management)

___ Percentage of management time in relation to the total session (management time/total session time)

II

Exploring Behavior Management Approaches

When the proactive methods discussed in chapters 2 and 3 are ineffective, other behavior management approaches are needed. Part II examines numerous approaches that will help you manage behavior in physical activity settings. In chapter 4, we give you an introduction to the behavioral approach and describe the behavior-change process, including how to select, observe, and analyze a behavior and how to implement an appropriate behavioral intervention. Chapter 5 delves deeper into the behavioral approach as we explore ways to maintain and increase desirable behaviors using reinforcement methods. In chapter 6, we conclude our review of the behavioral approach by discussing how to decrease or redirect inappropriate behaviors through the prudent application of corrective methods. In chapter 7, we look at the humanistic approach, including responsibility, conflict resolution, and self-evaluation methods. In chapter 8, we discuss different biophysical approaches, including how to deal with stress-related behaviors, behavioral disabilities, behaviors modified by medications, and nutritional issues. In chapter 9, we help you examine yourself in light of all you've learned in chapters 1 through 8. We show you how to lay a foundation for effective behavior management by following a 10-step process. Along with our suggestions for how to complete these tasks, we offer personal insights gleaned from our experiences. Think of this as a conversation in which we discuss the problems we face as physical activity professionals. As each situation arises think about how you would approach it based on what you have learned in this text. The goal is to design a behavior management program to fit your unique personality, circumstances, and participant needs.

Behavioral Approach

*I*n nature there are neither rewards nor punishments: there are consequences.

Robert G. Ingersoll, 1895

Ms.Cabraal,a student teacher,and Dr.Sumner,her university cooperating teacher,met to discuss a lesson Ms.Cabraal had just taught to one of her 7th-grade physical education classes. Dr. Sumner told Ms. Cabraal,"Overall the lesson went well today. Compared to the first time I observed your teaching 8 weeks ago, student activity time has certainly increased and the time you spend on management has decreased. Transitions between activities are clear and easy for the students to follow. You are addressing students more often by name and making more positive statements to them. I could tell the students understood and enjoyed the new drills and activities you incorporated into today's lesson. I attribute these positive changes to your increased organizational skills."

Ms. Cabraal smiled and said, "Thanks. I've been working on getting my lessons better organized on paper, and this has helped me with my class management and the ability to transition from one activity to the next. I'm also working hard to be consistent in having students follow the class rules. Things are starting to come together, and the students are feeling more comfortable with me."

Then Dr. Sumner asked about Steven, a student who talked out of turn quite a bit during the lesson.

Ms. Cabraal's smile quickly turned into a frown. "I've told him repeatedly that when others are speaking, he is to listen. Last week I even gave him a warning and a time-out, but it didn't seem to matter. In fact, he started making faces at the class while he was in time-out. He's a real pain!"

Dr. Sumner responded, "Sounds like the strategy you're using with the rest of the class is not working with Steven. Why don't you think back to the times he has talked out of turn and see if there's a pattern? Based on what you've told me and what I observed today, it seems like he's speaking out to get attention. As soon as you can have a meeting with Steven, get to know him better and find out what kinds of activities he likes. Perhaps have him tell you some of the rewards, class activities, or privileges he would like to earn. Remember, be positive but firm with him. Be sure to give him clear, definable examples of the way he's speaking out of turn so that he recognizes the problem behavior. From there, you can begin to map out a management plan with methods to reduce the number of times Steven talks out of turn. After you've developed your plan, come by my office and we can discuss it before you present it to Steven."

Ms. Cabraal replied, "Okay, I'll try."

In recent years, the behavioral approach has helped physical activity professionals promote responsible behavior, thereby promoting performance in physical education (Siedentop and Tannehill, 2000), sport (Weinberg and Gould, 2003), and recreation (Datillo and Murphy, 1987). This approach is the most widely accepted method of intervention used in physical activity settings today (Weinberg and Gould, 2003).

Understanding the principles of the behavioral approach can help you systematically manage behavior in physical activity settings. It will also help you increase the motivation of the individuals in your program. This approach allows you to identify behaviors to be changed, measure behavior, implement interventions, and evaluate the effectiveness of the intervention. Using this approach will help you avoid using interventions that aren't working and try others that may be more effective. Using this approach will help individuals see improvement in their own behavior and will motivate them to perform and learn. You will spend less time managing behavior and more time engaged in physical activity.

WHAT IS THE BEHAVIORAL APPROACH?

Advocates of the behavioral approach believe that behaviors are learned and, once clearly identified, they can be changed. The behavioral approach uses the principles of operant conditioning to change behavior. Operant conditioning is often referred to as the ABC (antecedent-behavior-consequence) approach. A relationship exists between the behavior and the action occurring before the behavior, called the antecedent, and the consequence that will occur after the behavior. Table 4.1 provides two examples of how to use the ABC approach.

Antecedents can stimulate behavior to occur, such as when you state, "Line up and get ready for warm-up exercises." By making certain statements you can stimulate or cue the individual's behavior.

Consequences follow the behavior and affect the probability that the behavior will increase or decrease in the future. Use pleasant consequences to develop, maintain, and increase positive behaviors (see chapter 5), and use unpleasant conse-

Table 4.1 ABC Behavioral Approach

A	B	C
Antecedent (before the behavior occurs)	Behavior (observable and definable)	Consequence (result of the behavior)
Line up and get ready for warm-up exercises.	Stand on your space and listen.	The first participant from each of the six squads to be quietly standing on his or her space will be one of the exercise leaders for today.
You have 1 minute to move into your soccer skill stations and begin practicing skills.	Independently practice at the soccer skill stations.	All participants who are independently practicing at the soccer skill stations will earn 15 minutes to play mini soccer games.

quences to redirect or decrease inappropriate behaviors (see chapter 6). We cannot emphasize enough that for consequences to be effective you must apply them consistently. Beyond this basic premise, make sure that a consequence only reinforces or punishes those participants who actually performed or did not perform the specific behavior. This ensures a fair and predictable physical activity setting.

BEHAVIOR-CHANGE PROCESS

In this chapter, we'll show you how to implement a plan to change an individual's behavior using the behavior-change process (see figure 4.1). The methods discussed in this chapter are most often used in the behavioral approach (chapters 5 and 6), but they can also be incorporated into the humanistic approach (chapter 7) and biophysical approach (chapter 8). To help you see how to tailor this information to your situation, we'll give you specific examples of the concepts applied in different situations. In the final section we'll examine methods for evaluating the behavior-change process to help you determine if a behavior has actually changed.

Here are the sequential steps in the behavior-change process:

1. Select, define, and prioritize the behavior.
2. Observe and record the behavior.
3. Develop and implement the behavioral intervention.

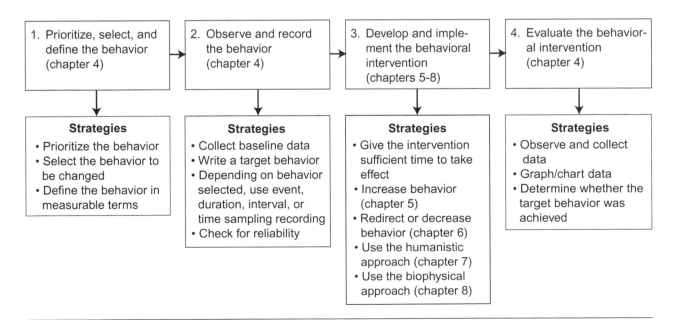

Figure 4.1 The behavior-change process.

4. Evaluate the behavioral intervention to determine the effectiveness of the program.

In the following material we'll look closely at each of these steps. Figure 4.1 and checklist 4.1 (on page 71) outline the key points of each procedure for you to use as a guide.

Select, Define, and Prioritize the Behavior

The first, critical step in the behavioral approach is to select or identify the behavior you wish to develop, increase, maintain, or decrease. Start by asking the following:

- "What behaviors do I want the individual or group to do?"
- "What behaviors will bring success to each individual or the group?"
- "What do I consider appropriate and inappropriate behavior?"

Naturally, you must first identify the behavior before you can measure it.

Define the Behavior

The behavior must be a measurable act, meaning you can observe and objectively identify it, such as throwing a Frisbee or standing in a designated space during warm-up exercises. Making the behavior measurable will also make it easy to record and help individuals set obtainable, clearly defined goals. Saying that an individual is "acting inappropriately" or "not acting responsibly" is simply too vague. Instead, you must describe

exactly what the individual is doing to act inappropriately or responsibly. For example, when acting responsibly, you might say, "The individual stands on her designated number during warm-ups," or "She turns in assignments on time." These are well-defined, measurable behaviors; they have a clear beginning and end (see figure 4.2). For other examples of immeasurable and measurable behaviors in physical activity settings, see table 4.2.

- Stand on designated number during warm-ups.
- Take turns.
- Share equipment.
- Hand a ball to a teammate when it comes in your court.
- Turn in assignments on time.
- Distribute and collect equipment.
- Lead warm-up exercises.
- Be a squad leader.
- Assist another individual or be a peer tutor.

Figure 4.2 Examples of defining responsible behavior.

Prioritize the Behavior

Where should you start when selecting behaviors? You may want to change so many behaviors exhibited by an individual or a group that it may be difficult to decide which behaviors to work on first. Initially, identify the most important behavior or two. This will help keep you and the individual or group from becoming overwhelmed and confused. Tracking one or two behaviors at a time will allow

Table 4.2 Immeasurable and Measurable Behaviors in Physical Activity Settings

Immeasurable behaviors	Measurable behaviors
Paying attention	Going from the warm-up to the first activity when the signal is given
Cooperating	Putting equipment away in the cart after completing an activity
Being helpful	Sharing equipment with a teammate during a session
Hustling	Touching each of the four cones during the running drill
Being responsible	Turning in a tennis-skills worksheet on time with all skills completed
Dribbling properly	Dribbling the basketball using the pads of the fingertips
Being disruptive	Running around instead of sitting in the designated area and listening to the next direction
Misusing equipment	Kicking a basketball during a basketball game
Interrupting	Not raising a hand and waiting for permission to speak

you to focus your attention on implementing an intervention plan that consistently reinforces the identified behaviors.

Following are guidelines for identifying inappropriate behaviors and prioritizing them from most to least important. When selecting behaviors, be sure to make behaviors that harm the participant or risk the safety of peers your first priority. Other high priorities are to maintain group control so that learning can occur and to increase behaviors that promote performance, such as listening to directions. Also important are social skills, such as the ability to participate cooperatively with peers. Based on your philosophy, you may decide to prioritize these behaviors differently, but this list is a good place to start.

When prioritizing behaviors, you don't have to select an inappropriate behavior to get positive results. Instead you may wish to promote a particular positive behavior. For example, reinforcing athletes who listen and watch a skill demonstration may help them focus and consequently improve their skill performance. Two other considerations when identifying and prioritizing behaviors include frequency (how often) and duration (how long). For example, inappropriate behaviors that occur infrequently or for a brief period of time may not warrant the time and energy it takes to fully develop a behavioral plan.

Observe and Record the Behavior

Identifying baseline behavior helps you determine what direction to take when designing the behavioral plan. It also helps you gather information about the behavior and look for patterns (i.e., when behaviors occur on certain days or in certain situations) that may help you develop an effective intervention plan. Determining baseline behavior means observing and recording the behavior before you intervene. You should determine the baseline behavior when setting your ultimate goal for the behavior, or the target behavior. For example, Coach Danielle is convinced that Penny, a talented athlete on her soccer team, is capable of scoring more goals. After collecting baseline information for 2 weeks on the number of successful soccer kicks on goal (definable behavior) that Penny can perform during each 5-minute warm-up session, Coach Danielle calculates a baseline average of 19. The scores are variable with a range of 29 for the high and 10 for the low. Next, Coach Danielle determines the target behavior by averag-

ing the recorded baseline behaviors and deciding on an appropriate intervention. She then has a discussion with Penny: "I've been keeping track of the number of successful goals you have kicked in the 5-minute warm-up for the last 2 weeks. You've averaged 19 goals during each warm-up, which is good. However, I think you could be more consistent and kick more goals. What do think is the number of successful goals you can kick in the 5-minute warm-up?" Penny and Coach Danielle decide that if Penny kicks at least 25 goals in the warm-up each day during the next 4 days, she can select and lead a soccer drill of her choice during Friday's practice.

Notice that in this example, the coach chose a measurable behavior to observe and manage. In addition, it was a behavior for which she could praise the athlete while encouraging her to do even better. The target behavior was kicking at least 25 goals in 5 minutes. If Coach Danielle had not taken a baseline measure, she might have set the target behavior, or number of successful soccer goals, too high or too low. A low number is too easy to obtain while a high number is too difficult and may cause frustration. Either way, an inappropriate target behavior or goal fails to motivate. Consider working with all individuals to help them set appropriate target behaviors or goals to keep them focused, challenged, and motivated.

You can use your observations and recorded baseline information to ascertain if an intervention is working. When Coach Danielle reinforced Penny's behavior by allowing her to select a soccer drill during Friday's practice, Penny increased her average number of soccer kicks on goal during the warm-up from 19 to 25. Coach Danielle was pleased that the plan was so effective and Penny was pleased with her improvement and consistency.

Observation and Recording Methods

Several methods are available for observing and recording individual or group behavior. As you read the following list of common recording methods and practices stemming from those methods, think about how you might tailor the ideas to your particular situation. The method selected depends on the nature of the behavior. First, you must ask yourself if you are determining the frequency or the duration of the event.

Frequency behavior. This is the number of times that a particular behavior or event occurs within a specific time period. Examples include counting the number of times Steven talks out of turn or the number of soccer goals Penny kicks in 5 minutes during soccer practice.

Duration behavior. This is the length of time in minutes or seconds that a behavior occurs, such as the number of minutes an individual is on task during warm-up exercises or when performing a skill. Use this method when the length of time engaged in the behavior is the best way to determine performance. For example, measure the amount of time in minutes or seconds a participant is on task and attempting layups during a 4-minute basketball drill. You can convert duration results into percentages by dividing the total amount of time engaged in the desired behavior by the total time observed. For example, a participant who correctly attempts layups for 3 minutes during the 4 minutes of the drill is on task and correctly performing for 75% of the time: 3 minutes (180 seconds) divided by 4 minutes (240 seconds) = 75%.

Both frequency and duration recording can be a continuous recording of the behavior, where you observe during the entire period and count the number of times or minutes the behavior occurs. However, continuous recording may take too much time. Another option is to record the frequency or duration of the behavior for short periods of time and then predict the frequency or duration of the behavior for the entire period of time. You can use interval recording for both frequency behaviors and duration behaviors and time sampling for duration behaviors (Siedentop and Tannehill, 2000).

Interval frequency recording. Observe and record the number of times the behavior occurs during each predetermined observation session (interval). For example, observe John for 5 minutes at a time during four specific or randomly chosen times during a 60-minute recreation session. During those 5-minute intervals count the number of times John pokes at or pushes another individual. If you observe John and see that during the intervals he pokes 4 times, 6 times, 2 times, and then 3 times, you know that in a 20-minute (4 × 5 minutes) period he poked other individuals 15 times. You would then predict that in the 60-minute session, John is poking 45 times (15 × 3 = 45).

Interval duration recording. Observe and record the duration of the behavior during each specific or randomly chosen observation session (interval). For example, observe 2-minute intervals on five separate occasions during a 50-minute basketball class and record the amount of time the individual is on task. Then add up the number of minutes the individual is on task during the five recorded 2-minute sessions (total 10 minutes)

and determine the duration of the individual's on-task behavior. For example, if the individual was on task for 8 minutes (480 seconds) out of the total 10 minutes (600 seconds) of observation, the individual would be on task for a duration of 80 (480 seconds divided by 600 seconds = 80) or 80% of the time.

Individual time-sampling recording. This method is used to predict the amount of time an individual does a particular behavior during a specified period of time when it takes too much time to observe and record continuously during the entire time period. To use time sampling, predetermine specific or random times to observe. For example, during a 30-minute soccer practice, you might decide to look up every 3 minutes to see if Carlos is participating in practice. You can set a beeper to go off every 3 minutes as a reminder and mark on a time-sampling chart whether Carlos is participating or not. If in 10 observations Carlos was participating 6 times, you can predict that during this practice Carlos was participating 60% of the time.

Group time-sampling recording. This method is used to measure the behavior of a group by scanning the entire group at specific or random intervals of time. It can be used to record the group's duration behaviors. For example, you might observe the group once every 5 minutes and record the total number of players in a group of 15 who are engaged in performing basketball drills during a 30-minute practice. You can then determine the percentage of players engaged in basketball drills. For example, 12 out of 15 players are engaged in the basketball drills, or 80% (12/15 = 80) of the players, during the first observation. Repeat this procedure every 5 minutes for a total of six times during a 30-minute practice. Average

Table 4.3 Group Time Sampling Percentage of Players Engaged in Drills

Observation	Players engaged in drills	Total players
1	12	15
2	9	15
3	6	15
4	12	15
5	13	15
6	15	15
	67	90

67/90 = 74% on task

the percentages for each observation and predict the percentage of players engaged in the basketball drills for the entire team during the 30-minute practice (see table 4.3).

To save time, develop observational recording charts that are easy to use for you and others who are helping with the program. For example, consider enlisting the help of teacher aides, assistant coaches, managers, trainers, peer tutors, older participants, and parents (Weinberg and Gould, 2003). Figure 4.3 is a sample frequency recording chart with information that Ms. Cabraal from the example at the beginning of the chapter has filled in for Steven. See worksheet 1 in appendix A for a blank form you can photocopy for your own use. To use it, merely cross out a number each time the behavior occurs, then circle the total number of times the behavior occurs on a particular day.

Measurement Reliability

We can define reliability as the degree to which two or more independent observers agree on what they see and record (Siedentop and Tannehill,

2000). Unreliable measures can give you inconsistent information, leading you to make wrong decisions when designing behavioral interventions and your overall program.

To ensure your data are reliable, make sure the data are collected by at least two observers in one session of observation. When reliability is poor, you may need to define the behavior more clearly or the observers may need more training. Refer back to the sample measurable behaviors in figure 4.2. For example, we defined on-task behavior as, "The individual correctly attempts layups." Correctly attempting a layup was clearly defined and agreed on by the observers. Observer 1, using the technique of interval recording, recorded the individual correctly attempting basketball layups 8 times, while observer 2 observed the individual correctly attempting layups 9 times. The formula to calculate the interobserver reliability between two observers is as follows: Take the lower frequency observation (observer 1) and divide it by the higher frequency observation (observer 2). In other words, 8 divided by 9 = .89, or 89%.

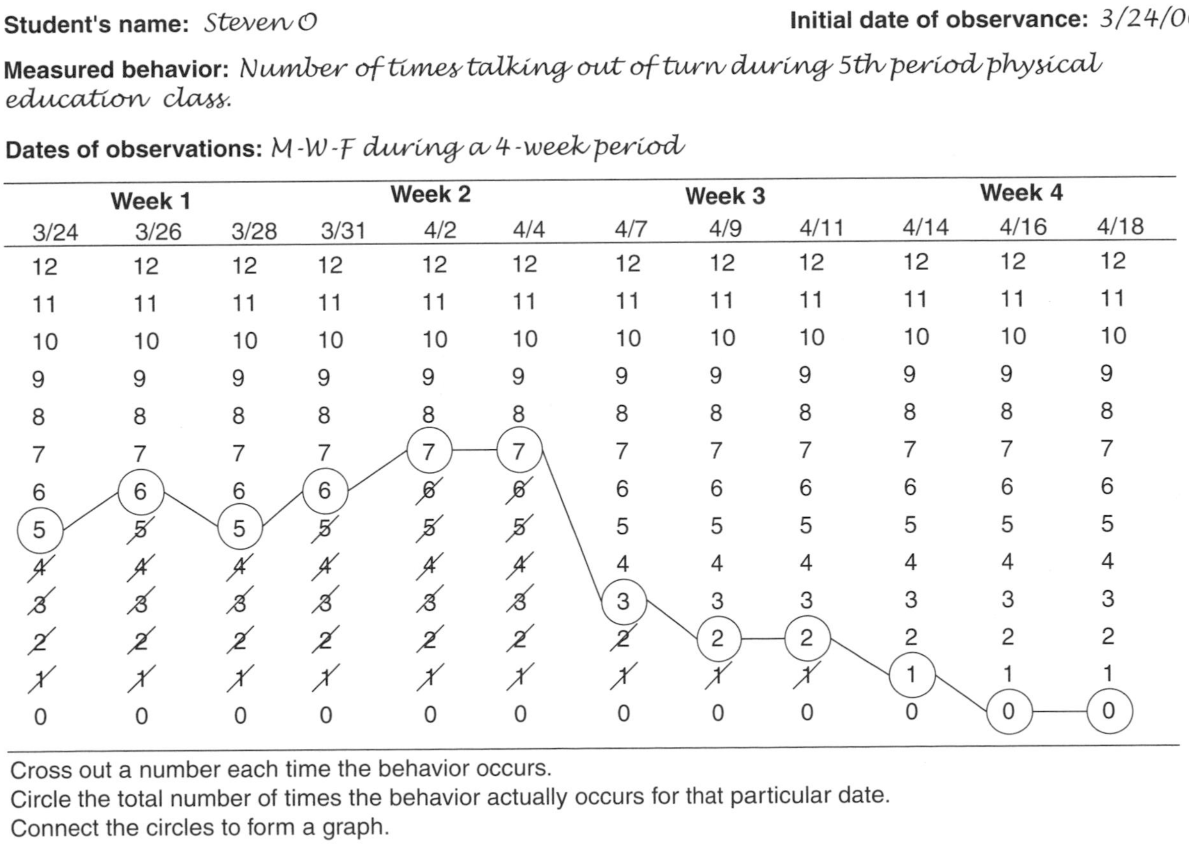

Student's name: *Steven O*

Initial date of observance: *3/24/06*

Measured behavior: *Number of times talking out of turn during 5th period physical education class.*

Dates of observations: *M-W-F during a 4-week period*

Cross out a number each time the behavior occurs.
Circle the total number of times the behavior actually occurs for that particular date.
Connect the circles to form a graph.

Figure 4.3 Frequency recording chart.

Adapted from J.E. Walker and T.M. Shea, 1995, *Behavior management: A practical approach for educators*, 6th ed. (New York: Macmillan).

Therefore, an 89% agreement, or interobserver reliability, exists between the two observers. Acceptable reliability is usually a minimum of 80% (.80) or above, but this can vary depending on the particular behavior you are measuring. You can also videotape the session so you can concentrate on instruction during the session. Later the observers can observe the videotape and calculate interobserver reliability (Boyce, 2003).

Implement the Behavioral Intervention

The intervention is the heart of the behavior-change process. In the previous basketball layup example, the coach promoted on-task behavior by reinforcing those individuals who correctly practiced the basketball layup. You can choose a variety of behavioral methods to develop, maintain, increase, redirect, or decrease the behavior. To increase a desired behavior you can use prompts, the Premack principle, a contract, or other reinforcement methods discussed in chapter 5. To redirect or decrease an undesirable behavior you can use extinction, time-out, response cost, or other consequences discussed in chapter 6.

Many behavioral interventions fail because the physical activity professional does not give the plan sufficient time to take effect or does not implement the plan consistently. Behavior change does not always occur immediately. In fact, some inappropriate behaviors may escalate at first as the individual rebels against the change in your approach. You must be consistent and patient when intervening, allowing at least three sessions for changes to begin to take place. In general, behavioral interventions are quite simple to design. However, it is also an art to successfully change an individual's behavior and maintain the change over time.

IN THE TRENCHES

A Behavior Curriculum
Eric Sell, Certified Adapted Physical Education Specialist (CAPE), Salt Lake City School District

The Adapted Physical Education Program in the Salt Lake City School District needed a system for measuring and tracking nonsocial behaviors of students with an identified emotional disorder. In addition, the district's core curriculum standards outlined the teaching of social behaviors. Current trends in education such as accountability, data collection, and opportunity for reflection on both teaching and student learning were considered. A behavior curriculum was adapted from Hellison's social responsibility model. This model includes sequential levels that empower students to take responsibility for their own behavior and is discussed in detail in chapter 7.

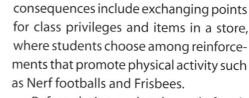

The acronym SPORT, meaning self-control, positive interaction, others, responsibility, and trying, was developed and defines what students focus on during each class meeting. Students can earn up to 5 points if they exhibit all five behaviors. Students ascend a level system similar to Hellison's social responsibility model as they are successful. Positive consequences include exchanging points for class privileges and items in a store, where students choose among reinforcements that promote physical activity such as Nerf footballs and Frisbees.

Before, during, and at the end of each class session, students dialogue with the teacher regarding their behavior. This system applies behavior theory principles in that a class consists of an antecedent (start class with reflecting on what SPORT means), a behavior (yes or no for each letter), and a consequence (success or nonsuccess dialogued and recorded).

Student behaviors are formatively recorded by the staff and kept in a database. The behaviors (data points) are charted by the teachers to show behavior trends. This charting allows the teachers to reflect on the teaching–learning relationship and provides a visual reference for student reflection. The teachers share this information with parents at the student's individualized education program (IEP) and other meetings.

Evaluate the Behavioral Intervention

You must evaluate the intervention to determine if it was effective. Did it actually contribute to the desired behavioral change? Two key questions to ask during evaluation are, "Was the target behavior achieved?" and "Is the individual or group now displaying the target behavior?"

To answer these questions you must examine the behavior data you collected. Graphs are a helpful evaluation tool. They clearly display data and the level of change in the behavior during the intervention, helping you detect small degrees of change that you may otherwise have missed. In addition, graphs can show if the behavior did not change at all or if it worsened. They provide simple, effective, and unbiased feedback about the behavior. An easy way to develop a graph is to connect the circled numbers on the frequency recording chart (see figure 4.3).

However, you must keep graphs simple if they are to be useful. Remember Steven, the boy who often spoke out of turn in the opening scenario of this chapter? Ms. Cabraal could draw a graph of Steven's behavior as illustrated in figure 4.4, which is based on data she recorded in figure 4.3. The graph shows Steven's baseline behavior followed by the change, which shows a decrease in the behavior after the administration of the behavioral intervention. How did Ms. Cabraal get Steven to improve? After meeting with Steven to discuss the situation, she determined that Steven wanted to be a class exercise leader and help collect equipment, so she selected these two privileges as reinforcers (intervention). To interpret the graph in figure 4.4, first examine the information collected in the

frequency recording chart in figure 4.3 on page 65. This shows the baseline data of how often Steven spoke out of turn in class during a 2-week period. Steven spoke out of turn an average of six times per class period, and the behavior was escalating. With Dr. Sumner's help analyzing Steven's baseline data (figure 4.4), Ms. Cabraal determined that Steven might not be able to immediately stop speaking out of turn.

Ms. Cabraal developed the following behavioral intervention. During the first week of the behavioral intervention, for each class session that Steven spoke out of turn no more than three times, he was allowed to help collect equipment after class. During the second week of the behavioral intervention, for each class session that Steven did not speak out of turn at all, he was able to not only help collect equipment but was also given the responsibility of being the exercise leader at the beginning of the following class period. Throughout the intervention Ms. Cabraal also complimented Steven for listening during instruction and for not interrupting, thereby reinforcing the positive behavior even more.

The graph shows that Steven's tendency to speak out of turn greatly lessened the first week and completely stopped by the end of the second week of the intervention (figure 4.4). Specifically, during the first week of the intervention, Steven spoke out of turn an average of fewer than three times per class session. Thus, at the end of each class period he was allowed to help collect equipment. During the first day of the second week, Steven spoke out of turn once and therefore was not allowed to collect equipment or be the exercise leader. Immediately after that class, Ms. Cabraal met with Steven to discuss his behavior, reminding

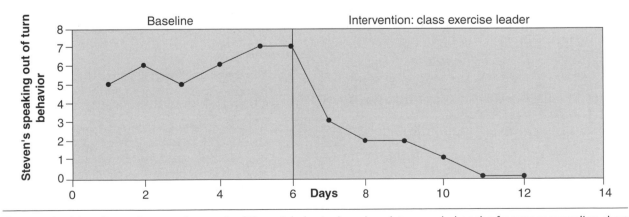

Figure 4.4 A baseline-to-intervention graph of Steven's behavior based on data recorded on the frequency recording chart in figure 4.3.

him that he needed to completely stop speaking out of turn if he wanted to continue to collect equipment and be the exercise leader. During the next two class sessions, Steven completely stopped speaking out of turn and was able to resume collecting equipment as well as become the exercise

leader (see figure 4.4). Ms. Cabraal also noticed that since Steven stopped speaking out of turn, he was paying better attention to instruction and consequently his class performance was improving. She pointed out this improvement to Steven in a follow-up meeting and also explored with

HOW TO DESIGN A BEHAVIOR MANAGEMENT LINE GRAPH

Use the data from figure 4.3 that includes the number of days (12) and Steven's behavior for each of the 12 successive days during baseline 5, 6, 5, 6, 7, 7 and intervention 3, 2, 2, 1, 0, and 0.

1. Open Excel: Go to the Start menu, scroll to the applications, and click on Microsoft Excel.

2. Using the data in the previous paragraph (or figure 4.3 in the text), make two columns. Column 1 is in cell A1 and is labeled "Days." Beginning in cells A2 to A13, number the days 1 through 12. Column 2 is in cell B1 and is labeled "Speaking-out behaviors." Below cell B1, input the data beginning with 5 in cell B2 and ending with 0 in cell B13. Highlight all of the data.

3. Go to Insert and then Chart. Select an XY (Scatter) and highlight the third graph down on the left side. Click Next.

4. The beginning of the graph will appear. Click Next.

5. Name each item by clicking in the Chart title (give chart a title), Value (X) axis (days), and Value (Y) axis (behavior).

6. Click the grid lines tab and ensure that no boxes are checked in the Value (X) and Value (Y) boxes. This will eliminate the grid lines. Then click Finish.

7. Resize your chart to fit the entire size of the page by clicking and dragging the corners. Your chart needs to take up almost the entire sheet. Ensure that it does so by going to File and then Print Preview. If it takes up the page, close the preview and continue.

8. Highlight the box labeled "Series 1" and delete it by using the delete key on your keyboard.

9. Click on View and then Toolbars. Make sure there is a check next to "Drawing."

10. Locate the drawing toolbar and click on the text box icon.

11. To format your X and Y axis labels and title, click on them. You may adjust the font type, font size,

and move them around. Before continuing to the next step, move the X axis title, "Days," up. This will give you room to type in a figure legend.

12. Click below "Days" on your graph and a text box will appear. Type your figure legend below "Days," such as, "Figure 4.4, a baseline-to-treatment graph of Steven's speaking-out-of-turn behavior."

13. Next you will develop phase lines. First, locate the drawing toolbar and click on the line icon.

14. Your phase line goes at the end of the 6th day of collecting baseline data. Place a phase line on the graph by clicking and holding as you drag your line down. Note: The line begins at the top of the graph. Pull it down through the sixth dot, which is day 6, on the bottom of the graph. Hold the shift key down while dragging to keep the line perfectly straight.

15. Using the text box icon on the drawing toolbar, label each side of your phase line. The left side is labeled "Baseline" and the right side is labeled "Intervention: class exercise leader."

16. Your graph is complete and should look similar to the graph in figure 4.4.

17. Printing: Remember to click on your graph so that the little black boxes surround the box. Click the Print Preview tab. If you like what you see, click Print. Click Close to return to your original page.

Summary

- Your complete line graph needs to include a title, X and Y axis, phase lines, condition labels, and a figure legend.

- After you have successfully completed the graph, choose a behavior in your physical activity program and develop a graph for it. Be sure to include a title, an X and Y axis, phase lines, condition labels, and a figure legend. Be sure to give your graph a title.

Figure 4.5 These directions will help you develop a simple line graph using Microsoft Excel®.

him other ways to work toward more responsible behaviors in class that could eventually lead to him becoming a peer tutor.

Figure 4.4 is a simple baseline-to-intervention graph that includes measurements from baseline and intervention. This involves charting the baseline phase during which the intervention is absent and an intervention phase during which the behavioral intervention is introduced. For more information on ways to chart and graph behaviors, see Cooper, Heron, and Heward's *Applied Behavior Analysis* (1987). In addition, computer graphing programs such as Excel make graphing data quite simple. Figure 4.5 provides step-by-step directions on how to design a simple behavior management line graph using Microsoft Excel to evaluate an individual's behavior.

Additional questions to consider when evaluating the behavioral intervention include the following:

- Was the intervention long enough to achieve the desired behavior?
- Was the behavior change substantial?
- Were there any intervening variables or influences that could have caused the behavior change, such as outside sources or environmental factors?
- Is it likely that the behavior change is permanent?
- Can the behavior change be generalized to other settings?
- Was the behavior change at the expense of other behaviors?
- What might you do differently during the process the next time?

SUMMARY

The behavioral approach is based on the principles of operant conditioning, which involves systematically modifying the environment to develop, increase, maintain, redirect, or decrease a behavior. In the ABC approach, you take advantage of the fact that relationships exist among the behavior to be changed, the actions occurring before the behavior (antecedent), and the consequences following the behavior. Follow these steps to apply the behavior-change process:

1. Select, define, and prioritize the behavior.
2. Observe and record the behavior.

3. Develop the behavioral intervention.
4. Evaluate the behavioral intervention to determine effectiveness.

The heart of the behavioral-change process is the intervention, during which you administer different methods of behavior modification. In general, behavioral interventions are quite simple to design, but it is both a science and an art to develop, administer, and maintain a behavioral plan that will effectively change the behavior of the individual or group over the long term. Use checklist 4.1 on page 71 to get started. In the next chapter we'll examine methods to increase desirable behaviors using the behavioral approach.

WHAT DO YOU THINK?

1. Think of a behavior you want individuals in your program to exhibit, such as hustling, listening, or cooperating, and make it into a clear, definable behavior.

2. Discuss different methods for observing and recording behaviors (i.e., frequency, duration, interval, and time-sampling recording). For each method, justify why and when you would use that particular method over another method. Provide an example for each method that is appropriate to your physical activity role.

3. Describe interobserver reliability and calculate interobserver reliability by observing a skill or behavior of an individual in your setting.

4. Consider an individual or group who is displaying a behavior you would like to change. Outline a behavioral intervention plan to change that individual's or group's behavior. First, select and define the behavior. Next, collect baseline data by observing and recording the behavior. Determine your target behavior and develop a behavioral intervention to change the behavior and collect intervention data. Use the recording chart in figure 4.3 as a model for collecting the information (baseline and intervention behavior), use worksheet 1 in appendix A to record the data, and then construct a graph following the directions in figure 4.5, which is similar to the graph in figure 4.4. Based on the graph and information evaluate the intervention for effectiveness.

CASE STUDIES

For each of the three case studies in chapter 1 on page 13, select methods described in this chapter and discuss in detail how you would implement each of the methods to manage the behavior. After you have developed your own methods, read the following suggestions, which are only some of the many creative ways you might apply the information covered in this chapter.

CASE 1
Hector, a Disruptive 3rd Grader

▸ Clearly define and prioritize Hector's inappropriate behaviors.

▸ Prioritize his four main problem behaviors: not standing or sitting on his assigned spot in the gym for any length of time, running when he should walk, having difficulty following a series of directions, and becoming easily upset.

▸ Observe and chart Hector's behaviors during class to determine what may cause the inappropriate behaviors.

▸ Meet with Hector and his classroom teacher to develop a positive management plan (see chapter 5) for correctly performing each of the behaviors: staying on his assigned spot during attendance and the warm-up, walking from one activity area to the next when requested to do so, listening to and following all teacher directions, and remaining calm. Work on reinforcing

the highest priority behavior first and then add additional behaviors over time.

CASE 2
Ashante, an Instructor in Charge of Weight-Room Cleanup

▸ Clearly define and give examples of what constitutes the weight room being safe and clean. Stress safety to the group as the top priority.

▸ If necessary, develop a charting or recording procedure that participants follow to keep the weight room clean.

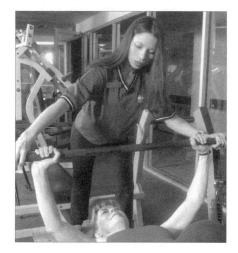

CASE 3
Molly, an Overly Aggressive Soccer Player

▶ Meet with Molly and discuss how arguing and especially fighting are serious problem behaviors that will be handled immediately, making sure she recognizes that this type of behavior is unacceptable. Be clear with Molly that these behaviors will be dealt with immediately with consequences based on the league's policy and the team rules.

▶ Have Molly define and give you clear examples of good and poor sportsmanship.

▶ Consider charting Molly's poor sportsmanship to determine if there is a pattern of occurrence.

▶ End the meeting on a positive note by explaining to Molly that you are confident she can demonstrate good sportsmanship during all practices and games.

Checklist 4.1 Designing the Behavioral Approach

Rate yourself in regard to the following statements.

	Consistently	Inconsistently	Never
Selecting and defining a target behavior:			
I choose a measurable behavior (see table 4.1 and figure 4.2).	☐	☐	☐
I define objectively what I will observe.	☐	☐	☐
I prioritize the behaviors.	☐	☐	☐
Observing and recording the behavior:			
I pinpoint the behavior and, depending on the behavior, use frequency or duration recording.	☐	☐	☐
When appropriate I use time sampling or interval recording.	☐	☐	☐
I check for interobserver reliability.	☐	☐	☐
I plan the intervention to maintain, increase, or correct the behavior using checklists 5.1 and 5.2 in chapter 5 and checklists 6.1, 6.2, and 6.3 in chapter 6, as appropriate.	☐	☐	☐
Evaluating intervention effectiveness:			
I observe behavior.	☐	☐	☐
I collect data.	☐	☐	☐
I make charts and graphs.	☐	☐	☐
I determine whether there was a sufficient increase or decrease in behavior.	☐	☐	☐

Behavioral Methods for Maintaining and Increasing Behaviors

*M*ost researchers suggest that 80 to 90% of reinforcement should be positive.

Weinberg and Gould, 2003

r. Shaw was sitting in his office thinking about his after-school recreation program for teenagers. During the past few months, he had observed escalating incidents of poor sportsmanship. Because of this, the previous week he reviewed the program rules with the participants and briefly discussed the importance of demonstrating good sportsmanship, providing clear examples of both positive and negative behaviors. He also took a few individuals aside who displayed poor sportsmanship and shared with them steps to take to improve their behavior. Yet with all this effort, poor sportsmanship continued to escalate. Specifically, he had observed the more athletic individuals putting down the individuals who were less skilled, including swearing at them and refusing to pass them the ball during the activities and games.

Such behavior does not promote a positive atmosphere where all individuals feel empowered to participate and learn. Based on past experience, Mr. Shaw knew the behavior would not go away without action on his part, and he wondered what to do. He wanted to use a positive approach as he felt this promoted better sportsmanship among the teenagers. He had read a book called *Character Education* that provided methods and strategies for team building and promoting sportsmanship (Glover and Anderson, 2003). As he considered some of the ideas in the book, he began to think of ways the group could demonstrate good sportsmanship.

First, Mr. Shaw thought about the characteristics of the individuals who attended the daily after-school recreation program. He knew that teenagers typically seek the approval of their peers. So he thought that having individuals work together in small squads of

five and earn points for demonstrating good sportsmanship might work. He wondered what to use for an incentive, then remembered that the group was always asking him for more time to play basketball games. He also decided to involve the group in the plan by having them discuss and vote on an additional reward. The squads who earned a certain number of points by demonstrating proper sportsmanship Monday through Thursday of each week earned the right to play basketball games on Friday and received another reward that the group voted on. Over the weekend, Mr. Shaw outlined the plan on a dry-erase board, defining and giving examples of good sportsmanship and how many points each squad needed by the end of Thursday's session to earn the rewards.

On Monday, Mr. Shaw discussed the plan with the group. The idea of earning more time to play basketball games and voting for an additional reward appealed to everyone. As the first week of the plan progressed, Mr. Shaw observed more and more participants demonstrating good sportsmanship, such as encouraging one another during activities and games. He noticed individuals in their squads reminding each other about earning more time to play the basketball games and receiving the additional reward. By Friday, all but one of the squads had earned the rewards. On Friday, the squad who did not earn the reward practiced the activities presented throughout the week while the other squads played basketball games. After Friday's session, Mr. Shaw encouraged the members of the squad to earn enough points next week in order to receive the reward. Mr. Shaw realized he should have implemented this plan months ago when the program first started!

In this chapter we'll discuss behavioral methods you can use to increase desirable behavior. These methods are based on the relationships among the antecedents or events that occur before the behavior, the actual behavior, and the consequences or events that follow the behavior. This concept of operant conditioning was first introduced in chapter 4. The positive methods we'll discuss in this chapter have not only been successful in alleviating inappropriate behavior (French and Silliman-French, 2000; Siedentop and Tannehill, 2000) but also in enhancing skill performance

(French and Lavay, 1990; Weinberg and Gould, 2003) and responsible behavior (Hellison, 2003; Rink, 2002) in various physical activity settings. We'll focus on different types of reinforcement and provide methods with examples of how to give positive reinforcement to maintain and increase desirable behaviors.

WHAT IS REINFORCEMENT?

We can define positive reinforcement as offering something valued as a consequence of a desired behavior, resulting in an increase in the frequency of that behavior. Naturally, to be motivating the reinforcer must be something the individual wants. For example, when a teacher asks a question (antecedent) and the student responds with the answer (behavior), the teacher reinforces the student's answer with praise (favorable consequence). The student will continue to answer questions if you reinforce her efforts with positive statements. The behavior of answering questions is strengthened by the favorable consequence of the teacher's praise and will likely occur again. However, the player who is yelled at by the coach to stop taking low-percentage shots most likely will not try that type of shot again to avoid the coach's criticism. Figure 5.1 and checklist 5.1 (page 91) provide the reader with best practices for administering positive reinforcement.

Unfortunately, many people confuse positive reinforcement with bribery. Bribery is the use of gifts to corrupt, manipulate, or entice someone to do something illegal, unethical, or wrong (Sprink, 1996). In contrast, reinforcement is given only after the appropriate behavior is demonstrated. Reinforcement occurs frequently in everyday life. For example, when the physical activity professional states, "Thank you for holding the door open for the group. That was nice of you," chances are the individual will hold the door open again.

It is all too easy to unintentionally reinforce behaviors you don't wish to increase. For example, each time Michelle makes noises during warm-up exercises, Coach Sayers tells her to stop. Michelle may enjoy the attention she is receiving from Coach Sayers and find it reinforcing because attention is what she wants, so her noisemaking increases. Coach Sayers is better off ignoring the inappropriate behavior and praising Michelle when she is quiet and performing the warm-up exercises. Positively reinforce the desired behavior and when appropriate, ignore the undesirable behavior.

Identifying Potential Reinforcers

The most important aspect of an effective reinforcer is that it is idiosyncratic or desired by the individual or group you are targeting. Successfully identifying potential reinforcers and keeping up with the changing preferences of each individual is an ongoing process, especially since what one individual finds reinforcing may not be reinforcing to another. In addition, just because individuals respond favorably to specific reinforcers one week does not necessarily mean the same reinforcers will be effective the following week. Thus, it is important to have a variety of highly motivating reinforcers available to help you keep up with changing individual interests. It also helps to observe the individual or group during physical activity to see what type of activities and equipment they choose. Simply asking the individual or group what reinforcers they enjoy also works

---

- The reinforcement is contingent on the individual or group demonstrating the appropriate behavior.

- Individualize the reinforcer to meet the unique needs of each individual or group. For the reinforcer to have meaning, it must be perceived as valuable.

- Choose age-appropriate reinforcers.

- Be patient in implementing the reinforcement plan. The desired behavior or performance you wish to increase may not happen immediately.

- Reinforce the individual or group immediately once you observe the desired behavior. This is especially important when they are first learning the behavior.

- Pair social reinforcers with tangible reinforcers. This helps the individual or group associate the social reinforcers with the tangible reinforcers, making it easier for you to eventually phase out tangible reinforcers.

- Use physical activity reinforcement when possible (see figure 5.2 and worksheet 2).

- Choose the reinforcement method that requires the least amount of intervention to change a behavior. In other words, reinforce as little as possible to achieve the desired results.

- Reinforce less once the target behavior or performance reaches a satisfactory level. Design a schedule where you gradually reduce the frequency of reinforcement (see figure 5.4).

Figure 5.1   Best practices for administering positive reinforcement.

because when the individual or group is involved in the decision-making process, they have a feeling of ownership and the strength of the reinforcer increases (Siedentop and Tannehill, 2000). To determine who prefers what type of reinforcer, consider using preference scales or lists, surveys or questionnaires, participant or parent interviews, or direct observation. To help you get started, worksheet 2 in appendix A provides a sample reinforcement preference survey.

Catch Them Being Good

It's easy to fall into the habit of noticing only the negative and ignoring the positive behaviors. To avoid making only negative or corrective comments, videotape or audiotape a session and review the tape, calculating the number of positive statements you made. Work toward making at least five positive statements to every corrective or negative statement. Also, don't just recognize and reinforce the highly skilled individuals. Try to catch all individuals being good. This is also called positive pinpointing.

Provide positive statements that reinforce appropriate behavior. You can help individuals internalize appropriate behavior if they understand why the behavior is appropriate. For example, it is appropriate to cover your mouth when you cough so you won't spread germs. You want individuals to choose to behave in appropriate ways not because there will be negative consequences if they don't but because they value appropriate behavior and internalize the consequences. It also helps if the individuals are involved in the decision making of what is and is not appropriate behavior (Rink, 2003), as discussed in chapter 3. Examples of positive statements are provided in the next section.

TYPES OF POSITIVE REINFORCEMENT

There are many types of positive reinforcement. Primary reinforcers are those that satisfy a biological need, such as food when hungry or water when thirsty. Secondary reinforcers are types of reinforcement that individuals have learned to like, such as shooting a basketball successfully or receiving stickers or a trophy. Examples of secondary reinforcers are listed in figure 5.2. You can also send parents notes, certificates, or letters to acknowledge an individual's appropriate behavior or skill (see figure 5.3)

Extrinsic and Intrinsic Reinforcement

Reinforcement can be extrinsic or intrinsic. Extrinsic reinforcement comes from an outside source, usually in the form of a reward such as a trophy or sticker. It makes the desired behavior more tangible to individuals who may not be intrinsically motivated. Intrinsic reinforcement resides internally within the individual and is the most sophisticated type of reinforcement. It is an internal, intangible feeling of accomplishment such as taking pride in successfully completing a task. For example, an individual may be motivated to perform an aerobic routine because she feels a sense of accomplishment, not because she receives an award. Advocates of intrinsic reinforcement worry that if individuals are extrinsically rewarded, for example with certificates when they successfully complete a skills challenge, they may feel a sense of accomplishment but may not be motivated to complete more skill challenges without the extrinsic rewards.

Studies have provided mixed results on whether extrinsic reinforcement undermines intrinsic reinforcement. Different types of intrinsic and extrinsic reinforcement exist along a continuum ranging from unmotivated to extrinsic motivation to intrinsic motivation (Weinberg and Gould, 2003). Not all individuals are intrinsically motivated and some initial extrinsic motivation in the form of a reward may be necessary. However, physical activity professionals need to strive to assist individuals to move from being extrinsically to intrinsically motivated by empowering them to take responsibility for their behavior. When appropriate, you can schedule individuals off extrinsic reinforcers. More on reinforcement schedules appears later in this chapter.

Now we'll take a closer look at different kinds of positive extrinsic reinforcers, including social, tangible, physical activity, and privilege reinforcers. Figure 5.2 lists reinforcers that have proven to motivate participants. However, do not limit your selection of reinforcers to this list, but begin to develop your own with the help of the individuals in your group.

Social Reinforcement

Social reinforcement requires little preparation and can be either nonverbal or verbal. Nonverbal reinforcers do not include words. Examples are a smile or a high-five. More examples of nonverbal reinforcement appear in figure 5.2. Remember,

Social Reinforcers: Nonverbal

- Smile, grin, nod, or wink
- High-five, thumbs up, applause, or pumping the arm in the air
- Arm around the shoulder, a pat on the back, or a hug
- Individual's photo on a "superstar" chart
- Individual's appropriate behavior, skill, or fitness chart posted
- Participant(s) of the Week or Month posted

Social Reinforcers: Verbal

Positive General

- "Wow, nice running!"
- "Great shot!"
- "Excellent pass."

Specific Positive Statements

- "Terrific swimming, you're kicking your feet more!"
- "Excellent, squad 5 is the first to be lined up and ready for the first drill."
- "Ralph, thank you for listening and following directions."
- "Nicole, way to go—you made 8 out of 10 free throws!"
- "Red squad, I appreciate your group taking responsibility to set up the exercise stations."
- "Terry, thank you for helping James with his forward roll."
- "Great, the Celtic squad was able to get the equipment put away, and now there's time to play Frisbee golf."
- "Did everyone on the team see how Sharon helped Charlie roll up the mats? She has been selected as exercise leader for her efforts."

Tangible Reinforcers

- Stickers, decals, or stamps
- Trading cards, pictures, or posters (sport stars or action heroes)
- Models or puzzles
- Simple, inexpensive games or toys
- Trophies, certificates, or medals
- Reading or coloring books
- Money (PE Bucks)
- Note home to parents
- Special t-shirt (e.g., defensive player of the week, hustle award)

Physical Activity Reinforcers

- Earning the use of equipment such as juggling scarves, a scooter board, or exercise equipment
- Participating in activities, games, or sports

Privileges

- Being a squad or exercise leader or team captain
- Distributing, setting up, or collecting equipment
- Being a peer tutor to another individual
- Demonstrating a skill, activity, game, or sport
- Choosing a favorite activity or a partner
- Assisting with activities, grading, taking attendance, or helping with locker-room procedures
- Performing an errand
- Participating in a field trip (e.g., to a sporting event)
- Receiving a visit from a local coach or athlete
- Allowing the most responsible individuals or squads extra time in an activity

Figure 5.2   Examples of social reinforcement, tangible reinforcement, physical activity reinforcement, and privileges.

the opposite gender or certain cultures may incorrectly interpret an arm around a shoulder or a pat on the back by a physical activity professional. Be aware of your organization's policy on touching individuals.

Verbal reinforcers include words or statements. They can be general or specific, and they should be sincere. A general statement would be,

"Good effort." However, for a verbal statement to have meaning, it needs to include a specific, objective comment that reinforces the desired behavior. Specific feedback provides individuals with information about the response (Petray-Rowcliffe, Williams, Lavay, and Hakim-Butt, 2002), such as, "Good running with your knees high!" or "You all lined up quickly in your squads and are

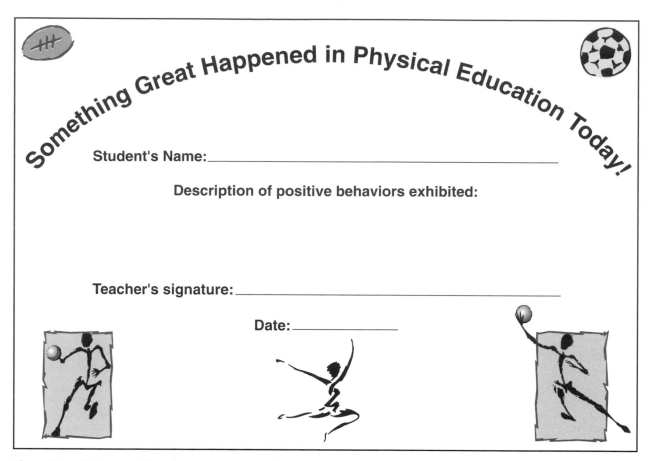

Figure 5.3 Giving a certificate is a great way to reinforce good behavior.

now ready for the next drill!" Positive specific feedback statements can be motivational by providing information on their progress, such as, "Jeff, that was an excellent run. Since last month you have lowered your time in the mile by 50 seconds!" Don't just reinforce the individual's outcome but also the effort. For example, you might say, "Tanya, I know during the past few weeks you've been staying after practice to work on your shot and I see that it is starting to pay off!" For additional examples of positive verbal statements, see figure 5.2.

Tangible Reinforcement

Tangible reinforcers are consumable or material objects an individual wants, such as food, stickers, medals, or certificates used as consequences to increase the desired behavior (see figure 5.2). For example, Susan Alexander, an adapted physical education specialist in Santa Ana, California, provides her students with PE Bucks and 500 Mile Club certificates to reinforce fitness participation and exemplary behavior (see In the Trenches).

If you cannot immediately give tangible reinforcement, you may wish to use a token economy system that delays the reinforcer. An explanation of this system appears later in the chapter. Tangible reinforcers need to be paired with social reinforcers so that the individual associates the social reinforcers with the tangible reinforcers and eventually you can phase out the tangible reinforcers. Reinforcement occurs along a continuum from material objects that may at first be more powerful to the individual than intrinsic reinforcers. Tangible reinforcers also can be expensive, so when possible, use inexpensive reinforcers that are more natural to the environment such as physical activity.

Physical Activity Reinforcement

Physical education, sport, and recreation activities can be reinforcing in themselves. You can reinforce appropriate behavior with physical activity such as playing with a favorite piece of equipment or participating in a favorite game or sport contingent on performing the desired behavior (see

PE Bucks

Susan Alexander, Adapted Physical Education Specialist, Santa Ana Unified School District

The setting is a self-contained high school adapted physical education program that includes students in grades 9 through 12 who have moderate to severe cognitive and physical disabilities and severe behavioral disorders. The adapted physical education program philosophy is modeled after schoolwide expected learning outcomes that focus on creating self-directed learners who will become responsible members of society. Students enter my classes expecting me to tell them what to do. That expectation fuels defiance and sets me up to be the typical nagging teacher. If our goal is to create self-directed learners, the tables must be turned, especially at the secondary level. I accomplish this by using a sound behavior management plan, providing motivational methods, and conducting student self-evaluation and reflection. Initially, a great deal of time must be invested in teaching students the skills and providing them with the tools they need to manage their own learning.

The foundation for what happens in class is a proactive behavior management plan that establishes the standard of behavior that I expect of everyone in the class, including the instructor and the paraprofessionals. Students buy into the plan by being actively involved in developing the class rules and consequences at the beginning of the school year. Students then create silent hand signals that represent each of the class rules and use them to convey their feelings to others if they feel threatened or disrespected. Using silent signals avoids verbal confrontations and behaviors that may escalate beyond what is acceptable. The instructor and paraprofessionals also use the silent signals as a reminder to students who are off task.

It would be nice if all my students were intrinsically motivated to be physically active and improve sport skills. Unfortunately, most of my students seem to be lacking that motivation gene, so I must constantly develop programs and activities that motivate them to work toward their individual goals. Choice and self-pacing are key ingredients because we all know that teenagers need to feel like they are in control of what's happening.

PE Bucks are a successful motivational strategy I use throughout the school year. They look like play money with my picture in place of the president's and are color-coded in denominations of 1, 5, and 10. Students accumulate bucks by going the extra mile to help others, by demonstrating outstanding leadership or teamwork, or by participating in physical activity outside of school. They also receive a buck for every 10 minutes of fitness training they complete during class. Students collect PE Bucks throughout the year and use them to purchase items at an end-of-the-year luncheon and auction that is hosted by the adapted physical education staff.

Students tend to straggle in from the locker room at the beginning of the class period, so I created the Bonus Miles program to provide a structured activity for students to begin as soon as they arrive. They can earn extra fitness miles (PE Bucks) by exercising on a piece of cardio equipment until all students have arrived. Each student writes the time they arrive at class next to their name on the board, and when I call "Time," they compute their bonus-mile minutes and record them in their personal fitness log. The sooner students get to class and begin working, the more bonus miles they accumulate.

Other successful strategies that help students take responsibility for their learning and develop physical activity goals include the following:

- Writing the daily schedule on the board
- Having the Student of the Week lead warm-up exercises and cool-down stretches

(continued)

- Posting visual aids to help students remember warm-up, cool-down, and circuit sequences

- Posting task cards at fitness stations so that students can choose exercises that meet their fitness and interest levels

- Teaching students the lifelong benefits of physical activity

- Teaching students to check their own heart rate during exercise or use perceived exertion to determine whether they are working at the optimal level

- Helping students learn to pace themselves during physical activity

- Conducting group discussions, called fireside chats, at the end of class or when a problem occurs

- Teaching relaxation techniques to help students cope with stress

- Daily brief discussions with the teacher about each student's behavior as they leave the class

figure 5.2). The group can vote on the desired equipment, activity, game, or sport.

Physical activity reinforcers not only serve as an effective form of reinforcement but also may improve performance. For example, let's say that if a recreation fitness group completes all their exercises, they earn the right to participate in a cardio kickboxing class. Not only is their good behavior reinforced, they also receive physical fitness benefits from the activity. This type of reinforcement should not be viewed as free time but must have some instructional purpose, and the physical activity reinforcer must be earned. The Premack principle discussed later in the chapter provides more ways to use this approach (see page 83).

Physical activity reinforcers are usually free or inexpensive because the equipment or activity is already available as part of your program. When you consider that certain individuals may not respond to social reinforcers and that tangible reinforcers can be expensive, this form of reinforcement is an attractive alternative. In addition, focusing on earning physical activity reinforcers will make it easier for individuals to develop a greater appreciation for intrinsic rather than extrinsic rewards. After all, achievement itself can be an intrinsic reward. For example, you can assist individuals in setting personal goals and have them keep track of their progress. Seeing their results written down is concrete evidence of progress and can be intrinsically reinforcing.

Privileges Reinforcement

Earning a desired privilege can be motivational and is usually inexpensive. Examples of privileges include distributing equipment, being a squad or exercise leader, receiving a visit from a star athlete, and being a peer tutor. Together you and the individuals can determine a list of reinforcing privileges. Other privileges that can reinforce appropriate behavior are located in figure 5.2.

REINFORCEMENT MENUS

A reinforcement menu is a list of items that individuals can choose from when they earn a reinforcer. Display a menu of reinforcers such as the items that appear in figure 5.2 where everyone can easily see it. For some individuals, simply viewing the reinforcement menu on a locker room wall, bulletin board, dry-erase board, or outdoor facility can be quite reinforcing. Reinforcement menus can be paired with public posting, discussed later in this chapter. You can post pictures on a menu for nonreaders. To maintain motivation, change reinforcement menu items as needed. Whenever possible, empower individuals to choose the reinforcers to place on the menu. To develop reinforcement menu items you can use some of the examples from figure 5.2 and the reinforcement preference list in worksheet 2 (appendix A).

REINFORCEMENT SCHEDULES

You can use different reinforcement schedules to administer reinforcement, depending on individuals' needs. For example, continuous reinforcement means you immediately follow every occurrence of the behavior with a reinforcer. This type of schedule is most appropriate when an individual is in the initial stages of learning a behavior or skill. Once the individual has acquired or established the behavior, you must work to systematically decrease the reinforcer before its effectiveness fades. Adjusting the frequency helps assure that the reinforcement remains effective. Follow a schedule by which you gradually and systematically delay the reward for demonstrating the behavior. Figure 5.4 provides definitions and types of reinforcement schedules to follow.

POSITIVE REINFORCEMENT METHODS

In this section we'll examine proven, positive methods used in different physical activity settings to develop, maintain, or increase positive behavior. The Creating a Positive Climate for Learning section of PE Central (www.PEcentral.com) provides additional examples of positive reinforcement methods. When administering these methods, remember to offer the reinforcement only after the individual exhibits the desired behavior.

Which method will work best? The answer depends on the situation and the individual or group, but a good practice is to choose the method that requires the least amount of reinforcement to change the behavior. When possible, pair the reinforcement methods discussed in the following sections with a social reinforcer to help you phase out the reinforcer. For example, pair a tangible reinforcer with a smile and brief explanation why the individual earned the reinforcer so that ultimately you can fade the tangible reinforcer and use only a social reinforcer.

There is no such thing as a quick fix that will work with all individuals in all situations! Simply put, not everyone will respond in the same way to these methods. In addition, a reinforcement method that is effective at first may not work as well later. Thus, you must develop a wide repertoire of reinforcement methods and then tailor your behavior management program to the particular individual or group, maintaining interest and increasing desirable behavior. Always bring a variety of methods to the program, or as Hellison would say, "Have a big fat bag of tricks" (2003).

Prompting

A prompt is a cue or reminder to get an individual to perform a desired behavior. You can give a prompt before or during the behavior. Prompts

- **Continuous reinforcement.** The reinforcement is provided each time the appropriate behavior occurs.
- **Intermittent reinforcement.** The reinforcement is provided at specific times when the appropriate behavior occurs. Some type of schedule is followed.
- **Ratio reinforcement.** The reinforcement depends on the number of times the behavior is demonstrated.
  - *Fixed-ratio reinforcement.* The behavior is reinforced after a specific or predetermined (fixed) number of times the behavior occurs—for example, rewarding an individual for every five volleyball serves successfully completed.
  - *Variable-ratio reinforcement.* The behavior is reinforced after a variable number of times the behavior occurs, and the schedule of reinforcement is constantly changing—for example, reinforcing the participant the third time she correctly performs the volleyball serve, then rewarding her on the fifth correct serve. There is an average number of times that she is reinforced for correctly performing the skill (e.g., 4 times).
- **Interval reinforcement.** The reinforcement depends on the period of time in which the behavior occurs.
  - *Fixed-interval reinforcement.* The behavior is reinforced after a specific, predetermined period of time the behavior occurs. For example, the athlete is reinforced for every 15 minutes he is on task swimming laps in the pool.
  - *Variable-interval reinforcement.* The behavior is reinforced after a variable period of time the behavior occurs. For example, the athlete is reinforced for remaining on task swimming laps in the pool after 8 minutes, then 12 minutes, and then 10 minutes.

Figure 5.4 Reinforcement schedules.

can be verbal, physical, or environmental. Verbal prompts need to be positive and remind the individual of the expected behavior. For example, instead of saying, "Don't run around and don't talk," say, "Remember to sit in your designated area and listen for the next direction." You need to then reinforce those individuals who perform the desired behavior. A physical prompt physically conveys to individuals what kind of behavior you expect, such as tapping their arm to remind them to transition to the next activity. An environmental prompt can be posting the rules or routines as a reminder of the expected behaviors. Another example is putting up posters with motivational slogans to increase exercise or skill performance (Weinberg and Gould, 2003).

Shaping

Some new behaviors may be too difficult at first for certain individuals to successfully complete. If so, use a task analysis or rubric to break the behavior down into smaller, well-defined parts or steps. You can then shape the behavior by reinforcing the performance of each small step or approximation of the expected behavior. For example, say that the desired behavior is to have the individual put equipment away in the equipment cart. This behavior can be shaped in a progression as follows: Reinforce the individual

for picking up the equipment; then reinforce the individual for walking with the equipment to the cart; then reinforce the individual for putting the equipment in the cart. Many examples of rubrics or task-analyzed behaviors and skills exist in the literature (for instance, refer to Lieberman and Houston-Wilson, 2002).

Once the individuals perform the desired behavior consistently, gradually fade and eliminate the steps. The goal is for each individual to eventually perform the behavior without a reinforcer.

Token Economy System

In physical activity settings, it is not always convenient to immediately give tangible reinforcers. A token economy system is a delayed method of reinforcement. In such a system, individuals receive a token immediately following successful performance of the desired behavior. Later they exchange the tokens for a reinforcer (see figure 5.5). You can use the reinforcement schedules previously discussed in figure 5.4 to schedule such exchanges.

Whatever you choose to use as tokens, you need to be able to easily dispense them and to quickly record their use. Consider using points, stamps, poker chips, tickets, stickers, smiley faces, or marbles. Be sure individuals cannot access the same type of tokens outside the pro-

Figure 5.5   The token economy system is a delayed method of reinforcement that allows the participant to exchange the token for a desired reinforcer.

gram. For young children you can use seasonal theme tickets. For example, in October you could use a ticket with a picture of a ghost, pumpkin, or witch, and in February you could use a ticket with a heart on it. To keep track of each individual's tokens, use a group reinforcer pocket chart with names displayed on the pockets. Write the individuals' names on the tickets in ink to keep them from "borrowing" others' tickets. For older participants, record checkmarks on a point card. Teach responsible behavior by having individuals keep track of their own points with minimal monitoring. If you have a problem with individuals adding checkmarks they have not earned, have trustworthy individuals, perhaps squad leaders, add checkmarks, or periodically oversee this procedure yourself. Worksheet 3 in appendix A shows a sample weekly physical activity point card for middle or high school students. They can earn 1 point for following each of the class rules, which they check off in the appropriate blank on the card.

Premack Principle

The Premack principle states that you can use highly reinforcing activities to promote less popular behaviors (Premack, 1959). When administering the Premack principle remember to use "when and then" statements. The Premack principle is also known as "Grandma's rule," that is, "When you eat all your vegetables, then you get your dessert!" An example of the Premack principle is when individuals successfully complete five volleyball skill stations (less popular behavior) during the first 25 minutes of practice, then they can play a volleyball game (more popular behavior) for the remainder of the practice. Those who do not finish during the first 25 minutes do not earn the game reward and must continue to participate in the skill-station activities.

The Premack principle is effective because you can use activities that the individuals desire as an incentive. Refer to figure 5.2 and worksheet 2 (appendix A) in selecting highly desirable reinforcing activities.

Public Posting

This method involves publicly posting the names of individuals who have successfully performed the desired behavior. When possible, consider choosing a behavior that everyone is capable of performing. For example, everyone can be successful at improving a behavior such as transitioning from one activity area to the next, but some may fail to measure up when it comes to performing a particular motor skill. If they cannot perform the behavior, they may become discouraged and lose motivation. The idea is to acknowledge as many participants as possible. You can recognize appropriate behavior by posting the Participant of the Week or Month, for example. Be sure to check your organization's policy for publicly posting names.

Mary Ann Shaff, a teacher at Paul Elementary School in Paul, Idaho, uses public posting to promote good sportsmanship among all students in her physical education classes (see In the Trenches for more information).

Public posting combined with physical activity reinforcement greatly reduced the physical education transition time of students at one middle school. After observing and recording the timing of

---

IN THE TRENCHES

Promoting Sportsmanship
Mary Ann Shaff, Physical Education Specialist, Paul Elementary School, Paul, Idaho

I have started a Sportsmanship Club this year. I discussed at the beginning of the year what good sportsmanship is. At the end of the physical education period I ask each group who they felt were good sports that day. I also watch and if one of the students they identify is one I also noticed, they get their name up on the wall in the gym on a laminated sport ball. At the end of our grading period, all the students in the club whose names are on the wall get a sportsmanship award. Then the names are wiped off and we start over for the next grading period.

one of her classes, Ms. Dawson-Rodriques realized that her students were spending too much time transitioning from the locker room to the warm-up area and from the warm-up area to the first activity of the day. She met with her class and explained that students who transitioned from the locker room to their squad lines for the warm-up and from their squad lines to the first activity site in a certain amount of time would be reinforced by having their names publicly posted on the physical education bulletin board in the gymnasium. In addition, students would earn physical activity reinforcement based on the number of times their name was posted. She provided a list of possible activities and had students circle three of their favorite activities. Activities chosen by the class are listed in worksheet 2 in appendix A.

Almost immediately most of the students responded by getting to the warm-up area and the first daily activity during the allotted time. It was simple for Ms. Dawson-Rodriques to note the few students who did not make it on time and to post the names of all the other students. There was a decrease of 40 seconds in transitioning from the locker room to the warm-up area and a decrease of 18 seconds from the warm-up squad lines to the first teaching site. Student behavior improved as students focused on teacher expectations more. Many of the students remarked how they liked having their names posted on the board for all to see and participating in activities voted on by the class (Dawson-Rodriques, Lavay, Butt, and Lacourse, 1997). Since then, Ms. Dawson-Rodriques has continued to successfully use public posting with physical activity reinforcement in her classes.

Physical activity professionals who do not have access to a room or gymnasium and want to post behavior management information can use a trifold display board. Trifold poster boards are a portable, economical, and practical way to post such behavior management items as rules, motivational slogans, and folders for reinforcement stickers, tokens, and certificates. Worksheet 4 in appendix A provides a sample behavior management trifold poster board that has been developed and used by Barbara Lawrence, a teacher in the Los Angeles Unified School District (Lavay et. al 2003).

Contract

A contract can be either a verbal or a written agreement between two individuals that states the desired behavior or performance improvement over a specific period of time. Written contracts are usually more effective because the terms are recorded for all parties to see. You can design a contract to meet the needs of a particular individual or an entire group. You can write simple contracts to include only the behavior to be worked on and the reward to be earned (see figure 5.6), or you can write more detailed contracts (see figure 5.7). The range of responsibility for contracts will vary from the physical activity professional developing the contract and monitoring its effectiveness to the individuals planning their own contract with you and monitoring the contract themselves. In general, relate the amount of responsibility you give individuals in developing and implementing a contract to the level of personal responsibility and maturity they display.

Following are additional guidelines for developing and implementing contracts (French and Henderson, 1993; Weinberg and Gould, 2003):

- Be sure the contract is suitable. Ask yourself, "Are the terms attainable by the individual or group?" Set realistic goals with dates for when desired behaviors are to be met.
- Have all parties involved sign the contract, including the individual, parent, yourself, and any other professionals (i.e., teachers, coaches) that may have a vested interest in the individual.
- Have a third person read and sign the contract. Give each signing person a copy of the contract.
- Be positive. List accomplishments or behaviors the individual or group will perform.
- Be sure the reinforcement is highly prized by the individual or group and not easily obtained outside the conditions of the contract.
- Enforce the contract consistently and systematically, giving reinforcers only if earned and immediately following compliance with the contract terms.
- If necessary, consider small incremental accomplishments (i.e., shaping) to help the individual or group successfully perform the desired behavior. This allows for frequent rewards in the beginning. As behavior improves, you can gradually delay rewards.
- Include a bonus clause with an additional reward to reinforce outstanding behavior or performance and help motivate the individual or group.

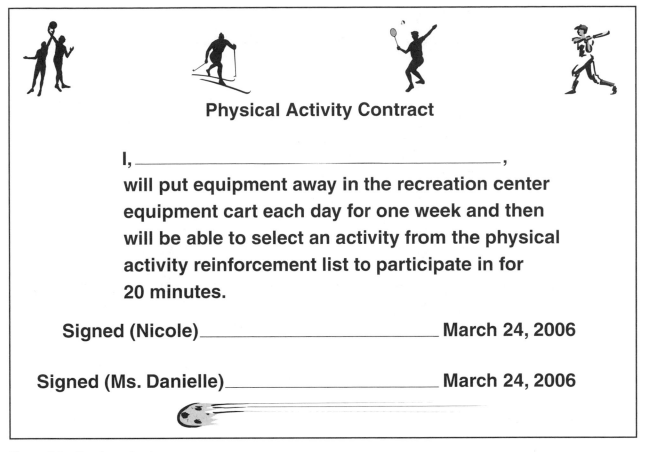

Physical Activity Contract

I, _____ ,
will put equipment away in the recreation center
equipment cart each day for one week and then
will be able to select an activity from the physical
activity reinforcement list to participate in for
20 minutes.

Signed (Nicole)_____ March 24, 2006

Signed (Ms. Danielle)_____ March 24, 2006

Figure 5.6 Simple contract.

- If the initial contract is ineffective or if you can see that the individual or group is not going to be able to meet the terms, renegotiate the contract.
- Use checklist 5.2 (page 91) when developing and implementing contracts.

Following is an example of how to effectively implement a contract in a youth sport program. Coach Richards, a youth volleyball coach, posted the names of different athletes and their specific responsibilities for helping with practice for the week (i.e., distributing and collecting equipment) in the recreation center gym. Shannon, a 12-year-old on the team, consistently forgot when it was her turn to perform her assigned duties. Coach Richards recognized that Shannon had attention-deficit/hyperactivity disorder (ADHD) and he patiently reminded her when it was her turn. Shannon tried hard and wanted to please, but she began to get frustrated because the coach had to remind her every time it was her turn.

The next season Coach Richards decided to try a different approach. At the beginning of the season, he spoke with Shannon's parents, who were helpful in explaining the medication Shannon was taking for ADHD. Coach Richards decided to meet with the parents and Shannon to discuss the problem of her forgetting to complete her assignment. Shannon's parents suggested that Coach Richards try using a written contract with Shannon. She was familiar with contracts because Ms. Stein, her classroom teacher, successfully used them to get Shannon to complete school reading assignments. The parents mentioned that because of Shannon's information-processing difficulty and short attention span, he would need to keep the contract simple. During the meeting, they also ascertained that Shannon would like to have Clayre, a teammate and friend who lived in her neighborhood, as a partner for volleyball drills.

When designing the contract, Coach Richards wasn't sure that Shannon could remember her assignment for 5 consecutive days to receive her reward, so they decided that if she successfully completed her assignment 4 out of 5 days without Coach Richards reminding her, she would be rewarded. Coach Richards also explained to

Group Physical Activity Contract

I,————————————————, understand and agree with the following **Weekly Grading Point System in Physical Education Class.** I understand I can earn points toward my grade each day of class by following this point system. I also understand that when I earn 100 points I can choose the Friday Sport Option Day from the sports and activities reinforcement list.

• 2 points for dressing properly for physical education class

• 2 points for following and participating in all class instructions given by the teacher

• 2 points for performing all the required exercises during the 10-minute warm-up stations

• 2 points for completing the performance skill worksheet during the 40-minute lesson

• 2 points for cooperating with classmates by sharing equipment, taking turns, and putting equipment away

You can earn a total of 10 points for each class meeting. The following is the weekly grading system:

GRADING SYSTEM – 5 DAYS	
Grade	**Points**
A	50-45
B	44-40
C	39-35
D	34-30
F	below 30

————————————————
Student's signature

————————————————
Physical educator's signature

————————————————
Parent's signature

Figure 5.7 Detailed behavior contract that involves a token economy.

Shannon about a special bonus clause through which she could receive an additional reward for successfully completing her assignment of distributing and collecting the volleyballs for 5 consecutive days.

Coach Richards explained the contract to Shannon. Shannon, Coach Richards, and Shannon's parents agreed to the contract and signed it (see figure 5.8). Shannon kept a copy of the contract in her gym bag. The contract was effective as Shannon remembered to distribute the equipment to teammates 4 out of 5 days and only forgot to collect equipment 1 day. Having Clayre as an activity partner not only motivated Shannon to remember her responsibilities but also helped her stay on task during practice drills. Coach Richards decided to have Shannon continue the contract for another 2 weeks.

Group Contingencies and Positive Behavior Games

A group contingency is the presentation of a highly desired reinforcer to a group of individuals based on the behavior of the group as a whole or one person (Vogler and French, 1983). A group contingency is usually effective with individuals who seek peer approval more than the approval of the physical activity professional. It can effectively build team and community spirit in groups (Glover and Anderson, 2003; Patrick, Ward, and Crouch, 1998).

The most common group contingency involves having everyone in the group earn a desired reinforcer depending on the behavior of the entire group. When using a group contingency, first consider whether or not every individual in the group is capable of earning the reinforcement. This helps ensure that individuals do not place undue peer pressure on any one individual or group of individuals. If an individual or squad consistently demonstrates negative behavior and ruins the chances of the entire group earning the reinforcer, assign those individuals to another group or design a different contingency plan.

In another type of group contingency, you and the participants develop a group goal and

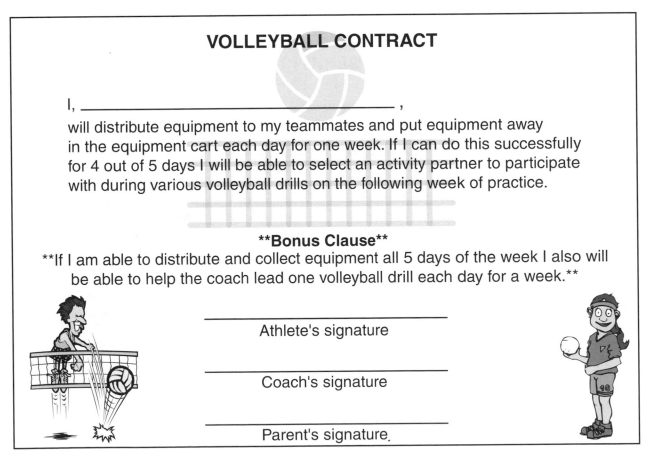

VOLLEYBALL CONTRACT

I, _____ ,

will distribute equipment to my teammates and put equipment away in the equipment cart each day for one week. If I can do this successfully for 4 out of 5 days I will be able to select an activity partner to participate with during various volleyball drills on the following week of practice.

Bonus Clause
If I am able to distribute and collect equipment all 5 days of the week I also will be able to help the coach lead one volleyball drill each day for a week.

_____
Athlete's signature

_____
Coach's signature

_____
Parent's signature

Figure 5.8 Shannon's contract.

participants work individually to earn the desired reinforcer. This method helps eliminate the competitiveness of the group contingency described earlier. Figure 5.9 provides examples of positive behavior games using group contingencies.

NEGATIVE REINFORCEMENT

We can define negative reinforcement as a reinforcer used to increase a desired behavior by encouraging individuals to perform that particular behavior in order to avoid something they dislike. Both negative and positive reinforcers produce similar results: an increase in a desired behavior. The methods, however, are quite different. Positive reinforcement results in an increase in a desired behavior by presenting the individual with something valued, called a pleasant stimulus, after the individual has exhibited the behavior. In contrast, negative reinforcement results in an increase in a desired behavior because you have removed something the individual perceives as unpleasant and wishes to avoid, called an aversive stimulus (Loovis, 2005). For example, a student in physical education class wants to avoid losing points off her class grade (aversive stimuli) by performing all her warm-up exercises (increase in behavior). The student recognizes that this is the only way to avoid receiving a lower grade. A student who doesn't want to sit in the bleachers and write a report (aversive stimuli) will dress for physical education class (increase in behavior).

Negative reinforcement is often confused with punishment, or corrective methods. Corrective methods decrease a behavior by either presenting an aversive stimulus or removing a positive stimulus. For example, if you make a student sit in time-out (removing them from the positive environment) to get the student to stop talking out of turn (decreasing a behavior), you are using a corrective method. If you take away a player's tokens (removing a positive stimulus) to get the player to stop misusing equipment (decreasing a behavior), you are also using a corrective method. Simply put, use corrective methods to redirect or decrease an undesirable behavior and negative reinforcement methods to increase a desired behavior. We'll further investigate corrective methods in chapter 6.

POSITIVE BEHAVIOR GAMES

Flip Chart Game

This game uses a flip chart or a scoreboard that participants can easily see. Have the team vote on possible physical activity reinforcers. Explain to the team that while playing this game, they have the opportunity to earn 10 minutes participating in the physical activity they voted for. Say, "Today 10 times during practice I will scan the team, and each time everyone on the team is on task and participating in the practice drills, I will reward the team by giving you a point on the flip chart (or scoreboard). For each point, you'll earn 1 minute of physical activity time, which we'll have at the end of practice. If any of you are not on task when I check, I will not give the team a point that time. But each time you are all participating, the team can earn a minute at the end of the practice for a possible total of 10 minutes. At the end of the session, I will add up all the points and see how much time you earned as a team." If one individual in the group is consistently ruining the group's ability to be rewarded, that individual can work alone to earn the desired reinforcer.

Run the State Game

Form groups who race each other on a map of your state or from city to city (New York City to Los Angeles), or have the group develop their own route, which you display on a bulletin board. Allow participants to exchange each completed fitness item, such as running a lap or performing so many push-ups or crunches, for a certain number of miles on the map, depending on how long the route is and how quickly you feel the desired behavior needs to be reinforced. Represent each group on the map with a picture of a running shoe. If desired, award miles for good behavior, such as following class rules or getting to class on time, instead of or in addition to miles earned for fitness efforts. When a group reaches their destination, give them a reward. If necessary or desired, have each participant work individually to earn the desired reinforcer. Make this a cooperative activity by having everyone accumulate miles as a single group.

Figure 5.9 Positive behavior games where participants work individually to earn a reinforcer.

SUMMARY

Behavioral methods help maintain and increase desirable behaviors. Choose the method that requires the least amount of intervention but is still effective in achieving the desired behavior. Reinforcement methods include positive reinforcements, such as social reinforcers, tangible reinforcers, physical activities, and privileges; prompts; shaping; token economy systems; the Premack principle; public posting; contracts; group contingencies; and negative reinforcement. Use these methods singly or in combination as you see fit.

There is no quick fix for creating positive behavioral change. Use a variety of methods, adapting them when necessary in order to maintain individuals' interest, thereby increasing desirable behavior. Refer often to checklist 5.1 as you experiment with what works for you. But don't get so caught up in using these methods that they become ends in themselves; instead, think of them as ways to help you meet your goal in assisting individuals to take responsibility for their behavior.

WHAT DO YOU THINK?

1. What does "Catch the person being good" mean? Provide an example of how you can implement this method in your everyday physical activity setting.

2. Provide specific examples of how you can use different positive reinforcement methods (social reinforcers, tangible reinforcers, privileges, physical activity) to motivate individuals. Develop examples of reinforcers such as those in figure 5.2, but make them specific to your own situation.

3. Discuss the pros and cons of extrinsic and intrinsic reinforcement.

4. Give examples of how you can implement the following positive methods to increase desirable behaviors: prompts, token economy, Premack principle, public posting, contracts, and group contingencies and positive behavior games.

5. Develop a reinforcer preference list and a point exchange system specific to your own setting.

6. Discuss what is meant by choosing methods that require the least amount of intervention.

7. Why does an effective instructor need a variety of methods, or as Hellison (2003) states, "A big fat bag of tricks"?

CASE STUDIES

For each of the three case studies in chapter 1 on page 13, select methods described in this chapter and discuss in detail how you would implement each of the methods to manage the behavior. After you have developed your own methods, read the following suggestions, which are only some of the many creative ways you might apply the information covered in this chapter.

CASE 1

Hector, a Disruptive 3rd Grader

▸ Expect good behavior. Praise Hector whenever he demonstrates appropriate behavior.

▸ Determine the types of activities or privileges Hector likes by talking with him, his teacher, and his parents.

▸ Meet with Hector and his classroom teacher to develop a point system through which he may

(continued)

Case Studies   *(continued)*

earn points for performing the desired behaviors (i.e., standing at his assigned area during warm-ups). Develop an activity or privilege that he can trade points for. Write the behaviors and how many points he needs to earn to receive reinforcers in simple terms on a chart or index card for Hector to keep in his locker or classroom desk. Include a bonus clause that allows Hector to earn additional points he can trade for time to work with you on motor skills after class. This privilege not only serves as an effective reinforcer but may also improve Hector's skill deficits. Each day before class, review the point system with Hector until he understands and remembers it.

▶ In conjunction with the reward system, establish a structured teaching approach with Hector as discussed in chapter 3.

CASE 2
Ashante, an Instructor in Charge of Weight-Room Cleanup

▶ Verbally reinforce individuals who follow the weight-room rules and routines.

▶ When individuals demonstrate safety in the weight room, post their names on a safety-first poster, make them a squad leader, or give them additional workout time.

▶ Use verbal or poster prompts to remind participants to put weight equipment away in the proper storage area.

▶ Use the Premack principle, explaining that if the group keeps the weight room clean each session (behavior that is less desired) there will be additional time to work out (behavior that is more desired).

▶ Develop a group contingency where everyone must work together to clean up the weight room by the end of the session to avoid spending additional time during the next session cleaning up the weight room (negative reinforcement).

CASE 3
Molly, an Overly Aggressive Soccer Player

▶ Have a meeting with Molly and explain that she is a good person and athlete and that you are confident she can demonstrate good sportsmanship to her teammates and opponents.

▶ Develop a group contingency to help reduce Molly's aggressive behavior of arguing and fighting, which will be effective as long as she seeks peer approval. For example, if Molly does not argue during practices or games, then the team can earn certain privileges.

▶ Develop a contract with Molly where she can earn certain privileges for exhibiting honorable sporting behavior in practices and games.

▶ If Molly continues to fight and argue, combine rewards for demonstrating appropriate behavior with corrective methods described in chapter 6.

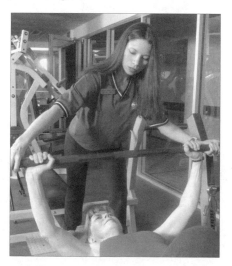

Checklist 5.1   Administering Positive Reinforcement

Rate yourself in regard to the following statements.

	Consistently	Inconsistently	Never
I make reinforcement contingent on the individual or group demonstrating the appropriate behavior.	☐	☐	☐
I individualize reinforcers to meet the unique needs of each individual.	☐	☐	☐
I am patient with my plan to increase positive behavior.	☐	☐	☐
When I see the desired behavior, I reinforce the individual immediately.	☐	☐	☐
I pair social reinforcers with tangible reinforcers so that I can eventually phase out the tangible reinforcers.	☐	☐	☐
On the continuum of reinforcement methods, I choose the method that requires the least amount of reinforcement to change a behavior.	☐	☐	☐
Once the individual or group performs the behavior, I reinforce less often.	☐	☐	☐

Checklist 5.2   Developing Behavioral Contracts

Writing a contract

_____ The contract is fair to and suitable for all involved.

_____ I have designed the contract positively, stressing what will rather than what will not be done.

_____ I have ensured that the rewards for compliance are highly prized by those involved and hard to obtain otherwise.

_____ I have listed rewards for small, incremental accomplishments, gradually delaying rewards over time.

_____ I have included a bonus clause.

_____ If this is a subsequent contract, I have made it more difficult than the previous one.

_____ The contract includes dates that the agreement begins and ends.

Enforcing a contract

_____ I have ensured that all involved understand the conditions of the contract.

_____ The contract is signed by all involved, possibly including parents.

_____ I have given each signing person a copy of the contract.

_____ The contract begins as soon as possible after signing.

_____ I give reinforcers immediately after individuals have earned them.

_____ I enforce the contract consistently and systematically.

Following up

_____ If the initial contract seems ineffective or I see that an individual cannot succeed, I renegotiate the terms accordingly.

CHAPTER

Behavioral Methods for Decreasing Inappropriate Behaviors

***U**nfortunately, many coaches attempt to motivate their athletes predominantly through intimidation, criticism, sarcasm, guilt, and physical abuse. Although these methods often are effective in the short term, they typically backfire in the long term.*

Weinberg and Gould, 2003

Ms. Jackson had just completed her first two softball practices as the coach of a team of 8- to 10-year-old girls. She was frustrated because some of the girls were goofing off and not doing the drills as instructed. She remembered that in a class in her training program her professor had said time-outs could be effective in decreasing inappropriate behaviors. To think through the situation, Ms. Jackson wrote a description of the behaviors she wanted to eliminate. She decided to have anyone who exhibited any of the described inappropriate behaviors sit out for 1 minute for an observational time-out. She explained her plan to the girls at practice on Monday, telling them the specific behaviors that would result in a time-out. As is typical, the girls thought of this plan as a game and at first behaved inappropriately simply to see what time-out was like. They soon realized, however, that they did not like sitting in time-out, watching the other girls having fun practicing softball. Soon the undesirable behaviors disappeared almost entirely.

To create an environment that is conducive to learning, you must implement management methods that occur along a continuum (see figure 6.1). The first step is to use the proactive management methods described in chapter 3 to prevent behavior problems. Then use reinforcement methods described in chapters 4 and 5 to increase the frequency of appropriate behaviors.

There are times, however, when individuals ignore positive efforts and continue to exhibit disruptive behaviors, interfering with their own and others' opportunity to learn and perform. According to Charles (2002), there are five types of misbehavior. Following they are listed in descending order of severity:

1. Aggression—physical or verbal attacks on others
2. Immorality—unethical behaviors such as lying, cheating, or stealing
3. Defiance—refusing to do what is requested
4. Disruption—talking out of turn, interrupting, or clowning around
5. Goofing off—being off task, leaving the assigned area, or not doing the drills in the intended manner

If inappropriate behaviors occur, use methods to decrease them, such as differential reinforcement or corrective methods.

Punishment is a term often used to describe consequences that are implemented to decrease the future occurrence of a behavior. The strict definition of punishment is the infliction of a penalty for a crime or wrongdoing that generally connotes retribution rather than correction, a harsh or injurious treatment. We think that this term is too harsh for educational settings, so we have chosen to use the term *corrective methods*.

In this chapter, we'll continue discussing the behavioral approach by elaborating on methods to decrease inappropriate behaviors. Specifically, we'll examine five methods: differential reinforcement, withdrawal of a reinforcer, presentation of an aversive stimulus, physical restraint, and requirement of an aversive behavior. To help you tailor these methods to your own situation, we'll give specific steps and examples. Then we'll discuss the possible side effects of using more severe methods to decrease inappropriate behavior as well as guidelines for using these methods cautiously yet effectively.

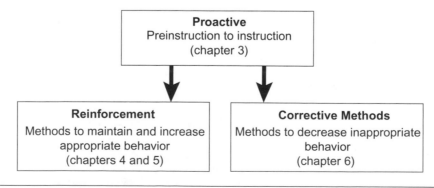

Figure 6.1 Behavior management methods from prevention to correction.

DIFFERENTIAL REINFORCEMENT

Sometimes you can decrease an inappropriate behavior by using differential reinforcement. Differential reinforcement is a positive way to decrease inappropriate behavior by reinforcing an appropriate behavior.

There are four types of differential reinforcement.

1. **Differential reinforcement of incompatible behavior (DRI)** is reinforcing a behavior that is incompatible with the problem behavior, meaning the individual could not do both behaviors at the same time. For example, if Trevor is talking to Mark while the coach is giving instructions, the coach could ask Trevor to demonstrate the instep kick and reinforce him using social praise for his demonstration. Demonstrating a kick is incompatible with talking to Mark.

2. **Differential reinforcement of alternative behavior (DRA)** is reinforcing a behavior that is an alternative to the problem behavior. The individual must choose to do the alternative behavior and get reinforced for it. For example, if Trevor is talking to Mark during instructions, the coach could ignore Trevor until he stops talking and then verbally praise him when he is listening.

3. **Differential reinforcement of a low rate of behavior (DRL)** is using reinforcement when a problem behavior occurs less often than a specified amount in a period of time. For example, say the group leader collects baseline data on the number of times Alex uses inappropriate language in a 30-minute recreational activity. The average number of times the inappropriate language occurs is 10. The group leader would then tell Alex that if she decreases the number of inappropriate words to 5 or fewer during the activity, she can play a game of her choice. The group leader keeps track of the number of times Alex says an inappropriate word and reinforces her if she meets the goal. The goal is set each time to gradually decrease the number of inappropriate words until Alex is not saying any inappropriate words during the entire activity.

4. **Differential reinforcement of the omission of behavior (DRO)** is using reinforcement when problem behavior does not occur during a specified period of time. Using the same example, the group leader gets baseline data on the average length of time that Alex participates in the activity without saying an inappropriate word for 30 minutes. If the average length of time is 5 minutes, then the leader would say to Alex, "If you can participate for 8 minutes without saying an inappropriate word, you can choose the game at the end of the activity." The leader keeps track of the number of the inappropriate words Alex says during the 8-minute time period and reinforces Alex if she meets the goal. The length of time can be gradually increased until Alex participates the entire 30 minutes of activity without saying an inappropriate word.

Differential reinforcement has been successfully used to increase appropriate behaviors and decrease inappropriate behaviors. If these methods do not work, then corrective methods can be used. Often these methods can be used in combination with differential reinforcement to strengthen the probability of success.

CORRECTIVE METHODS

You can administer corrective methods in four basic ways:

1. Taking away something the individual likes, known as withdrawal of a reinforcer
2. Presenting something the individual does not like, known as presenting an aversive stimulus
3. Physically restraining the individual
4. Requiring individuals to do something they dislike, known as requiring an aversive behavior

These methods range from mild to severe (see figure 6.2). The continuum is not as linear as it

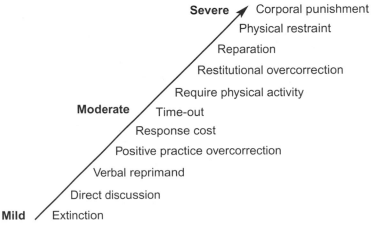

Figure 6.2   Continuum of corrective methods.

appears, as each method can be administered mildly or more severely. For example, seclusion time-out could mean placing an individual in another room for 3 minutes (a mild seclusion time-out) or kicking the individual out of the program or off the team indefinitely (a more severe seclusion time-out).

Withdrawal of a Reinforcer

There are three methods of withdrawing a reinforcer: extinction, or planned ignoring, response cost, and time-out. These are considered mild to moderate corrective methods (see figure 6.2). Let's examine each method in detail.

Extinction, or Planned Ignoring

Extinction, also called planned ignoring, is withholding a reinforcement when an inappropriate behavior occurs in order to decrease the occurrence of that behavior in the future. In other words, the reinforcement for a previously reinforced behavior is discontinued. To extinguish an inappropriate behavior, you must first identify the behavior, determine what is reinforcing it, and determine how to take the reinforcer away. For example, Jose was making duck noises (inappropriate behavior) while the coach, Ms. Hannigan, gave instructions. Ms. Hannigan decided to ignore the duck noises (withdrawal of the reinforcement) and continue with the instructions. Eventually, Jose stopped making the noises because he was not being reinforced. If the behavior is benign, of short duration, and does not interrupt the group, it is usually best to ignore it. Examples of behaviors that usually should be ignored include talking quietly and quickly to a friend, continuing briefly to perform an activity when the coach has asked players to come in, not paying attention, walking around the group, and so on. Sometimes all it takes is a look to get the individual to stop doing the behavior.

Consider the following variables when using extinction:

- The greater the magnitude of the reinforcer, the greater the resistance to extinction. If individuals really like the reinforcer, they will continue the behavior for a longer time after the reinforcement stops.
- The longer the behavior has been reinforced, the more resistant it will be to extinction. In other words, an entrenched behavior is usually harder to extinguish than a new behavior.

- The more frequently the behavior has been extinguished, the more quickly extinction will occur.

Although extinction may appear easy to administer, it can get complicated:

- Sometimes it is difficult to identify what is reinforcing the individual's behavior.
- If the physical activity professional is the reinforcement source, then it is relatively easy to extinguish the behavior. But often the source of reinforcement is another person, such as a classmate, player, peer, or parent, who is not as easy to control.
- Extinction is gradual. Moreover, undesirable behavior will increase before it decreases.
- Never use the extinction method to eliminate behaviors that are harmful to the individual or others. You cannot simply ignore dangerous behavior.

During extinction, look for appropriate behaviors the individual exhibits and reinforce those behaviors. You can also reinforce the appropriate behaviors of other individuals. For example, while ignoring Jose's duck noises, compliment Carlos for listening to directions quietly: "I like the way Carlos is listening and sitting quietly." Leaving off an additional comment such as "Why can't you do that too, Jose?" can be difficult, but such a comment can reinforce inappropriate behavior by giving Jose attention and is not part of a positive climate. So simply let peers serve as models of good behavior. Meanwhile, be patient: Extinction can be very effective when used appropriately.

See checklist 6.1 to make sure you are using extinction appropriately (page 112).

Response Cost

For this method, you must take away a reinforcer. This method is common in everyday life. A child may lose his allowance for not cleaning his room, an employee may have her pay docked for coming in late, or a driver may get a speeding ticket and have to pay a fine for going over the speed limit. Sometimes the reinforcer is a privilege such as going to a game after school or losing free time.

Response cost can easily be applied in different physical activity settings. For example, if an individual behaves inappropriately, you can take away such things as points toward her grade; activities that are reinforcing such as playing in a soccer game at the end of practice; privileges such as attending basketball games, soccer matches, swimming meets, football games, or field trips; free time by requiring the individual to stay after school or practice for a detention; or the individual's next turn in a game or activity. See In the Trenches for one way to use response cost in a physical activity setting.

Response cost is used in sport in a variety of ways. In basketball, when a player commits a foul he loses his opportunity to play the game (see figure 6.3). In football, when a foul is committed the offending team loses yardage.

Response cost works well with a token economy (see chapter 5). An individual gets tokens for good behavior, but the physical activity professional can take the tokens away if the individual misbehaves. The individual then has fewer tokens to turn in for prizes or fun activity time.

Figure 6.3   Fouling out is a response cost in basketball.

IN THE TRENCHES

Response Cost
Penny Davis, Special Physical Educator, Salt Lake School District

How I use corrective techniques in my classes depends a great deal on the classroom dynamics. When I am working with a group that has a healthy competitive attitude, I use group consequences with response cost. I give all the warnings before we start the activity so that everyone is equally accountable. For example, in a relay, if the direction is to skip and a team member decides to run, the whole team needs to sit down and they lose the opportunity to participate and earn points for that race. Then I repeat the race, allowing the team member to make a better choice. When the student makes the appropriate choice to skip, I reinforce the student and team for their good choices. As much as I do not want to decrease activity time, I also do not want to reinforce inappropriate behaviors. Following through with set consequences greatly increases appropriate behaviors and decreases inappropriate behaviors.

Another corrective method I have found effective in my classes is the use of verbal reprimands. To make this method effective I must first earn the respect of the students. With verbal reprimands, I give quick, quiet, specific commands that are between the student and me. My goal is not to embarrass anyone. I strive to create a friendly and supportive environment in which the children can play, have fun, and improve their fitness and motor skills. I find that one-to-one attention with verbal reprimands actually makes the student feel special and noticed. In return, the student's appropriate behaviors almost always increase and their inappropriate behaviors decrease because they seek my approval. This would probably not be the case if I did not earn the respect of the students beforehand.

Guidelines for Using Response Cost

1. Reinforcers must be available for good behavior that the individual exhibits instead of the inappropriate behavior. When an individual performs a desirable behavior, such as serving as a peer tutor for another individual who is having trouble on an assignment, notice the behavior and reinforce it with social praise and perhaps extra points.

2. An individual must have access to the reinforcer before you can withdraw it. If the individual already has a low grade, taking more points away will not mean much. Likewise, if the individual could not attend the soccer match anyway because of parental restrictions, then taking away that privilege is meaningless.

3. The reinforcer must be important to the individual. If the individual does not like basketball, taking away the privilege of playing in a basketball game is meaningless.

4. Keep the withdrawal of reinforcers to a minimum. If you take reinforcers away too frequently, the individual will feel defeated and stop caring about the reinforcers.

5. Make sure the individual understands beforehand which behavior is causing you to take the reinforcement away. If, for example, you are going to take away the privilege of playing in a group game for getting into verbal confrontations, tell everyone of this possibility before the activity begins.

6. Refrain from chronically warning, nagging, or threatening the individual. It is far more effective to simply administer the response cost when the misbehavior occurs than to threaten the individual with the consequence. Warnings often prolong the misbehavior as the individual will expect a number of warnings before being corrected and will use all the warnings possible, often making a game out of it and seeing how many times misbehavior can occur without a consequence.

7. Be careful not to debate the administration of the response cost once the misbehavior occurs, trying to justify your response. Never give in when an individual tries to debate with you about the misbehavior with such pleas as, "I'm sorry, I didn't mean to do it"; "I won't do it again"; or "Please, just give me one more chance." This too becomes a game. Calmly state the consequences and resume your work with the other individuals.

8. Be careful not to become emotionally involved. For example, individuals often try to make you feel guilty for correcting them. Don't buy into this ploy. Detach yourself from the situation and say, for example, "You chose to throw your bat when you struck out, so you will miss a turn at bat." Then refocus on the entire class or team.

9. When possible allow natural or logical consequences to take place. For example, when an individual is showing off during an activity or game, she is likely to miss a turn, which is probably more of a consequence than if you had required her to sit down and miss a turn.

10. Be consistent. Whenever the individual exhibits the inappropriate behavior, make sure you administer the consequence. If individuals get away with misbehavior without consequences, inappropriate behaviors will increase instead of decrease.

Time-Out

To use this method, remove individuals from a reinforcing environment for a certain period of time when they exhibit an inappropriate behavior frequently. The three types of time-out are observational, exclusion, and seclusion. Another equally important but different type of time-out is self-time-out.

1. **Observational time-out.** Remove the individuals from the activity for a certain period of time but allow them to watch others participating and behaving appropriately. This method is effective if the individuals enjoy participating in the activity, and coaches use it when they substitute players for players who lost their temper on the field, allowing the replaced players to sit out and cool down. The rules of some games give extended time-outs for misbehavior. For example, in basketball, if players commit 5 fouls, they must sit out the rest of the game; in soccer, if players exhibit poor sportsmanship, the referee can give them a red card, banning them from playing the rest of the game. See figure 6.4.

2. **Exclusion time-out.** Remove the individuals from the activity by having them sit on the side of the field where they cannot see the activities of the others. The exclusion time-out can take place in any area away from where everyone else is playing,

Figure 6.4   Getting a red card in soccer means a time-out for the rest of the game.

such as a bench, drawn circle, or bleacher, as long as the group leader can still see the individuals in time-out.

3. **Seclusion time-out.** Have the individuals leave the setting completely. This method works best when the time-out area has little visual and auditory stimulation and no one else is around. However, you must ensure that the area is supervised, safe, and properly lit and ventilated. Some options for this type of time-out area are the office or another room where the individual can be supervised. Coaches and recreation specialists sometimes send children home, but this method should only be used in extreme cases such as aggressive or violent behavior. If this method is used, the individual should be escorted home by another adult. The parents should be home and should be informed of the inappropriate behavior.

4. **Self-time-out.** The intention of time-out is to allow the individuals to cool off, gain self-control, think about the behavior, and realize that what they did was unacceptable. Guide the individuals to find their own way to gain control and use it for the time-out. Children and adults need to learn how to deal with their anger and frustration and may need to be taught an alternative behavior. Encourage individuals to take their own time-out when they feel they are losing control. Children as young as 3 years old can learn the concept of self-time-out. It is unreasonable to expect everyone to gain self-control in the same way. Methods for gaining

self-control include walking, running, taking deep breaths, yoga, singing, and so on. See chapter 8 for an explanation of relaxation techniques. Finally, you need to offer methods that are compatible with the setting. For example, if certain individuals throw the bat when they strike out, they should take four deep breaths, put the bat in the rack, and walk around the park. Once they learn how to control their emotions and practice their time-out, instruction and learning can occur.

After the individual has learned an alternative behavior, consequences for the misbehavior may still be necessary. If someone called a teammate a name, he will be required to apologize to his teammate. If she threw the bat and broke it, she will pay for the bat. If he dumped the card game on the floor at the recreation center, he will be required to pick it up. White and Bailey (1990) suggest that children feel better about themselves when they are required to pay their dues and take responsibility for their behavior. Without an available means of righting a wrong, individuals begin to think of themselves as "bad." That negative thought often leads to behavior consistent with that belief.

In effect, time-out provides time to reflect on inappropriate behaviors and to calm down and figure out solutions to problem situations (White and Bailey, 1990). If the physical activity professional gradually gives individuals the responsibility for knowing when to take a time-out and finding solutions to the problem, that teaches them a valuable lesson in taking responsibility that they will use throughout a lifetime.

See checklist 6.1 to check your effectiveness in using these methods (page 112).

Presentation of an Aversive Stimulus

An aversive stimulus is one that is unpleasant to the individual. Two of the most common methods of presenting aversive stimuli are direct discussion with the individual and verbal reprimands. These are considered mild corrective methods. The third method, corporal punishment, is the most severe aversive stimulus.

Direct Discussion

Before implementing any corrective method for a misbehavior, it is critical to determine why the individual acted inappropriately. Arrange a private meeting with the individual to determine reasons for the misbehavior. Begin the discussion with a statement such as, "Andrea, you usually listen when I am giving instructions, but today you were arguing with Jami when I was talking. Has something upset you?" Listen carefully to the response and then restate the response in your words to verify your understanding of it. If you have accurately stated the response, the individual will feel validated and understood. If you have restated it incorrectly, the individual has the opportunity to restate the response so that you understand it. Identification of what is upsetting often helps individuals express their feelings in a safe environment and deal with those feelings in a positive way (Hichwa, 1998). After discussion, you must determine if a consequence is still necessary. If so, you must agree upon an

Guidelines for Using Time-Out

1. Inform the individual which behavior elicited the time-out; for example, say, "Felix, you threw your bat; sit in time-out for 1 minute."

2. Individuals may try to talk you out of the time-out by saying, "I'm sorry. I'll be good." Administer time-out in a consistent and matter-of-fact manner and do not discuss or negotiate the time-out with the individual. When an undesirable behavior occurs, state the rule they violated, for example, "No hitting," and send the individuals to time-out. Say nothing else; give no explanation. If you do negotiate, they will try to negotiate each time they misbehave and it becomes a test of wills.

3. Make sure that the time-out is not reinforcing. For example, some individuals like to be alone or to sit in the hall and interact with others who pass by, so being alone or in the hall may actually be more reinforcing than participating in the activity they were required to leave.

4. Make sure the individuals are not getting out of a situation that they don't like. Time-outs may be negatively reinforcing, that is, the individuals get out of doing an activity they don't like to do, such as running sprints or doing warm-up exercises. In such a case you are actually reinforcing the misbehavior, and the next time they run wind sprints, it is likely that Katerina will again talk with Isabel so that they can go to time-out instead of running sprints.

5. Specify the amount of time for the time-out in advance. It should not be too long or it will lose its effectiveness. One to 5 minutes is sufficient.

6. Wait until disruptive behavior stops before starting to time the time-out. If, for example, individuals have a temper tantrum and scream obscenities, wait until they calm down and stop screaming before you start timing the time-out.

7. When the time-out is over, have the individuals take responsibility by stating the rule that they broke and developing a plan to keep from breaking that rule again.

8. Make sure that after the time-out the individuals return to the task they were engaged in when the inappropriate behavior occurred so that they cannot use time-out to avoid doing tasks they don't like.

9. When individuals are not in time-out and are engaged in appropriate behavior, be sure to reinforce the appropriate behavior they are exhibiting. Say, for example, "Marcus, I sure like the way you put the bat down by the dugout." Be sure to use an enthusiastic, sincere tone of voice.

10. Encourage individuals to take a self-time-out by selecting their own way of timing out within the limits of the situation, such as walking or jogging around the soccer field, taking deep breaths, popping aluminum cans, and so on.

appropriate one and enforce it. See chapter 7 for more on this topic.

Verbal Reprimand

A verbal reprimand involves telling individuals that the behavior they exhibited is unacceptable and why it is unacceptable. This is followed by telling or asking the individual what they need to do instead. For example, if someone is interrupting you when you are giving instructions, you might say, "Joy, interrupting is impolite. It makes it dif-ficult for others to follow my instructions. Please wait until I am finished to ask your question."

Verbal reprimands are widely used because they are easy to administer and they are rela-tively effective when used appropriately (Hen-derson and French, 1990). However, when used inappropriately, verbal reprimands can lead to guilt, decreased self-esteem, and the perception of being attacked (Sands, Henderson, and Kilgore, 1999). For these reasons you must know how to administer effective verbal reprimands.

Guidelines for Administering Verbal Reprimands

1. Try nonverbal reprimands such as hand signals first.

2. Be specific. Tell the individual exactly what inap-propriate behavior you are reprimanding. Then encourage the individual to behave appropri-ately and include a statement of the appropriate behavior in the reprimand. Using "I" messages is often effective. For example, "Karl, when you are bouncing the ball, others cannot hear my instruc-tions. Please give me the ball. I get upset when I have to repeat my instructions."

3. Use proximity control (see chapter 3) by moving closer to the person who is behaving inappropri-ately and giving the verbal reprimand.

4. Reprimand the behavior; do not degrade the indi-vidual as a human being (Henderson and French, 1990). Say, for example, "Interrupting is impolite" rather than "You are impolite."

5. Avoid sarcasm. Some adults use sarcasm to chastise or cut down an individual in an attempt to con-trol behavior. Using words as a weapon of control, however, can alienate the misbehaving individual as well as the others in the group. Many times an adult unconsciously slips into this method or con-siders it a form of joking that gets the point across. However, sarcasm is usually not considered funny by the individuals on the receiving end and could negatively affect both their self-image and their status with their peers. In short, it is not a behavior builder. Sarcasm is detrimental to both the target of the sarcasm and to the overall climate of the group.

6. Always praise the desired behavior when the indi-vidual performs it. For example, say, "I like how you held the ball and paid attention while I was giving instructions." Avoid the temptation to add "for once," and you've reinforced the positive behavior.

7. Reprimand immediately after the behavior occurs. A delayed reprimand loses its effectiveness.

8. Be firm but gentle. Make sure the individual under-stands that you disapprove of the behavior.

9. If the individual or others may be harmed by the behavior, remove the individual to a time-out.

10. If necessary, back up the reprimand with a loss of privileges (response cost). For example, say, "Throw-ing a bat is unacceptable behavior. You will miss your next turn at bat."

11. Be calm. Getting upset only compounds the prob-lem and shows the individual a poor role model.

12. Avoid embarrassing the individual in the presence of others; take the individual aside whenever pos-sible. This is difficult in coaching, but it is critical. Sometimes when players are criticized in front of their teammates, they withdraw and their perfor-mance decreases (Sands, Henderson, and Kilgore, 1999). Before reprimanding, try using nonverbal reprimands such as the time-out signal, a finger to the lips, a stern look, and so on.

13. Do not use guilt! For example, do not say, "I'm disap-pointed in you, I never thought you would get into a fight."

14. Observe the individual's reaction to the reprimand to determine if it is aversive. Sometimes an indi-vidual finds the attention of an adult reinforcing even if it is in the form of a verbal reprimand. If the individual's behavior does not decrease with this method, try another method.

15. Always follow through. If you tell individuals they will have to sit out a turn for using inappropriate language, make sure they sit out.

16. When it's over, it's over. Do not keep reminding the individual of the misbehavior.

Corporal Punishment

Corporal punishment is using physical force with the intention of causing an individual to experience pain, but not injury, for the purpose of correction or behavior control. Some school districts define corporal punishment as touching an individual for the purpose of discipline, starting with putting your arm on an individual's shoulders to discuss a problem and including dragging an individual into time-out. Corporal punishment is the most severe corrective method (see figure 6.2) and it is the authors' opinion that it is never appropriate.

Organizations and institutions vary in their policies on corporal punishment. Some policies do not allow adults to touch individuals for any reason. Be sure you know what these policies are before you begin working. Whatever the policy, it is never appropriate to hit someone. When an individual is exhibiting aggressive, dangerous, or destructive behavior, the best solution is to get yourself and others away. The second option is to follow your organization's physical restraint policies to protect yourself and others.

Corporal punishment in schools is prohibited in all developed countries of the world except parts of the United States, parts of Canada, and one state in Australia. Schools are the only institution in the United States in which striking a person is legally sanctioned. It is not permitted in penal or mental institutions or in the military (www.stophitting.com). As of 2005, 28 state legislatures had passed laws prohibiting corporal punishment in the schools. Since these rulings, the number of individuals struck each year in the public schools has decreased from 1,521,896 (3.5% of all individuals) in 1976 to 342,038 (0.7% of all individuals) in 2000 (U.S. Department of Education, 2000). See table 6.1 for a list of states that have banned corporal punishment. For more information, see www.stophitting.com.

Researchers have shown that corporal punishment is used more often on individuals who are poor, are an ethnic minority, or have disabilities. In addition, boys are hit more often than girls. Schools that use corporal punishment typically have more vandalism, more truancy, more student violence, poorer academic achievement, and higher dropout rates (www.stophitting.com). Corporal punishment has also been linked to juvenile delinquency and adult criminal behavior of a violent nature. Individuals often experience rage and indignation that they do not express because of their fear of punishment. Later that repressed anger may exhibit itself in aggressive behaviors,

an inability to empathize, and a tendency to be either controlling or submissive (Imbrogno, 2000). Psychological side effects of corporal punishment include feelings of alienation, depression, and suicidal tendencies.

In states that still allow corporal punishment in schools, district administrators retain the discretion to prohibit the practice in their district. Make sure you know your district's or organization's policy regarding corporal punishment (see an example of a district policy in figure 6.6). In districts where corporal punishment is banned, if pain is inflicted on the student as a result of punishment, a parent or student could sue the teacher, school, and district for infliction of emotional or physical harm.

See checklist 6.2 to check your use of aversive stimuli (page 113).

Physical Restraint

You must avoid touching an individual when you are angry. However, physical restraint may be appropriate when you are unable to get away from a violent individual or when you need to stop a violent individual from hurting herself or others.

You must know how to properly restrain an individual. The preferred method is to stand behind

Figure 6.5   An effective method of physical restraint.

© Hester L. Henderson

the individual and hold the individual's wrists with the arms crossed over the chest (see figure 6.5). When using physical restraint, hold the individual firmly but not roughly, giving a sense of protection but not punishment. Speak softly to the individual, telling her you will hold her until she calms down. Hold her until she calms down and you feel she is in control.

Policies regarding physical restraint will be found in the same book as policies regarding cor-

poral punishment and may vary from institution to institution. Obviously, if the policy forbids adults to touch individuals, then physical restraint is not an option. Find out what your organization's policy is regarding this and other methods of discipline. Finally, we recommend attending any available training specifically related to using physical restraint.

The Massachusetts Department of Education has developed regulations to ensure that every

Table 6.1   States That Have Banned Corporal Punishment

State	Year	Present statute
Alaska	1989	AK stat. section 11.81.430
California	1986	CA educ. code section 49000
Connecticut	1989	CT gen. stat. section 53A-18
Delaware	2003	DE educ. code title 14, sec. 702
District of Columbia	1977	Board of education rule
Hawaii	1973	HI rev. stat. section 298-16
Illinois	1993	IL school code section 24-20
Iowa	1989	IA code section 280.21
Maine	1975	ME rev. stat. section t. 17-a 106
Maryland	1993	MD educ. code. ann. section 2305
Massachusetts	1971	MA ann. laws ch. 71, section 37G
Michigan	1989	MI comp. laws section 380.1312
Minnesota	1989	MN stat. section 127.45
Montana	1991	MT code ann. section 20-4-02
Nebraska	1988	NE rev. stat. section 79-4, 140
Nevada	1993	NV rev. stat. ann. section 20-4-302
New Hampshire	1983	NH rev. stat. ann. section 626:6
New Jersey	1967	NJ rev. stat. section 18A:6-1
New York	1985	NY penal law section 35.10
North Dakota	1989	ND cent. code section 15-47-47
Oregon	1989	OR rev. stat. section 339.250 (8)
Rhode Island		All local boards have banned
South Dakota	1990	SD codified laws section 13-32-2
Utah	1992	UT school code section 534-11-802
Vermont	1985	VT stat. ann. t. 16 section 1161a
Virginia	1989	VA code section 22.1-279.1
Washington	1993	WA rev. code section 9A.16.100
West Virginia	1994	WV code section 81A-5-1
Wisconsin	1988	WI stat. section 118.31

Dates listed are when the law was enacted, unless otherwise noted.

www.stophitting.org/laws/legalinformation.php

SAMPLE SCHOOL DISTRICT POLICY ON CORPORAL PUNISHMENT

Granite School District
Salt Lake City, Utah

Administrative Memorandum Number Six

Corporal Punishment

It is the practice of the district that incidents which involve corporal punishment or the use of physical force by school authorities to correct unacceptable behavior should be avoided. While the law is clear that the schools do act in loco parentis, and while the courts have upheld teachers who have, under certain circumstances, used corporal punishment, the complications which arise out of such incidents suggest extreme care should be used before using any physical force.

If school staff find themselves in a situation where they think that circumstances may result in physical action against a student, they should refer the student, situation permitting, to the administrative offices. Hopefully this action will result in a satisfactory resolution of the student behavior involved without using corporal punishment.

The above is not meant to rigidly prohibit physical action if provoked and/or warranted, such as actions taken in defense against physical attack by a student or to protect the life or safety of another student or staff member. These examples are more descriptive of self defense than of corporal punishment. Clearly our district position is not to engage in acts of physical aggression toward students which could be defined as corporal punishment.

Loren G. Burton,

Superintendent

Figure 6.6 Granite School District's policy on corporal punishment.

Reprinted, by permission, from Granite School District, 1992, *Administrative Memorandum Number Six on Corporal Punishment* (Salt Lake City, UT: Granite School District).

---

student is free from the unreasonable use of physical restraint. Physical restraint can be administered only when needed to protect a student or member of the school community from imminent, serious, physical harm. For more information on how this state established regulations for using physical restraint, see www.doe.mass.edu/lawsregs/603cmr46.pps.

Requiring an Aversive Behavior

There are several ways to require individuals to do something aversive to reduce inappropriate behavior, including requiring a physical activity or extra work, reparation, and overcorrection. These methods are considered moderate corrective methods (see figure 6.2).

Requiring Physical Activity

When individuals misbehave, too often physical activity professionals require the individuals to perform a physical activity such as running a lap, running wind sprints, performing sit-ups, or doing push-ups. However, using physical activity as a corrective method can create a negative attitude toward physical activity. The result may be that the individuals perceive physical activity as something to avoid. Another concern is that in some states where corporal punishment is illegal, using exercise as punishment is categorized as corporal punishment so it is against the law to use this method (Himberg, 2000). To check if using exercise as a corrective method is illegal in your state, consult your state's office of education. See figure 6.7 for one state's position statement on the use of physical activity as punishment.

Another common corrective method is assigning extra work. If an individual misbehaves, physical activity professionals may assign extra work to that individual such as writing a paper on why good sportsmanship is important or writing "I will exhibit good sportsmanship while playing on this team" 100 times. This method, although noble in its intent, may also teach individuals that writing is negative and should be avoided.

We do not condone using physical activity or extra work to correct behavior because it defeats

ON THE USE OF PHYSICAL ACTIVITY AS PUNISHMENT

The California Association for Health, Physical Education, Recreation and Dance is committed to the development of positive attitudes toward activity and active lifestyle habits in children and adults.

One of the prime goals of physical education programs is to provide students with positive experiences that will motivate them to pursue and develop active lifestyles. CAHPERD supports the California Physical and Health-Related Fitness Test and the objectives of teaching youth about the importance of fitness and an active lifestyle to their health.

The practice of utilizing physical activity (running laps and doing calisthenics) as punishment develops student attitudes that are contrary to the stated objectives of CAHPERD.

Teachers do not punish children with reading and then expect them to develop a joy for reading. Neither should teachers punish with exercise and expect children to develop a love of activity.

Not only is the use of physical activity as punishment contrary to the philosophy of CAHPERD, it is illegal. The California State Education Code states that "No person employed or engaged in a public school shall inflict, or cause to be inflicted, corporal punishment upon a pupil." The code defines corporal punishment as "the willful infliction of, or willfully causing the infliction of,

physical pain in a pupil." Punishing a child with lap running or push-ups imposes both physical and mental stress on a person. The physical and psychological damage is immeasurable.

Therefore, CAHPERD takes a position opposing the use of any form of physical activity as punishment in school and recreational programs.

The President of CAHPERD, M. Kathryn Scott, says:

> If a child is required to do push-ups or run laps, this should be done as part of an organized program in which all children are performing these activities as part of a conditioning aspect of the program. To single out students and have them perform push-ups or run laps as a form of discipline is contrary to sound educational practice. It is not going to teach discipline or respect. Unruly individuals, required to perform acts causing pain or discomfort, are not going to change behavior. This form of discipline does not address the actual behavior problem, but instead creates a deep-rooted dislike for any physical activity, which over a period of time will be more detrimental to the child's long-term health. That is a lot to sacrifice for what will be achieved in a few minutes of disciplinary lap running. (Letter to Superintendent Honig, August 10, 1989; see www.pesoftware.com)

Figure 6.7   California's position statement on using physical activity as punishment.

Reprinted, by permission, from CAHPERD, *Position Statement on the use of Physical Activity as Punishment* (Sacramento, CA: California Association for Health, Physical Education, Recreation and Dance). www.nospank.net/exerc2.htm. Accessed 4-20-05.

the goal of creating a positive attitude toward physical activity and promoting the desire to lead healthy, active lifestyles. Having a student or player run a lap for being late is not an uncommon practice, and we must think about the negative consequences of using physical activity to correct misbehavior (French, Lavay, and Henderson, 1985). When the individual is running the lap, is he thinking about how enjoyable physical activity is or is he thinking about how much he hates it?

Reparation

In this method individuals pay for misbehavior with money or time. If an individual breaks her hockey stick after she misses a goal, she must either pay for the hockey stick or do work such as picking up trash around the grounds a speci-

fied number of hours to pay for it. If working is the consequence you choose, have a conference with the parents and the child to explain the philosophy behind the consequence. Review school district or organizational policy to assure that the method is acceptable. It might be appropriate at the conference to ask the parents to suggest alternative methods. We have found that parents often want to pay for the equipment to get the child off the hook. This is only acceptable if the parents then make the child work to earn the money to repay them; otherwise the child has only learned that her parents will bail her out when she misbehaves.

Overcorrection

In overcorrection appropriate behaviors are taught and encouraged while inappropriate behaviors are decreased. Individuals must assume responsibility for their behavior by recognizing the effects of their inappropriate behavior on others and being willing to correct that behavior. The two types of overcorrection are restitutional overcorrection and positive-practice overcorrection.

Restitutional overcorrection is a method in which individuals have to rectify the situation by returning the environment to an improved state. For example, if individuals throw trash on the playing field, gym, or recreational facility they will be required to pick up all the trash in that area. If individuals steal something, they will be made to return the stolen object and apologize to the person from whom they took the object. This method works best if the consequence is immediate and if it relates to the inappropriate act.

Positive-practice overcorrection is a method in which an individual or group of individuals repeatedly practices performing a behavior appropriately as a consequence of performing it inappropriately. For example, if students come into the gym and are noisy and playing around, the physical educator might have the class practice going out of the gym and walking in quietly and sitting in their assigned place. If the players on a Little League baseball team are not paying attention when the coach is explaining how to slide into home base, the coach might have each player describe how to slide and then demonstrate the proper slide. After each player has repeated the instructions and demonstrated the slide several times, the probability that the team will not pay attention to the coach next time is decreased.

See checklist 6.3 to determine your effectiveness in requiring aversive behaviors (see page 114). Also see the You Can Handle Them Web site in appendix B for a list of over 100 inappropriate behaviors and different methods to manage them.

NEGATIVE SIDE EFFECTS OF SEVERE CORRECTIVE METHODS

Corrective methods are perhaps the most widespread method of controlling behavior (Weinberg and Gould, 2003). They are used frequently because of their immediate results. If a severe enough method is used, the probability is high that the undesirable behavior will stop immediately. So if stopping the undesirable behavior is our only goal, we would conclude that we should use the most severe method every time an individual exhibits an undesirable behavior.

Unfortunately, the solution to misbehavior is not that simple. When severe corrective methods are used to the exclusion of milder or positive methods, we run the risk of damaging individuals physically, emotionally, psychologically, and spiritually. Because our primary goal as physical activity professionals is to create an environment in which individuals feel safe, are willing to take risks, are motivated to learn, and take responsibility for their behavior, we must not make them feel threatened by extreme corrective methods, nor should we subject them to the possible negative side effects. In other words, if our goal is to create a learning environment in which individuals feel safe, secure, and nurtured so that they are more likely to enjoy physical activity and adopt it as a lifestyle as adults, we must avoid using severe corrective methods. (See figure 6.2 for a continuum of methods to decrease misbehavior.) Several researchers have examined the effects of using severe corrective methods. In the following sections, we'll look more closely at some of these effects.

Increased Fear

If you correct individuals often, they will come to fear you. This fear may cause them to withdraw emotionally and therefore stop performing and learning. Avoidance behaviors such as skipping class, school, or practice may result. The individual who is corrected often soon learns how to escape correction by lying. A 2nd grader was once asked by her physical educator, "Samantha, where is your homework assignment?" Fearing correction for not doing her assignment, she responded, "I did it, but I erased it."

Correction can also arouse a fear of failure. When an athlete has been maligned by the coach for striking out, he may try harder to get a hit the next time he is at bat, but instead of being motivated by the desire to be better or to win, he will be motivated to avoid defeat. Some fear improves performance, but there comes a point when that fear becomes destructive to the athlete's performance and the athlete chokes under pressure (Sands, Henderson, and Kilgore, 1999). The athlete focuses more on the consequences of making mistakes than on what needs to be done to be successful. This focus may make the athlete tentative and hesitant in a game where confidence and assertiveness are critical for peak performance. Smith and Smoll (1990) indicate that athletes not only have a high fear of failure but also are more likely to get injured, enjoy the sport experience less, and drop out. When we create a fear of failure through corrective methods, we increase the likelihood that the individual will make the very mistakes we are trying to prevent.

Decreased Motivation to Learn

When you use corrective methods frequently, you create an unpleasant, aversive learning environment. These methods can cause individuals to be hostile and resentful, and their desire to think, learn, and function appropriately may be impaired. The desire to cooperate with you, peers, or teammates may decrease and their sense of personal responsibility may diminish as you take more responsibility for controlling their behavior. It may also affect their ability to build positive relationships with others.

Increased Emotional Disturbance

Individuals can experience emotional harm from severe corrective methods. Some common side effects are social deviancy, rigidity, regression, and other forms of behavior demonstrating poor adjustment. Individuals who are victims of emotional assault frequently feel attacked, vulnerable, and highly defensive. Other potential emotional effects include pessimism, depression, constriction of thinking, and psychosomatic diseases such as speech disorders, lags in physical development, and failure to thrive.

When individuals are corrected, they sense a lack of empathy and love from the person administering the correction. Over time, there seems to be a cumulative effect. The results may be low self-esteem, self-destructive behaviors, apathy, withdrawal, and depression. Individuals who are frequently corrected typically have low self-esteem because they feel they can't do anything right. The lower the self-esteem, the more likely the individuals are to misbehave, and a vicious cycle begins.

An individual who is corrected may receive the message, "I am a bad person because I misbehaved." Whenever you reprimand an individual, ensure that the reprimand is specific to the behavior rather than the person who committed the behavior. For example, if an individual threw a bat, you might say, "Throwing the bat is unacceptable. I'm afraid someone will get hurt," instead of asking, "Why are you being such a poor sport?"

Sometimes adults use guilt, either knowingly or unknowingly, to try to make individuals behave a certain way. Guilt is a strong emotion and often it will control an individual's behavior. For example, when Bobby misbehaves and you say, "Bobby, how could you have done such a horrible thing?", Bobby's goodness is in question and he feels ashamed of himself. This has a detrimental effect on Bobby's self-esteem and in the long run may lead to more misbehavior.

Increased Aggression and Misbehavior

Violence begets violence. Children learn by copying adult behavior. Those who are corrected harshly, frequently, and seemingly unnecessarily may become angry at and feel revengeful toward the person correcting them. Some may even resort to violence and aggression and vandalize the school, recreation center, or playing field or get into fights in and out of the physical activity setting. In addition, every pain inflicted on a child, whether emotional or physical, may be passed on sooner or later to someone else younger and more helpless (see figure 6.8).

© Human Kinetics

Figure 6.8 Individuals may pass pain on to someone younger and more helpless.

Failure to Solve the Behavior Problem

Individuals who are corrected for a misbehavior will generally refrain from the behavior in that situation only and will often display the same behavior in another environment. For example, if an individual is corrected for aggression at practice, she will not be aggressive at practice but may become more aggressive at home.

The effects of correction for one behavior may generalize to related behaviors that you do not want to suppress. If, for example, you reprimand someone harshly for talking while you are giving instructions, the individual may not talk during group discussion or when asked a question.

Individuals often identify the correction with the person who administered it instead of with the inappropriate behavior, and they will misbehave again when that person is gone. Ironically, often the misbehavior will occur at a higher rate than before.

Severe corrective methods affect different people in different ways. Several factors determine the effect these methods have on an individual:

- **Individual's self-esteem.** Individuals who already have low self-esteem will experience a greater negative effect. The message they get is, "Your behavior was bad," but the individual often translates this as "I am bad," which is harmful to the individual's self-concept.

- **Individual's perception of the adult.** Correction has a much stronger effect if the individual views the adult as an important person.

- **Method used.** The more severe the corrective method, the stronger the effect. In the continuum of methods to decrease misbehavior (see figure 6.2), the methods toward the top tend to have a more negative effect.

- **Frequency of corrective methods.** When someone is corrected frequently, often the method becomes less effective and eventually fails to redirect the behavior. It is as if the individual becomes immune to being corrected, becoming callused or withdrawn and less responsive to the person administering these methods.

- **Nature of corrected behavior.** If individuals are corrected for a mild infraction of the rules, the feeling of being watched too closely may cause them to not care and quit trying to obey the rules or become personally responsible.

All too often we want the individual who is displaying an inappropriate behavior to stop the behavior immediately, and we may be tempted to use severe corrective methods to stop a mildly inappropriate behavior. If we don't make sure that the corrective method fits the infraction, the individual may feel that the consequence was unfair and will likely exhibit disapproval by acting out in some other inappropriate way.

GUIDELINES FOR USING CORRECTIVE METHODS

Whenever possible, use positive methods to manage behavior. Severe corrective methods, even when used with the best intentions, may affect individuals negatively. To minimize the negative effects of corrective methods, follow these guidelines.

1. **Establish rules and expectations.** Don't apply consequences if you haven't told the individuals what behaviors are inappropriate and what the consequences will be. Send a list of rules, expectations, unacceptable behaviors, and consequences home so that parents will know what behaviors are expected of their children (see chapter 3).

2. **Maintain self-control.** Do not lose control over your own emotions. The problem will only become worse if you lose control. When emotions are high, the likelihood of finding a rational solution to the problem is not very high. Instead, you should model appropriate behavior.

3. **Avoid confrontations.** Do not confront individuals, especially in front of their peers. Adolescents in particular tend to function as members of a group and are quite protective of each other. By confronting one adolescent, you may lose the respect of the others as well as of the adolescent you are confronting.

4. **Make sure the severity of the method fits the behavior.** When children and adolescents exhibit extremely undesirable behaviors such as acts of aggression or immorality, you must deal with the behaviors more strongly than with milder forms such as defiance, disruption, or goofing off. You must know how to use a variety of methods to decrease these behaviors. The first step is to determine the nature and degree of the behavior and make sure the method you use is a fair consequence for the severity of the inappropriate behavior. Specifically, the question to ask yourself is, "Given the severity of the behavior, which corrective method is appropriate?" The method must fit the infrac-

tion. This seems like a simple concept, but it is often one of the most difficult decisions to make. If the corrective method is too harsh, the individual will perceive it as unfair. If it is too lenient, it may not change the behavior. With experience you will learn which methods are most effective with each individual. The rule of thumb is to err on the side of leniency and move up the continuum. For example, if a player throws the bat after striking out in practice, you may assign an observational time-out for 10 minutes. If the player throws the bat again in practice, you can assume that the previous method was not severe enough to change the behavior, so you would use a more severe method such as not allowing him to play in the next game. For a continuum of corrective methods see figure 6.2.

5. **Make sure the behavior was intentional.** It is also important to distinguish between unintentional and intentional disruptions. You must not treat individuals who accidentally make a mistake and those who misbehave on purpose in the same manner. For instance, you should treat someone who accidentally hits you with a ball differently from someone who intentionally hits you. Sometimes intentions are obvious, sometimes not, so be perceptive and accurate or you may be accused of being unfair.

6. **Specify the behavior that warranted correction.** When an individual behaves inappropriately, make sure that you specify which behavior brought about the consequence. For example, you might say, "Hitting is an inappropriate behavior, so you must sit out for 5 minutes."

7. **Administer the method immediately.** Do not allow an individual to exhibit inappropriate behavior for too long, giving the behavior a chance to increase in intensity.

8. **Ensure that you use the methods fairly.** If one individual misbehaves and you reprimand her, you must do the same for all others who exhibit the same behavior. It is easy to overlook misbehavior from someone who is generally well behaved and to correct someone who is always in trouble. You must avoid this so that individuals see that you are fair.

9. **Be consistent.** As with all methods for redirecting disruptive behaviors, you must be consistent in your use of corrective methods. What is wrong today must be wrong tomorrow, and the consequences must be the same. If you are not feeling well or are having a bad day, you may be tempted to correct individuals for a behavior that you may not correct them for tomorrow when you are feeling better. Individuals need to know that the consequences of a behavior will be consistent from day to day.

10. **Correction does not inherently teach alternative replacement behaviors (Vollmer, 2002).** When an individual receives a consequence for an inappropriate behavior, the professional rarely discusses what the individual should have done instead. This is a key component when using correction; you must make sure individuals know what behavior they should have exhibited. For example, you might say, "Asad, you were throwing balls at Marcus when I asked you to clean up. You should have been picking up the balls and putting them in the bag. Come over here and pick up the bats and bases and put them away."

11. **Return to positive methods.** If correction is necessary, administer the consequences then return to a positive behavioral method as soon as possible. Reserve corrective methods for gaining immediate control over serious misbehavior but never use it as a primary method of managing behavior.

12. **Never hit!** Hitting is inappropriate in any situation. There are too many possible negative side effects of hitting an individual for it to ever be an approved method. In addition to the negative side effects the individual experiences, you must consider the issue of legal liability; corporal punishment is against the law in 28 states.

See checklist 6.4 to evaluate your effectiveness in using corrective methods (page 115).

Recreation specialists face a unique challenge when individuals in their programs misbehave. Their programs are in community settings that lack the structure and outside support of a school or athletic team. Parents often feel that since they are paying for their child to be in the program, it is the leader's responsibility to find positive ways to manage behaviors because the environment is supposed to be fun. Consequently, the specialist feels pressure to refrain from using corrective methods, and misbehaviors are often present and a source of frustration. Establish rules and expectations and notify parents of them as well as consequences before they are allowed to enroll their child in the program. This will make the program fun and safe for all.

SUMMARY

If physical activity professionals are concerned about the well-being of our students and participants, we must examine how we manage behavior.

To begin, we need to structure our setting so that behavior problems are prevented or decreased. Then we must use positive methods to increase appropriate behavior. We should use differential reinforcement when possible, and if corrective methods are necessary, we must use mild methods and follow appropriate guidelines. Through this process, we create a positive environment that is conducive to learning and enhances the emotional well-being of all individuals. See the continuum of behavior management approaches in figure 6.1.

There is no easy answer to behavioral problems, so you must develop a repertoire of methods to choose from for effectively redirecting undesirable behavior. When managing behavior, be sure to use the least amount of intervention possible. It is helpful to develop a continuum of corrective methods ranging from mild to severe (see figure 6.2). This will help you match the intervention to the severity of the behavior problem. In general, behavioral interventions are simple to design, but it is an art to administer and develop a behavior change that is maintained over time and doesn't have negative side effects. Refer often to checklists 6.1, 6.2, 6.3, and 6.4 to assess how you are doing.

WHAT DO YOU THINK?

1. Think about your own leadership style and make a list of ways you are correcting inappropriate behaviors.

2. Rate your perception of the methods' effectiveness (question 1) from 1 to 5, with 1 being not effective at all and 5 being very effective.

3. Take the methods on the list that you scored 3 or less on and look back through this chapter to find another method you could try. Collect baseline data on the frequency or duration of the inappropriate behavior for 1 week (see chapter 4), and then implement the new method for at least 3 weeks. Continue to collect data on the occurrence of the inappropriate behavior and compare the intervention data to the baseline data. Was the new method effective?

4. Look at the list of methods you made and see where on the continuum of corrective methods each falls, categorizing them as mild, moderate, or severe. Plan how you can use mild methods.

5. Think of a time when you used a more severe corrective technique. What were the negative effects it had on the individual? Was stopping the behavior immediately worth the negative side effects?

6. Think of the physical activity professionals that you have known in your lifetime. Which ones stand out to you as the best? Which ones stand out to you as the worst? List the corrective methods that each used. What do you notice about the ones you liked the best? The worst?

CASE STUDIES

For each of the three case studies in chapter 1 on page 13, select methods described in this chapter and discuss in detail how you would implement each of the methods to manage the behavior. After you have developed your own methods, read the following suggestions, which are only some of the many creative ways you might apply the information covered in this chapter.

CASE 1

Hector, a Disruptive 3rd Grader

▸ Have a discussion with Hector and explain why it is important for him to stay on task and perform the activities that you have planned.

▸ Use differential reinforcement of an incompatible behavior by asking Hector to help you monitor the performance of other individuals and check off their performance on a rubric checklist, then reinforce him for a job well done.

▸ Use differential reinforcement of the omission of behavior by watching Hector during class and reinforcing him for participating in the drills for a specified period of time, (i.e., after 10 minutes of participating, give him verbal praise for his participation).

▸ Use response cost by giving him 5 points at the beginning of each class. Every time he is off task, take a point away. If he has any points left at the

▶ end of class he can use the last 10 minutes playing his favorite game.

▶ When Hector is off task, use a verbal reprimand. Tell him, "Goofing off is unacceptable. You should be participating in the drills so that you can improve your performance. Now go over to station 1 and perform the drill."

▶ Verbally reprimand participants who leave equipment out when they use the weight room, telling them that it is important to put equipment away, why it is important, and that you want them to put it away.

▶ Use restitutional overcorrection by having participants who do not put the equipment away after they use the weight room clean up not only the weight room but also other areas of the recreation center.

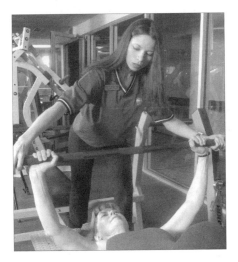

CASE 2
Ashante, an Instructor in Charge of Weight-Room Cleanup

▶ Use differential reinforcement of a low rate of behavior by setting a limit on pieces of equipment that may be left out at the end of the day, such as 6 pieces. Set a group goal such as, "We will leave 6 or fewer pieces of equipment out at the end of the day." Reinforce the participants in the weight room for meeting that goal by inviting them to a fun activity at the end of the week. Gradually decrease the number of pieces that are allowed to be left out until it is 0.

▶ Use response cost by telling the participants who use the weight room that if they leave equipment out, their privilege to use the weight room will be suspended for a week.

▶ Have a discussion with the participants who are leaving the equipment out and ask them to come up with reasons why it is important to put equipment away.

CASE 3
Molly, an Overly Aggressive Soccer Player

▶ Have a direct discussion with Molly and ask her what is going on. Ask her why she got in a fight. Try to find out if something is bothering her. Discuss with her why getting into fights with other players is not good sportsmanship.

▶ Use differential reinforcement of incompatible behaviors by praising Molly whenever she interacts with her teammates in a positive manner.

▶ Use differential reinforcement of a low rate of behavior by setting a limit on the number of negative interactions that Molly can have each practice, (i.e., 3 per practice). When Molly has 3 or fewer negative interactions, reinforce her. Gradually decrease the number of negative interactions allowed.

▶ Use differential reinforcement of omission of behavior by setting a time limit (i.e., 15 minutes). Be sure to get baseline data to see where to set

(continued)

Case Studies *(continued)*

this limit. If Molly can go for 15 minutes without a negative interaction, notice and reinforce her with verbal praise.

▸ Use response cost by giving Molly 3 points at the beginning of each practice. Each time she has a negative interaction with a teammate, take a point away. If she still has points left at the end of practice, she can pick her favorite drill to start the next practice.

▸ Use observational time-out. When Molly has a negative interaction with a teammate, have her sit on the sidelines and watch the others practice for a specified period of time.

▸ Teach Molly to take a self-time-out. Whenever she is feeling like she will lose control, have her pick an activity that will calm her down and allow her to gain control. When she joins practice again, reinforce her for participating appropriately.

▸ Use verbal reprimands for Molly when she has a negative interaction with a teammate, telling her why that type of behavior is inappropriate and giving her alternative behaviors.

Checklist 6.1   Withdrawing a Reinforcer

Rate yourself in regard to the following statements.

	Consistently	Inconsistently	Never
Using extinction or planned ignoring:			
I use extinction only for behaviors that are not harmful.	☐	☐	☐
I identify what is reinforcing the individual's behavior.	☐	☐	☐
I remove the reinforcer without calling attention to what I'm doing.	☐	☐	☐
I recognize that I cannot control the individual's entire environment.	☐	☐	☐
I reinforce appropriate behaviors displayed by other individuals.	☐	☐	☐
I expect extinction to be gradual and I am patient.	☐	☐	☐
Using response cost:			
I ensure that reinforcers for good behavior are available.	☐	☐	☐
I make sure the individual in question has access to the reinforcer.	☐	☐	☐
I choose to withdraw a reinforcer that is important to the individual.	☐	☐	☐
I keep withdrawal of reinforcers to a minimum.	☐	☐	☐
I explain ahead of time which behaviors will warrant a response cost.	☐	☐	☐
I refrain from warning, nagging, or threatening the individual.	☐	☐	☐
I avoid trying to justify my enforcement of a response cost.	☐	☐	☐
I am careful not to become emotionally involved when administering response cost.	☐	☐	☐
When possible, I allow natural or logical consequences to take place.	☐	☐	☐
I am consistent in using response cost.	☐	☐	☐

Using time-out:

	Consistently	Inconsistently	Never
I inform the individual specifically which behavior led to the time-out.	☐	☐	☐
I administer time-outs consistently and matter-of-factly.	☐	☐	☐
I make sure the time-out is not reinforcing.	☐	☐	☐
I make sure the individual is not getting out of a situation she doesn't like.	☐	☐	☐
I specify the period of time for time-out in advance.	☐	☐	☐
I wait until the disruptive behavior stops before starting to time the time-out.	☐	☐	☐
After the time-out, I have the individuals state the rule they broke and then tell how they'll avoid breaking the rule in the future.	☐	☐	☐
After the time-out, I have the individuals return to the task they were engaged in when the inappropriate behavior occurred.	☐	☐	☐
After the time-out I reinforce appropriate behavior when the individuals exhibit it.	☐	☐	☐
I encourage individuals to take a self-time-out by selecting their own way of timing out within the limits of the situation.	☐	☐	☐

Checklist 6.2 Presenting Aversive Stimuli

Rate yourself in regard to the following statements.

Using direct discussion:

	Consistently	Inconsistently	Never
I arrange a private meeting with the individual.	☐	☐	☐
I first determine the cause of the misbehavior by asking the individual.	☐	☐	☐
I listen carefully to the response.	☐	☐	☐
I am nonthreatening.	☐	☐	☐
I show sincere concern for the individual.	☐	☐	☐
If still necessary, I set and enforce a consequence for the behavior.	☐	☐	☐

Using verbal reprimands:

	Consistently	Inconsistently	Never
I try nonverbal reprimands, such as hand signals, first whenever possible.	☐	☐	☐
I make it clear to the individual exactly what behavior is unacceptable and why.	☐	☐	☐
I include a statement of what the appropriate behavior would have been.	☐	☐	☐
I use proximity control when giving a verbal reprimand.	☐	☐	☐
I reprimand the behavior, not the individual.	☐	☐	☐
I avoid using sarcasm.	☐	☐	☐
I praise the desired behavior when the individual performs it.	☐	☐	☐
I reprimand immediately after the behavior occurs.	☐	☐	☐
I am firm but gentle.	☐	☐	☐
If the behavior is potentially harmful, I remove the individual to time-out.	☐	☐	☐
If necessary, I back up the reprimand with a loss of privilege (response cost).	☐	☐	☐
I remain calm.	☐	☐	☐
I avoid degrading or embarrassing the individual.	☐	☐	☐
I avoid trying to make the individual feel guilty.	☐	☐	☐
I observe the individual's behavior to make sure the reprimand is having the intended effect.	☐	☐	☐
If the reprimand is not effective, I try another method.	☐	☐	☐

(continued)

	Yes	No	
I always follow through.	☐	☐	☐
When it's over, it's over, and I avoid reminding the individual of the misbehavior.	☐	☐	☐

Using physical restraint:

	Yes	No
I am aware of my institution or organization's policy regarding physical restraint.	☐	☐
I avoid touching individuals when I'm angry.	☐	☐
I use physical restraint only when I cannot get away from a violent individual or to stop him from hurting himself or others.	☐	☐
I stand behind the individual.	☐	☐
I hold the individual's wrists with arms crossed over the chest.	☐	☐
I hold the individual firmly, not roughly, giving a feeling of protection until he calms down.	☐	☐
I speak softly to the individual telling him I will hold him until he calms down.	☐	☐
I will hold him until I feel he is in control.	☐	☐

Avoiding corporal punishment:

	Yes	No
I am aware of my institution's or organization's policy regarding corporal punishment.	☐	☐
Regardless of the policy, I agree that it is never appropriate to hit an individual.	☐	☐
I get myself and others away from a violent individual.	☐	☐
If necessary, I use physical restraint to protect myself, the individual, or others.	☐	☐
I understand the negative side effects of corporal punishment.	☐	☐

Checklist 6.3 Requiring Aversive Behaviors

Rate yourself in regard to the following statements.

	Consistently	Inconsistently	Never
Requiring physical activity as punishment:			
I have read my institution or organization's policy about using physical activity as a corrective method.	☐	☐	☐
I avoid requiring physical activity as a consequence because it may give individuals a negative attitude toward physical activity.	☐	☐	☐
Requiring reparation:			
I review school district or organizational policy to assure that using reparation is acceptable.	☐	☐	☐
When I use reparation, I inform parents of the misbehavior and the consequence.	☐	☐	☐
If helpful, I hold a conference with the parents and individual to determine the reparation.	☐	☐	☐
I encourage parents to support the consequence rather than bailing their child out.	☐	☐	☐
Using overcorrection (restitutional and positive practice):			
I apply overcorrection immediately after the offense.	☐	☐	☐
I ensure that the consequence relates to the inappropriate act.	☐	☐	☐

Checklist 6.4 Using Corrective Methods

Rate yourself in regard to the following statements.

	Consistently	Inconsistently	Never
I establish rules and expectations as well as consequences on the first day and send a list of rules home for parents to see.	☐	☐	☐
I maintain self-control when using corrective methods.	☐	☐	☐
I avoid confrontations.	☐	☐	☐
I make sure the consequence fits the intention of the misbehavior.	☐	☐	☐
I make sure the behavior was intentional.	☐	☐	☐
I specify the behavior that warranted the consequence.	☐	☐	☐
I am fair. What is wrong for one individual must be wrong for others.	☐	☐	☐
I am consistent. What is wrong today is wrong tomorrow and the consequences remain the same.	☐	☐	☐
I make sure the individuals not only know that the behavior was inappropriate but also they know what the alternative replacement behavior is.	☐	☐	☐
I return to positive methods as soon as possible.	☐	☐	☐
I never, ever hit.	☐	☐	☐

CHAPTER

7

Humanistic Approach

All of us want to belong somewhere. When students do not feel accepted, for whatever reason, they are more likely to find negative places to belong. Gangs and other negative influences fill a need that so often is not met in positive settings. As educators we must create an environment in which students feel safe and accepted, an environment in which we are all learners together and where we feel a sense of togetherness— one where there are not "gotchas."

Tileston, 2000

Ms. Collier had been a teacher in Arlington County for 15 years. Because of her communication and behavior management skills as well as her successful track record working with students of diverse cultural backgrounds, she was asked to transfer to the district's new middle school, which would serve students of diverse backgrounds from the inner city. In this position, she would be responsible for developing the physical education program for grades 7 through 9.

At her previous school, Ms. Collier had successfully implemented some of the strategies of character education. After accepting the new teaching position, Ms. Collier read Glover and Anderson's book *Character Education* (2003) and busily planned ways to integrate these strategies into the new school's physical education program. She designed a bulletin board to depict the focus words and developed creative ways to implement the strategies throughout her curriculum.

During the faculty retreat in August, Ms. Collier gave an in-service workshop for the other teachers in the school to discuss the model so that the teachers would better understand her physical education program. She also suggested ways they could implement some of the strategies in their own classrooms.

Ms. Collier felt well-prepared for her new teaching position, and the year started smoothly. The students responded positively to her approach. At parent–teacher conferences just before winter break, a father told her that it was the first time his son actually looked forward to physical education class. He had even requested that his dad take him to the library to write a report on his favorite sport figure. The father asked Ms. Collier what her secret was for making the students so enthusiastic about her classes.

The humanistic approach to behavior management focuses on the development of self-concept, interpersonal relationships, intrinsic motivation, personal and social responsibility, and other qualities of good character. Physical activity settings are ideal for developing these traits. When programs are success-oriented, participants develop a positive self-concept and are more likely to become intrinsically motivated and strive to achieve their potential (Hellison, 2003).

When using the humanistic approach to deal with disruptive behavior, it is crucial to understand the psychological causes of behavior, develop a trusting relationship with the participants, and teach self-control. In this approach individuals must

- recognize that their behavior is a problem,
- recognize why it is a problem,
- understand what motivated the behavior, and
- determine through discussion with the physical activity professional alternative ways to behave in similar situations.

If you use the humanistic approach, your responsibilities include

- developing a safe, nurturing environment in which all individuals feel a sense of belonging (see chapters 2 and 3),

- understanding individual behaviors and feelings,
- listening to and then helping individuals understand their behavior and their feelings,
- teaching personal and social responsibility,
- encouraging individuals to learn, and
- helping individuals recognize that behavior limits are there to protect them, not punish them.

Many physical activity professionals shy away from the humanistic approach. Most have not been taught how to use the methods, so they do not feel qualified to use them. They think that only psychologists, therapists, counselors, or social workers should use the methods because they require more time, energy, and expertise than methods in the behavioral approach. In this chapter we will discuss several methods of the humanistic approach that have been used successfully in different physical activity settings and are well worth the time and energy they require (Hellison, 2003; Hellison and Templin, 1991; Stiehl, 1993). The humanistic approach helps the physical activity professional and the participant to analyze behavior and plan strategies to change it. In effect, this approach teaches participants to take responsibility for their behavior, a skill that will help them throughout life.

The National Association for Sport and Physical Education (NASPE) (2004) included the skill of demonstrating responsible behaviors in their content standards. Standard 5 states, "A physically educated person demonstrates responsible personal and social behavior that respects self and others in physical activity settings."

In this chapter, we'll examine a variety of methods, most of which concentrate on teaching individuals to accept personal and social responsibility, build character, and manage conflict. The methods and models have been successfully applied in physical activity settings. They include responsibility models, character education, self-evaluation, conflict management, and positive coaching.

RESPONSIBILITY MODELS

Responsibility models provide children with experiences that allow them to develop personal, social, and environmental responsibility, including "fulfilling our obligations, keeping our commitments, striving to do and be our personal and moral best, and nurturing and supporting one another" (Stiehl, 1993, p. 39). An assumption of these models is that children are capable of accepting responsibility for their actions as well as the consequences of their behaviors. Responsibility is a choice that is motivated internally. In addition, children who learn how to make more choices for themselves see that they are able to create opportunities for change and can design their own future (Stiehl, 1993). These models help children feel empowered, which helps them learn to act with a purpose and make responsible commitments to themselves, others, and their environment.

The responsibility models in this chapter are alternative curriculum approaches that use physical activity settings as a medium for teaching responsibility. Although behaviors will change as a result of using these models, the intent is to change perceptions, create responsibility, and build character, not merely to redirect disruptive behaviors.

Becoming Responsible

Morris and Stiehl have developed a program for becoming responsible that schools use to teach responsibility to children. In the program, the authors define responsibility as "taking care of ourselves, others, and our surroundings" (Stiehl, 1993).

Types of Responsibility

You can use this program to develop three types of responsibility: personal, social, and environmental.

Personal responsibility involves being able to

- make and keep agreements,
- set goals and create ways to achieve them,
- accept consequences of personal choices, and
- acknowledge personal accomplishments.

Social responsibility involves being able to

- communicate with others in a way that empowers them rather than demeans them;
- honor others' rights, dignity, and worth;
- work together toward common goals;
- negotiate problems and conflicts successfully; and
- create opportunities for others.

Environmental responsibility involves being able to

- become conscious of the various contexts in which we function;
- respect property and take care of equipment, the classroom, the school, and the larger community; and
- recognize the importance of taking care of the environment as well as influencing others to take care of the environment.

Steps of the Model

The becoming responsible model includes 3 steps:

1. Make individuals aware of language and behaviors that are irresponsible or that do not support the well-being of self, others, or the environment.
2. Offer alternative language and behaviors that are appropriate.
3. Give individuals a choice between irresponsible and responsible behavior.

Helping Individuals Become More Responsible

Suggestions for helping individuals become more responsible include modifying adult talk, participant talk, adult actions, and participant actions.

Adult Talk

You must become more aware of how your verbal and nonverbal language affects others. The positive messages you send to young people enhance their sense of self, helping them feel valuable and capable. You send messages to them through both words and actions. For example, when a child is listening to instructions, you might say, "Raja, thank you for standing quietly and listening to instructions." Rolling your eyes when someone says something silly has the opposite effect.

Participant Talk

When individuals blame other people or things for their behavior, they excuse themselves from personal responsibility. Then they feel they don't have to do anything about their behavior. A common phrase that points blame is "makes me," such as "Jessica makes me mad" or "McRay made me miss that goal." These phrases take control away from the individual. But they can learn to change the way they phrase their thoughts so that they take more responsibility for their feelings and behavior, thereby taking power and responsibility back. Teach participants to use "I" statements such as "I choose to be mad at Jessica" or "I missed that goal."

Adult Actions

You can create opportunities for responsible behavior by designing activities that nurture responsibility. The first step is to determine what responsibility means. Next, determine why responsible behavior is important. Specify what responsible behaviors are, and then give participants a list of responsible behaviors, such as coming to practice on time, working hard at practice to improve, doing all the activities at each station, and caring about the feelings of other participants. Encourage individuals to make a checklist of the behaviors for which they are willing to be responsible. This allows them to not only take responsibility for their behavior but also to evaluate their own behaviors. Then you and the participant can establish consequences for behaving irresponsibly, and after putting the plan into action reinforce participants for behaving responsibly and give consequences for behaving irresponsibly.

You can plan your activities or design your curriculum to include opportunities for teaching responsible behaviors. One way to do this is to plan activities that challenge a wide spectrum of abilities, offering a choice of activities and levels of difficulty within each activity. These activities can create teachable moments through which individuals may learn valuable lessons such as accepting the outcomes of their decisions, accepting the support of others, respecting the choices of others, and so on.

Participant Actions

It is important to provide individuals with opportunities to demonstrate responsible behavior through their actions. One method is to encourage them to participate in social responsibility activities that foster mutual support within a group, such as cooperative games (Grineski, 1996). Other effective methods include creating opportunities that require individuals to use conflict management skills and to deal with peer pressure (Glover and Anderson, 2003).

Projects

As individuals become more responsible for their behaviors and feelings, ask them to develop a personal responsibility project:

1. Think of an idea for a project.
2. Make a commitment, similar to setting goals and objectives. A commitment is a goal you have for yourself, such as "I want to improve my physical fitness so that I can be a better soccer player." An objective is the action the individual will take to fulfill the commitment, such as "I will jog for 40 minutes a day, 3 days a week, for 4 weeks." These objectives must be measurable.
3. Develop strategies for implementing your project, such as "When I get home from school on Monday, Wednesday, and Friday, I will jog to the park and back."
4. Establish time lines for achieving the goals and objectives, such as "I will accomplish these objectives in 4 weeks."
5. If you need help achieving the goals and objectives, identify individuals who can provide that help, such as "Coach can help me by keeping a jogging chart in her notebook that I can fill in when I am at practice for each day that I have jogged."
6. Implement your project (see figure 7.1).

Hellison's Personal and Social Responsibility Model

The teaching personal and social responsibility model was developed by Hellison (2003) to help young people

- develop themselves despite external forces,
- live by their values,

GOAL SHEET

Date _____

Goal 1

My goal is _____ .

Activities I can do to achieve this goal are _____

_____

_____ .

Ways I can measure my progress toward this goal are _____

_____

_____ .

I will achieve my goal by _____ (date).

Goal 2

My goal is _____ .

Activities I can do to achieve this goal are _____

_____

_____ .

Ways I can measure my progress toward this goal are _____

_____

_____ .

I will achieve my goal by _____ (date).

Figure 7.1   Sample goal sheet for a personal responsibility project (Stiehl, 1993).

- understand their connections with others, and

- respect the rights, feelings, and needs of others.

This model helps physical activity professionals teach responsible behaviors. Through the teaching personal and social responsibility model, Hellison provides a conceptual framework you present through various media, including posters, group discussions, personal discussions, written assignments, and any other means you can think of. But you will need to integrate the behavior management methods that we describe in this book to promote responsible behavior within the context of this model (see chapters 3, 4, and 5). Even so, you can expect that increasing responsible behaviors will decrease irresponsible

behaviors and therefore will decrease the need to use corrective methods (see chapter 6).

Challenges for Physical Activity Professionals

We live in an ever-changing world, and economic instability coupled with serious social issues such as violence, war, irresponsible sex, and easy access to illegal drugs have created a difficult environment for everyone. Although some individuals seem resilient or oblivious to all this, many others show signs of stress. Ironically, at a time when we face more challenges than ever, we are receiving less support and guidance in making decisions. Moreover, many individuals lack motivation and discipline. The challenges others face create challenges for us as physical activity professionals. It is our responsibility to help the people we work with meet these challenges and provide leadership for our changing world.

Teaching Responsibility

Hellison (2003) provides the following suggestions to help us in our quest to teach responsibility:

- Improve group control through role modeling and teaching self-control. You need to be a good role model and be in control of your feelings and actions (see figure 7.2). Individuals also need to learn self-control to avoid interfering with the rights of others at the recreation center, in the gym, or on the playing field.

- Help individuals develop personal responsibility. Expect them to take responsibility for their learning, for making wise choices, and for developing a meaningful and personally satisfying lifestyle.

- Help individuals lead more stable lives. Personal stability requires both a long-term commitment to satisfying activities and a sense of identity. Social stability requires cooperation, caring, helping, and a sense of community. Teach children to make commitments to others and to recognize their need for support and interdependence.

- Make the physical activity setting more effective by finding better ways to help individuals succeed and making the environment more personal.

- Find ways to meet individuals' needs and still maximize the time they spend in physical activity.

The physical activity setting is an excellent place to develop personal and social responsibility because the environment is interactive, fun, and provides many opportunities to explore emotions. Physical activities allow young people to demonstrate personal and social qualities while participating in games, skill practice, warm-ups, group discussion, and dialogue.

The purpose of this model is to provide opportunities for children to understand what responsibility means; know what to take responsibility for; learn how to take responsibility for their own development and well-being; and learn how to contribute to the well-being of others (Hellison, 2003).

Values for Personal and Social Responsibility

Because Hellison's model is intended to help children take more responsibility for their own well-being while becoming more responsive to the

Figure 7.2   Unless you control yourself, you cannot expect others to control themselves.

© Hester L. Henderson

well-being of others, you must teach them specific values. The two values Hellison (2003) relates to personal well-being are effort and self-direction. The two values related to social well-being are respecting others' rights and feelings and caring about others. Hellison places these values in a framework for the progression of levels, or goals. The levels represent values and behaviors in a progression so that you can build each value on the one before it. However, you may teach these values out of sequence with less emphasis on the progression. Develop your own levels that work for you and your setting.

Responsibility Levels

The five levels of responsibility are described in figure 7.3.

To develop responsibility in others, you must be willing to shift power and a significant portion of decision-making responsibilities to them. Help them get inside their heads and think about things. Changes in feelings, attitudes, values, and behaviors are more likely to occur if you think about, plan for, and model the same feelings, attitudes, values, and behaviors that you would like the individuals to have (Hellison, 2003).

The intention of the level system is to help individuals become aware of experiences; make decisions; and reflect on their thoughts, beliefs, and behaviors in a progressive manner (Hellison and Templin, 1991). Posting the levels for everyone to see will help them better follow the levels and will also motivate them to move up the levels (see page 83 in chapter 5 on public posting and worksheet 4 in appendix A). You can develop a catchy theme around the levels, such as Rounding the Bases to Responsibility (Lavay and Steinhaus, 1997). Using these levels as a framework can help you plan, teach, and evaluate your use of the teaching personal and social responsibility model. For individuals to progress through these levels, they must spend time in activities that expose them to opportunities to become more responsible. Hellison suggests the following six strategies for putting the levels into practice: awareness talks, levels in action, reflection time, individual and group decision making, group meetings, and counseling time.

Awareness Talks

The purpose of this strategy is to increase awareness of the levels. You can explain the levels at the beginning of a session or during warm-ups, starting with two levels and gradually adding the rest. Be brief; 1 or 2 minutes is sufficient. Introduce the basic concepts of the levels and discuss their relevance to the upcoming session. Then post the levels and refer to them when the individuals exhibit behaviors consistent (or inconsistent) with a level. Make sure that they are aware of

HELLISON'S SOCIAL AND PERSONAL RESPONSIBILITY LEVELS

Level 1: Respecting the Rights and Feelings of Others. Individuals maintain self-control and do not let their lack of control affect others. Individuals have the right to peaceful conflict resolution. Individuals have the right to be included; each individual deserves a turn and playing time.

Level 2: Participation and Effort. Individuals are self-motivated to participate. They explore and try new tasks. They persist even when the going gets tough. They accept the challenge. They participate in the program to gain a positive experience and they show effort to improve themselves. They practice and train to increase their skill and fitness levels.

Level 3: Self-Direction. Individuals are given responsibility to work independently and take that challenge. They set goals and work on them without supervision. They have the courage to resist peer pressure and do what they know is right. They demonstrate self-direction by learning to take more responsibility for their own well-being.

Level 4: Caring. Individuals act out of caring and compassion. They demonstrate inner strength to resist peer pressure, and they step up to be a leader. They have confidence without arrogance. They are sensitive and responsive to the well-being of others. They listen to others and respond appropriately, recognizing that others have feelings just like they do, and they learn to see things from another's perspective.

Level 5: Outside the Gym. Individuals take their sense of personal and social responsibility and try these ideas in other areas of life, practicing them at home, on the playground, and in the community. They become role models for others.

Figure 7.3 Posting the levels on a bulletin board for everyone to see will motivate your participants to move up the levels.
Adapted from D. Hellison, 2003, *Teaching responsibility through physical activity,* 2nd ed. (Champaign, IL: Human Kinetics).

their responsibilities. One way to do this is to have them develop respect rules (Hichwa, 1998), such as "Be helpful," "Use good listening skills," and "Accept others as they are" (see chapter 3 and the developing personal responsibility section on page 50 for more ideas).

Create opportunities for incidental teaching by developing one-liners to make individuals aware of how they are acting at a given time, such as "You can choose to do what someone else told you to do or you can think for yourself" or "The only person you have to change is yourself."

Levels in Action

Create chances for individuals to experience one or more of the levels while participating in physical activity. One way to do this is through direct questioning: "Who can tell me a way we could modify the game so that everyone can play successfully?" (level 1); "Show me another way to kick the soccer ball so that it goes between the cones" (level 2); "What is one goal you have for your own personal physical activity program plan?" (level 4); and "Tell me how you can encourage others to do their best when you play in your neighborhood this weekend" (level 5).

Reflection Time

Give individuals time to reflect on their feelings, thoughts, attitudes, intentions, and behaviors and to determine the level at which they think they are operating. This reflection can be accomplished through facilitated discussion, writing in a journal, or completing a personal responsibility project goal sheet (see figure 7.2). Have individuals state the levels they feel they are working on, giving the reasons for their evaluations. You may need to help by asking them specific questions, such as "Did you put anyone down in class?" (level 1); "Did you meet your goal at practice?" (level 3); or "Did you help anyone on the team?" (level 4). You can use this method at any time during the session or at the end.

Reflection can also be done as a group. Ask the group to give a thumbs-up if they did each of the actions you ask about. Then ask questions such as, "How well did you control your temper and mouth today?" (self-control); "How hard did you try today?" (effort); "Did you work on a goal today?" (self-coaching); and "Did you help someone learn something over the weekend?" (helping others). If they put their thumb up, it signifies yes; if their thumb is sideways it signifies a little; and if their thumb is down it means no and they need to work on that area (Hellison, 2003).

Another method for reflection is having individuals write in a journal about their actions for the day, including the behaviors they are proud of and the behaviors they need to work on. They could also write down what level they thought they were on today and why. Read the journals and give feedback either verbally or in writing.

Developing checklists is another reflection method. After the activity period give individuals a checklist about their behavior. Review the checklist and make appropriate comments to all individuals about their behavior or call a group meeting to discuss an issue if necessary. See figure 7.4 for a sample reflection checklist.

☐ Did you control your temper?
☐ Did you say something nice to someone else today?
☐ Did you try hard?
☐ Did you set a goal for yourself?
☐ Did you work on that goal?
☐ Did you help someone else do something?
☐ Did you help someone out on the playground or in the community?

Figure 7.4 Reflection checklist.

Individual and Group Decision Making

During the physical activity, you can have the group or individuals experience the levels in action by allowing them to practice decision making in the warm-up, drills, game, or closure. For example, you might have them play an inclusion game, such as following the all-touch rule for a six-person soccer game, or you might allow them to decide what drills they want to participate in to improve their soccer skills. Another way to provide experiences that allows individuals to work toward goals is to encourage them to develop fitness routines and perform them at their own pace. In addition, encourage them to serve as peer tutors to give them experience teaching and evaluating others. You can also incorporate self-paced challenges, which encourage individuals to work at their own rate and level, or have them work with a partner or in groups, such as having them develop and implement service projects.

Encourage individuals to negotiate and make choices in each of the levels. In level 1, for example, you might offer the choice either to stop calling another person names or to sit out of the game for a specified period of time. In level 2, consider allowing individuals to grade or evaluate themselves in selected areas. In level 3, guide individuals as they determine personal goals, for example, developing goals for each practice station. In level 4, you might let individuals choose a helping role, such as peer tutor or coach.

Group Meetings

When appropriate, hold group meetings so that individuals have a forum in which they can respond to issues that may arise. For example, if some are disgruntled about an umpire's call in a softball game, a group meeting may allow them to discuss their feelings about the call instead of showing poor sportsmanship. Holding group meetings allows individuals to express their views, raise issues, suggest solutions, lobby for their own interests, and share opinions and ideas about the physical activity program or class. Consider encouraging participants to evaluate the program or class and offer input on different topics, including making rules, telling how things are going, discussing the problems that have occurred, and coming up with possible solutions to the problems.

You can schedule these meetings on a regular basis or hold them as needed. Facilitate the discussion by asking specific questions such as "How can we protect the rights of everyone?" (level 1), "What is your opinion about the game?" (level 3), or "How can we resolve this issue?" (level 4). Questions like these are essential because they help the group feel empowered, giving them ownership in the program, and increasing their desire to work toward the goals. Establish rules of the meeting such as (a) all individuals have a right to share their opinions, (b) respect the opinions of others by listening, and (c) talk only when it is your turn. If the meeting gets out of hand you must regain control by reminding the group that each person's opinion is to be heard and respected. When needed, offer guidance such as giving advice about how to talk with each other or how to listen attentively. Be cautious about too much involvement on your part as everyone's voice needs to be heard and respected.

Counseling Time

Some physical activity professionals shy away from counseling, believing that it requires specialized training and takes too much time. However, on an informal basis you are probably already counseling the individuals in your program or class, so build time into your sessions for interactions with individuals or groups. Convey the individual's or group's strengths as well as areas for improvement. By demonstrating a genuine interest in each person you make sure they know they matter and you can check on how each individual or group is doing. In addition, you can evaluate levels of responsibility and ask if their choices worked and what they could do differently next time. Then encourage the development of a plan for change.

Make time to counsel all individuals, not just those who are in trouble or misbehaving. Counseling time may be a few minutes of discussion during the warm-up or cool-down, or for individuals who really need it, counseling can take place during a larger block of time such as recess, lunch, or after the physical activity.

When an individual or group practices social interaction with the levels in mind, they are more likely to incorporate these values into their lives. They feel empowered and purposeful, learn to make responsible commitments, strive to develop themselves, and understand how they are related to others (Hellison and Templin, 1991). The choices, however, rest with them.

The key to the success of this program lies in the relationship you establish with the individuals in your program. You must recognize and respect that each individual has strengths; has a voice, an opinion, and a perspective that needs to be heard; and has the capacity to make good decisions. The person who can use this model most effectively demonstrates the following qualities: listens and cares; has a sense of purpose; is genuine; is vulnerable; is intuitive; perseveres; self-reflects; has a sense of humor; and has a playful spirit (Hellison, 2003). To see if you have what it takes to use this model in your physical activity setting, answer the questions in figure 7.5.

The teaching personal and social responsibility model requires physical activity professionals to be confident enough in their abilities to be open to incorporating parts of the model in their programs if it makes sense to do so, vulnerable enough to share problems with others, reflective enough to analyze their own style, setting, and group, and creative enough to modify and change the model as needed (Hellison, 2003). If we want responsibility to be a way of life for the individuals in our physical activity program, we cannot ask them to take responsibility without giving it to them (Parker and Hellison, 2001).

TEACHING PERSONAL AND SOCIAL RESPONSIBILITY QUESTIONNAIRE

1. Do you like kids and can relate to them?
2. Do you try to treat all kids as individuals?
3. Do you spend time consciously focusing on each individual's strengths?
4. Do you listen to individuals and believe that their opinions are valuable?
5. Do you share your power with individuals?
6. Do you help individuals solve conflicts on their own?
7. Do you help individuals to learn to control their negative statements and temper, or do they rely on you to control them?
8. Do you help individuals include everybody in the activities so that they can do this on their own?
9. Do you give individuals opportunities to work independently and on their own goals?
10. Do individuals have a voice in evaluating each lesson, practice, and activity and in solving problems that arise?
11. Do individuals have opportunities to assume meaningful leadership roles such as teaching and coaching?
12. Do you emphasize transferring the levels to individuals' lives outside the physical activity setting?
13. Do individuals leave your program understanding what taking responsibility means and how it applies to them?

Figure 7.5 Answer the questions to determine if you have what it takes to use the personal and social responsibility model in your setting.

Reprinted, by permission, from D. Hellison, *Youth development and physical activity: Linking universities and communities* (Champaign, IL: Human Kinetics), 44-46.

Checklists 7.1 and 7.2 are helpful for assessing your teaching of personal responsibility (pages 138-139).

A number of curriculum options are available for implementing the teaching personal and social responsibility model. Your selection will depend on the needs of your program, the characteristics and needs of your participants, and your teaching, coaching, or leadership style. For examples of ways other physical activity professionals have used this model in their programs, see *Teaching Responsibility Through Physical Activity* (Hellison, 2003) and this chapter's In the Trenches. By reading what has worked for others, you will learn methods that might work for you.

CHARACTER EDUCATION

Character education is the deliberate effort to help others understand, care about, and act on core ethical values. These focused efforts must be made by families, schools, youth organizations, governments, and the media to help foster character development in young people (Glover and Anderson, 2003). If young people are taught core ethical values and are reinforced for caring for and emotionally supporting one another, appropriate behaviors will increase. By the same token, if methods are used to correct inappropriate behaviors, such behaviors will decrease.

Importance of Character Education

With the emphasis on students' GPA and their scores on college entrance exams, and most recently the accountability of schools in the No Child Left Behind Act, education is driven to focus more and more on preparing students for the tests. The irony is that once students graduate from school and join the hunt for a job, the emphasis shifts from wanting potential employees with heads filled with information to wanting individuals with certain skills. The *Fortune 500* newsletter (*Odyssey of the Mind* newsletter, 1995) listed the top 10 most important qualities desired of people in the workforce as teamwork, problem solving, interpersonal skills, oral communication, listening, personal and career development, creative thinking, leadership, goal setting and motivation, and writing.

Character Education in the Physical Activity Setting

The physical activity setting can teach all of the top 10 qualities listed by *Fortune 500*, but to do so we need to take a stand for teaching them over teaching facts. We need to convince governments, colleges, parents, school districts, and youth organizations that nurturing the well-being of the whole child is the goal, not simply teaching facts, sport

Putting the Responsibility Model Into Practice

Nick Cutforth, PhD, Associate Professor, Curriculum and Instruction, University of Denver

I've been a physical education teacher and professor for over 20 years and have always believed in the potential of physical activity to help kids take responsibility for themselves and others. As a doctoral student of Don Hellison in the 1990s I adapted his responsibility model and have used it in several extended day programs with kids in Chicago and Denver. Some of these programs are organized around specific sports such as soccer; others include a variety of activities such as fitness, team and individual sports, and cooperative games; and others focus more specifically on cross-age teaching and leadership development.

Photo courtesy of University of Denver

Three broad goals provide direction for my programs: *self-responsibility* for motivation and self-direction, *social responsibility* for respecting the rights and feelings of others and for being responsive to the needs of others, and *group responsibility* for cooperation and group betterment. To make clear what the kids are to take responsibility for, the goals of the model are presented to them as five levels of responsibility:

1. Respect the rights and feelings of others (including self-control, teamwork, cooperation, and peaceful conflict resolution).

2. Be self-motivated (explore motivation, try new things, and define success).

3. Have self-direction (develop, carry out, and evaluate personal goals).

4. Help others and work together for the group's welfare.

5. Implement responsibilities outside the gym (try out responsibilities in school, at home, and on the street).

I use several practical strategies to help kids become aware of these levels of responsibilities, experience them, and make decisions in relation to them:

- *Awareness talks* introduce the kids to the levels and remind them of their responsibilities.

- *Responsibilities in action* build responsibilities into the lesson so that the kids can experience and get a feel for them. For example, requiring that all teammates touch the ball before shooting in basketball helps them experience cooperation.

- *Individual decision-making strategies* are used at each level of responsibility. For example, someone who shows disrespect for others negotiates the consequences of this action, and if several kids are involved in a conflict, a time-out is called so that the kids can problem solve and reach a decision.

- *Counseling time* involves conducting brief, one-to-one meetings with all kids to check in and evaluate what has (or has not) been going on.

- *Group meetings* provide the opportunity for the kids to evaluate the program, the instructor, and each other as well as problem solve issues that arise and suggest ways to improve the program.

- *Reflection time* at the end of each lesson gives the kids the opportunity to self-evaluate the extent to which they were responsible (e.g., respectful, self-motivated) during the lesson.

Program evaluations indicate that the participants improve in self-control, self-direction, thoughtfulness, self-worth, maturity, and problem-solving. Their teachers also report that the participants exhibit enhanced interpersonal relations, teamwork, and sportsmanship. Both the kids and their teachers believe that participation in these programs helps young people become a more positive force in their schools and communities.

skills, active lifestyles, and strategies for winning games (Glover and Anderson, 2003).

As physical activity professionals, our mission is to create a positive environment where individuals can grow to understand what activity can do for them and be intrinsically motivated to participate in whatever activities they like. We are more likely to accomplish this mission if we can create a sense of community in our programs. Community implies an environment where people care for and support one another regardless of skill level. In this environment everyone is more willing to learn if the content is meaningful, they are involved in the learning, and they have a voice in the group (Glover and Anderson, 2003). Parents, teachers, coaches, and leaders have a responsibility to provide character education in order to create a sense of community.

In their book, *Character Education* (2003), Glover and Anderson provide information for creating a physical activity program centered on building character. This program addresses two of the NASPE content standards (2004). The first is standard 5: "A physically educated person demonstrates personal and social behavior that respects self and others in physical activity settings." By connecting kids with you and with their peers they will naturally take more responsibility for their own and others' well-being and development. Connected people appreciate and value what each person contributes to the team. The second standard the program addresses is standard 6: "A physically educated person values physical activity for health, enjoyment, challenge, self-expression, and/or social interactions." When people feel welcome, valued, and connected through physical activity, they will enjoy it more. This positive experience increases the likelihood that individuals will maintain a physically active lifestyle throughout life.

Character Education Methods

Glover and Anderson's character education provides character- and team-building activities to build character, enhance intrinsic motivation, and create enthusiasm for physical activity. These activities challenge and unite individuals in the pursuit of increased physical activity and honorable sporting behavior.

Unless we teach the participants in our programs how to be good teammates and good sports as well as give them opportunities to practice these skills, where will they develop these characteristics? There is evidence that most organized sport programs do not emphasize these skills. As physical activity professionals we need to be role models and demonstrate and encourage team building and good sportsmanship.

The first step in character education is to create a ritual at the beginning of each session that creates a welcoming atmosphere, promotes social relationships, builds character, empowers the participants, and makes learning and exercise fun. This ritual has three parts: the motivator, the huddle, and the warm-up.

The motivator is a way of greeting everyone with enthusiastic verbal and physical actions as they come in. Participants must feel welcomed and that others are glad they are there. The huddle is a group discussion about character-building activities. In the huddle, the group discusses *focus words,* which are words that represent values we want individuals to exhibit, such as respect, honesty, trust, integrity, and so on. Everyone tells what they think the word means and the leader facilitates a discussion about the word (Glover and Anderson, 2003). The warm-up consists of traditional warm-up activities as well as community-building activities done in teams. For more details on these games see *Character Education* (Glover and Anderson, 2003).

The character education program provides a number of team-building activities to use in physical activity settings. These activities allow individuals to listen to one another, solve mental and physical challenges, deal with failures and successes, share ideas, praise and encourage one another, physically and emotionally support one another, persevere, and start feeling a connection.

Several Web sites have information on character education, including the following sites in appendix B: www.cfchildren.org; www.cortland.edu/c4n5rs; and www.charactercounts.org.

See checklist 7.3 at the end of this chapter to see how effectively you are using character education methods.

SELF-EVALUATION

If individuals are to take an active part in their learning and development, they should be engaged in the evaluation process. If we are doing all the evaluating, they are not given the opportunity to reflect on their learning. Who knows more about how hard they have worked and how much they have improved than the individuals themselves?

Self-evaluation is a process where individuals compare their behavior to a set of criteria and then make a judgment as to whether the behavior meets the criteria or not. When the behavior meets the criteria, the individuals are reinforced either by themselves or by someone else. Self-evaluation systems have been successful in modifying a wide range of behaviors in settings ranging from preschool to high school (Glover and Anderson, 2003; Sainato, Strain, Lefebvre, and Rapp, 1990).

If a concept could be interpreted in several ways, such as good sportsmanship, you must first discuss behaviors that display the concept. These behaviors could include clapping for others when they make a goal; saying "Good try" when someone puts forth effort; helping others up when they fall even if they are on the opposing team; and so on. Then ask everyone at the end of the session to name one behavior they did today that showed good sportsmanship. Praise each person who reports a good deed. If the individuals know that they might be asked to give an example at the end, they are more likely to try to perform an appropriate behavior so that they can respond to your query.

You could use self-evaluation by having each person monitor and evaluate a target behavior. You could also use this method with a group as a whole or divided into teams. Your role is to guide each team in developing goals. One way to do this is to challenge the individuals to play the game without any putting down of other individuals. When participants are exhibiting the target behavior, reinforce them. When they look like they may want to say a put-down, give a physical cue such as a finger to the lips or the time-out sign (Glover and Anderson, 2003). At the end of a specific time, have each group evaluate their behavior to determine if they achieved the goal. The entire group or each team determines its rating. Then offer your rating of the group for comparison. Reinforce the group based on their behavior as well as their accuracy in evaluating their behavior. (See chapter 5 for a discussion on group contingencies.)

According to Salend, Whittaker, and Reeder (1993), group evaluation methods give individuals opportunities to achieve positive interdependence by creating a mutual goal related to their behavior. It fosters their dependence on each other to earn the reward by helping them learn how their behavior can contribute to earning the reward for the group. Additionally, it teaches them how to negotiate with each other to reach an agreement on the group rating.

See checklist 7.4 at the end of this chapter to monitor your use of self-evaluation.

CONFLICT MANAGEMENT

Conflict is natural. It occurs daily in everyone's life. Conflict is associated with destructiveness, antagonism, violence, and war. The understandable human reaction to conflict is avoidance (Mayer, 1995). However, when we avoid conflicts, the situation gets worse instead of better.

Conflict is neither good nor bad in itself. It is the manner in which we handle it that makes it positive or negative (Ohio Commission on Dispute Resolution and Conflict Management, 2001). When handled effectively, conflict can be a great learning experience for all involved. If handled ineffectively, anger and hurt are most likely the result.

The term *conflict management* refers to programs that teach concepts and skills for preventing, managing, and peacefully resolving conflicts. For young people to interact effectively with their peers, they must learn how to resolve conflict. These skills are not innate; they must be learned. They include listening, assertion, and collaborative problem-solving skills (Bolton, 1979). These skills are critical for developing and maintaining relationships with others. Ideally they are learned and nurtured in the home and reinforced once the child enters school and participates in youth sport or community recreation programs. Unfortunately, this is often not the case. How well children learn these skills early on will affect the quality of relationships they will develop later in life as well as the climate of our society.

Benefits of Managing Conflict

Conflict is threatening, yet it is inevitable when we interact with others. It takes courage to manage conflict effectively, but when we do, we can enjoy conflict's many benefits and prevent its potential destructiveness (Mayer, 1995).

Learning conflict management skills helps individuals

- develop the personal behavior management skills to take responsibility for their own behavior and accept the consequences of that behavior;
- act responsibly at school and in the community;
- respect others as individuals and as group members;
- develop self-control, self-respect, empathy, and teamwork;

- respect differences;
- become sensitive to others' feelings;
- solve problems before they escalate to violence;
- develop an understanding about interpersonal conflict and its consequences;
- increase the ability to recognize and nurture healthy relationships with people like and unlike themselves;
- improve verbal communication skills;
- improve listening skills;
- identify common interests;
- brainstorm multiple solutions;
- evaluate the consequences of different options; and
- agree on win–win solutions (Bolton, 1979; Lincoln, 2002; Ohio Commission on Dispute Resolution and Conflict Management, 2001).

Steps in Conflict Management

To resolve conflict, individuals must have good communication skills. There are 4 steps in the conflict management process.

Step 1: Identify your feelings and express those feelings in words (e.g., "I am feeling angry" or "I am feeling hurt"). Once you can do this, you are empowered and have gained a sense of control over your emotions.

Step 2: Discuss your feelings with the other person. When you are discussing your feelings, the other person is listening. Listening is the key to this process. The other person must learn to listen to gain information and understanding as well as show respect for your feelings. After you have a chance to share your feelings, the listener then mirrors or paraphrases what you said. This tells you that you were heard and that the other person understands how you feel. Mirroring allows you to clarify any points that the listener may have misunderstood. In this process it is important that the real source of the anger or hurt feelings be revealed.

Step 3: Both parties must agree to try to find a peaceful solution. To do this you must identify the issues, needs, and wants of each person involved. Then you both brainstorm to find mutually acceptable solutions. During this process emotions may run high. If they do, take a time-out to cool off, control emotions, and collect thoughts. Taking a walk, concentrating on something positive, jogging,

performing relaxation exercises, or taking deep breaths are all ways to cool down (Secor, 2001).

Step 4: Both parties must discuss the need to compromise to arrive at an equitable and fair outcome rather than allowing one party be right and one wrong.

Rules for Conflict Management

Rules are necessary for peaceful conflict management. The individuals involved should have a say in the making of these rules. Following is a sample list of rules.

- Both parties agree to the topic being discussed. Discuss related issues only. Unrelated incidents in the past may not be brought up.
- Select a neutral place to talk.
- Listen respectfully to each other.
- Keep an open mind.
- No name-calling or put-downs.
- The parties do not have to agree with each other. They can agree to disagree.

Methods of Conflict Management

Conflict management is difficult. We expect children to be able to do it, yet most adults are not very good at it. The learning curve is slow. Individuals should be encouraged to ask an adult for help when they feel they need it. The adult's role then is to guide the individual through the process:

- Ask what the individual did or said to stop the conflict.
- Suggest words the individual could use.
- Talk to both individuals to facilitate a solution.
- Remind them of the rules.

Even though we teach individuals to ask adults for support and encouragement through the process, our goal is to have individuals feel confident and empowered to use this process without adult intervention. If they experience a nonthreatening environment that encourages cooperation, promotes trust, and offers frequent group interaction, they will have more opportunities to practice their conflict management skills. They will have more reasons to choose conflict management rather than aggression to solve problems. Teaching ways to solve conflicts creates confident and caring individuals who will be more capable of developing meaningful relationships (Ohio Commission on Dispute Resolution and Conflict Management, 2001; Secor, 2001).

Talking Bench

An easy method that helps manage conflict and increase communication skills is the talking bench (Horrocks, 1978). The talking bench provides opportunities for individuals to resolve conflicts in the physical activity setting. To use this method, point out to the individuals that the causes of conflict are misunderstandings and mistakes. Then have the individuals sit on the talking bench, which is any place that they can sit down, talk, and listen. It could be on the bleachers, a park bench, or chairs off to the side (see figure 7.6). They then follow the 4 steps in the conflict management process. This method can increase interpersonal communication and understanding. Individuals are motivated to resolve the conflict because they want to return to the activity. However, you need to determine whether the individuals really understand the causes of the conflict or whether they are merely saying that they have found a solution to the conflict because they want to return to the activity. One method is to have the individuals report to you before they resume the

activity. Ask the individuals questions to determine whether they resolved the conflict:

- Did you determine how the conflict started?
- How did it start?
- Was the conflict started by a misunderstanding?
- Was the conflict caused by a misjudgment or a mistake that one or both of you made?

Create a dialogue similar to this:

- Andre, did you discuss your feelings with Raul?
- Raul, did you listen to Andre? Do you understand how he feels?
- Did you find a solution that is acceptable to both of you? What is that solution?
- Andre, is that solution acceptable to you? Raul, is it acceptable to you?
- What could each of you do to prevent this conflict from happening in the future?

If you are not convinced that the individuals are sincere in their resolution of the conflict, send them back to the talking bench to resume

Figure 7.6   The talking bench encourages communication to resolve conflict.

© Human Kinetics

discussing their differences of opinion. Horrocks (1978) believes that resolutions are more readily accepted when arrived at by the individuals rather than by an adult.

See checklist 7.5 at the end of this chapter to examine your effectiveness in teaching conflict management skills.

POSITIVE COACHING

Young people participate in sport primarily to have fun. Other reasons for participation include improving skills, doing something they're good at, getting exercise, being with friends, making new friends, and competing. Even with all the potential benefits, young people are dropping out of organized sport at an average rate of 35% a year. Some reasons for quitting include excessive competition, limited chances for successful participation, continual failure, poor sport etiquette, ridicule, sarcasm, embarrassment, intimidation, guilt, not having fun, too much pressure, overemphasis on winning, dislike of the coach, and physical abuse (Helion, 1996; Weinberg and Gould, 2003).

Because of the importance we place on sport, it helps shape our culture. We need to reclaim sport and use it to teach values and character.

How we conduct ourselves as coaches and players influences the kind of human beings we are and will become. Media coverage of poor coach conduct is not hard to find, including yelling at or berating players, motivating through intimidation and criticism, making players feel guilty about poor performances, and yes, even physical abuse. Cheating and dirty play are often encouraged and even glorified. We need to embrace a better way. We need to develop a more positive approach to coaching.

Creating a Positive Environment

How can physical activity professionals create an environment where individuals want to be; a place where they feel safe, connected, accepted, and competent; a place where they want to learn and succeed? The first step is to create an emotionally safe environment where individuals are not afraid to try because they know they will be accepted regardless of how they perform and they will be encouraged for trying rather than ridiculed for not succeeding. In this environment they are appreciated for who they are and not constantly compared to their peers.

Teaching Values

Positive coaching can build character by teaching values. Character will outlast any of the sport skills you teach your players. Common values that lend themselves to being taught in a youth sport setting include good sportsmanship, respect, mental toughness, positive attitude, self-esteem, responsibility, a lack of emphasis on winning, and honesty.

Good Sportsmanship

Good sportsmanship is one of the most important values youth sport teaches. Discuss, teach, and reinforce what good sportsmanship means beginning at the first practice and continuing throughout the season. Tell the players how much you value good sportsmanship, what your expectations are, and why it is important.

Sportsmanship is the unifying moral concept that describes good character in sport. It involves respect for teammates, for coaches, for the opponent, for the officials, and for the game (Clifford and Feezell, 1997). Coaches have a responsibility to practice, model, and teach good sportsmanship.

Point out and praise acts of good sportsmanship in practice and games. Other ways to reinforce these behaviors are by awarding more playing time and creating awards for good sportsmanship to give to players after games and at the end of the season.

Don't forget to look for good sportsmanship in the opposing team and point out those behaviors to your players. After the game congratulate the other team with compliments of good sportsmanship as well as good skills. Players must learn that the other team is just like them, kids who want to learn how to play the sport—they are not the enemy. Encourage the development of positive relationships with players on the other team. Share snacks after the game. Have the players get to know players on the opposing team after the game by engaging them in conversation.

Enlist the help of parents to reinforce the concept of good sportsmanship. Before the season starts, meet with parents and communicate the value you place on good sportsmanship. Encourage them to reinforce this value at home, and tell them the importance of being a role model for their children.

It is also important to communicate the importance of good sportsmanship to the fans. This can be done through a letter at the beginning of the season or by an announcement at the beginning of the game. Some organizations have developed an educational campaign to promote good sportsmanship. The coach can help in this process by being a good role model, making positive comments about sportsmanship after the game, recognizing fans for exhibiting good sportsmanship, and so on.

Establishing team rules and customs helps create team spirit and reinforces the concept of good sportsmanship. These rules must promote the idea that everyone on the team is a part of the effort directed toward the team's success, such as "All players must come to all practices" and "All players give 100% to improve their skills." Enforce these rules fairly and consistently. It should never be okay for some players to get away with breaking the rules. If star players are allowed to break a rule, they are showing disrespect for the team.

Develop clear guidelines for dealing with unsportsmanlike behaviors. Make it clear to the players that there will be consequences for rule violations, even at practice. Players have a hard time telling the difference if they are allowed to exhibit poor sporting behavior at practice but not in a game.

Respect

Another value sport can teach is respect: respect for the game, coach, players, officials, teammates, and opponents (Nakamura, 1996).

Respect for the Game

Players show respect for the game by playing their best and playing hard the entire time they are on the field. Hustling on and off the field also shows respect for the game. Respect the rules of the game; any form of cheating is unacceptable. Teach your players to be grateful for the opportunity to play.

Respect for the Coach

Because coaches are also teachers, they must know the game they are coaching. They earn the players' respect and are better able to improve their players' skill level if they are knowledgeable about the game's skills and strategies. Command respect from your players by having them address you as Coach. Require them to listen when you are speaking to them. Do not tolerate any signs of disrespect such as shaking their head, rolling their eyes, questioning your strategy, making derogatory comments, and so on.

Recreational sports often have volunteer coaches with little or no training in the sport they have volunteered to coach. They are often parents with an interest in their child's recreation pursuits. It is critical that the coaches attend a training workshop to learn game rules and strategies as well as how to teach the skills of the sport.

Respect for Players

Treat your players with respect. Interact with all players, get their input about the team, and value their comments and opinions. Be clear about your responsibilities as a coach. Be a good role model by demonstrating good sportsmanship and showing your respect for the game, officials, and opponents.

Respect for Officials

Show respect for the officials in the way you address them. Intimidating the officials is never okay. Do not lose your temper or argue with the official and do not let your players do so, either. Shake hands and thank the official after the game. When your team loses, do not blame the officials; instead, look for areas your team could improve and develop goals and strategies to get better.

Respect for Teammates

Players need to learn to build up, encourage, and support their teammates. At practice, encourage the players who are more skilled to work with players who need to learn and practice those skills. In a game, players should use words of encouragement after mistakes are made—putdowns are never acceptable. In the huddle, have your players compliment each other for plays well done. Expect all players to obey team rules; team unity is destroyed when the coach plays favorites.

Respect for Opponents

Encourage your players to cheer when an opponent makes a good play. It is not okay to clap when they make an error, and talking disrespectfully to the opponents is inappropriate. If players make a great play, they should not flaunt it, because this also shows disrespect for the opponents. It is fine to celebrate a great play, but not by taunting or rubbing it in. Teach humility. Make sure your players do not lose their temper or act immaturely when they make a mistake. Don't allow your players to become cocky if they are winning, and never run up the score on the opponent for any reason. This shows a lack of respect for the opposing team's coach and the players, and it also takes the fun out of the game for the losing team. If you are clearly winning, use the opportunity to put some of the players who are less skilled in the game. Have your players shake hands after the game and give sincere, specific praise for performance, such as, "That was a great shot at the buzzer." If your team lost, do not allow your players to make excuses for the loss, pout, or lose their temper—teach them to lose gracefully.

Mental Toughness

Another virtue players learn through positive coaching is mental toughness. Players should be taught to persevere, play hard throughout the game, and never give up. This is a valuable lesson for life.

Developing a Positive Attitude

Positive coaching instills a positive attitude in players. The players learn to approach problems as challenges, frustrations as learning experiences, and losing as an opportunity to improve. If players are being negative, teach them to reframe their statements in a positive way. Instead of saying "My bad," say "I will try harder next time." Instead of saying "I can't," say "I will work on being better at this" (Hunter, 2000).

Building Self-Esteem

Take many opportunities to build healthy self-esteem in your players. Address players by their name; "Hey you" is not okay. Treat your players with respect and value their opinions and feelings. Really listen to them: Nothing can make them feel more accepted, significant, and worthwhile than the coach listening to what they say (Nakamura, 1996). This not only helps build self-esteem but also can give you insight into issues in their lives that may be affecting their performance. Use positive statements to encourage them to improve their skills.

Teach players to value their mistakes and use them as motivation to improve. Teach them how to set personal goals that are challenging but attainable, and encourage them to achieve their goals for their own sake, not to please you. Be specific with your praise about their achievements so that they know exactly where they have made progress. Be honest and sincere; they will know if you are not. Recognize their achievements verbally, in writing, through certificates and awards, by making phone calls, and so on. This will instill pride in them.

Make sure your players know that how you feel about them as a person has nothing to do with how well they perform in the sport. Find and recognize strength of character in your players.

If players make a mistake, do not correct them publicly. Take them aside and ask them why they made the choice they did. They may have a good reason for making a choice that you could not see from the sidelines. Often they will admit they made a mistake, especially if you have made it clear that mistakes are for learning. Then ask them what they should have done instead. Let them come up with a solution, giving guidance only when needed. If several players made the same mistake, it may be appropriate to discuss that mistake in a team meeting as long as you are not singling out a player. Remember that for every correction you give, you should find five positive aspects to compliment.

Teaching Responsibility

Players should learn responsibility and have opportunities to take responsibility for their progress as well as their choices. At the beginning of every practice, allow players to set individual goals for themselves for that practice, such as run the wind sprints 5 seconds faster than last practice, score one more goal during the practice game, or make 6 of 10 free throws. After practice, provide a reflection time for players to think about, record, and discuss the progress they made toward their goals that day.

Use team goals as a means to evaluate the team, not the scoreboard. Have players determine team goals before each game, such as get more rebounds than the previous game, increase the number of attempted goals, play a tighter defense so as to allow fewer passes by the opponents, and so on. After the game, discuss whether they met the team goals. Praise progress toward these goals and taking the responsibility to achieve them.

Deemphasizing Winning

Make sure you examine how attached you are to the concept of winning, because this will determine how your players view winning and losing. Winning does not determine your worth. If you feel that it does, so will your players and their self-esteem will decrease with each loss. Instead, learn from each loss. Determine what skills the winning team had that you can work on, and use these skills to set goals for the next game. And even if you win, set goals. There are always skills to practice and new goals set for the next game (Hunter, 2000). We need to lose the "win at all cost" philosophy and replace it with an enjoyment of sport for all its benefits. Define winning as achieving personal and team goals, learning, connecting with others, making friends, having fun, and exhibiting good character.

Do not emphasize the score of the game. Often it is best to not even mention it. If a player asks the score, answer by pointing out the accomplishments of an individual or the team. For example, respond by saying, "It doesn't really matter who won, but I noticed you were really hustling out on the field. I am proud of you!" These types of statements send a message to the players and the parents that you value skill improvement over winning. Treat your players the same after a win as you do after a loss. Point out what the team did well in the game and emphasize those things.

Honesty

Be honest and never sacrifice integrity for a win. Cheating, dishonesty, and dirty play are never acceptable. Fair play should always be taught and encouraged, and you must model these values if you expect your players to learn them. Make sure they understand that success in sport is not merely achieving victory. Victory without sportsmanship, dignity, and honor is hollow (Clifford and Feezell, 1997).

Of all the opportunities to facilitate the physical and emotional development of young people, coaching is one of the most important. As a mentor, we can have an incredible influence on players' lives. We can build their self-esteem, increase their fitness, improve their skills and moral character, and create a positive attitude toward sport and life. It is not a responsibility to take lightly, and if you take it seriously it can be incredibly rewarding.

See checklist 7.6 to examine how effective your coaching methods are for building character. Several other checklists are designed to provide information on the coach's approach to character development, including the checklist at the Center for 4th and 5th Rs Web site (www.cortland.edu/c4n5rs/).

SUMMARY

The humanistic approach is based the psychological causes of individual behavior. To use this approach, work to develop a learning environment that is safe and nurturing, to understand individuals' feelings and behaviors, to build and

teach values, to encourage individuals to learn independently, and to help individuals understand that behavioral limits are meant to protect them. A number of models and methods use the humanistic approach and are particularly effective in a physical activity setting, including the becoming responsible model, teaching personal and social responsibility model, character education, self-evaluation, conflict management, and positive coaching. Refer often to our descriptions and practical examples of how to use these methods in physical activity settings as you design your own approach. Depending on your group's maturity, age, and size, you may need to modify the methods. Finally, use checklists 7.1 through 7.6 to review the concepts we have covered.

WHAT DO YOU THINK?

1. Think about your own teaching, coaching, or leadership style and list responsible behaviors. Rank them in order of importance, and think about how you would teach them.

2. How could you modify Hellison's teaching personal and social responsibility model to fit your situation? What would the level system look like? What teaching methods would be appropriate for your situation?

3. Do you think the physical activity setting is appropriate for teaching character? Explain your answer.

4. Briefly discuss five methods for building character that you could use in your setting.

5. Discuss how you could use self-evaluation in your setting.

6. Think about how you manage conflict. Using the concepts presented in this chapter, describe a conflict management method (or create a new one) that would work in your setting.

7. Think about your setting. Do individuals show respect? If yes, through what behaviors? How could you teach them to be more respectful?

8. Are you a good role model for your students in terms of demonstrating good character? Explain.

CASE STUDIES

For each of the three case studies in chapter 1 on page 13, select methods described in this chapter and discuss in detail how you would implement each of the methods to manage the behavior. After you have developed your own methods, read the following suggestions, which are only some of the many creative ways you might apply the information covered in this chapter.

CASE 1

Hector, a Disruptive 3rd Grader

▶ Discuss with Hector the behaviors you are concerned about. Focus on the behaviors one at a time, trying to get Hector to take responsibility for his behavior by asking questions pertaining to levels 1 through 3 of the personal and social responsibility model, such as the following:

> ▶ Why do you think you have trouble listening quietly while others are talking?

> ▶ Why do you think not listening quietly while others are talking might concern me?

> ▶ Why might it be important for you to learn how to listen quietly while others are talking?

▶ Give him specific examples of when he did not listen while others were talking and ask him what he could do to change this.

▶ Make sure Hector knows he is responsible for his behavior. Teach him what personal responsibility means. Introduce him to the levels of Hellison's teaching personal and social responsibility model, and when he is running around and not participating, ask him to identify the level he is functioning on.

▶ Reinforce Hector when he is participating in the activity and point to the level on the chart.

▶ Have Hector develop a personal responsibility project. Encourage him to set a goal to change this behavior, such as "Listen while others are talking 7 out of 10 times (70%)." Set up a self-evaluation chart for him in which he puts a +1 each time he listens quietly when others are talking and a –1 each time he does not listen. On Fridays, meet with him and evaluate his progress with him. If he listened quietly 70% of the time, give him the reinforcer; if he did not, give him the consequence.

▶ Follow the same procedure for the other three behaviors (not following directions, not waiting his turn calmly, and running when he should walk). If necessary, focus on only one behavior a week until Hector understands what behaviors you expect from him.

CASE 2

Ashante, an Instructor in Charge of Weight-Room Cleanup

▶ Discuss with the group environmental responsibility, which includes becoming conscious of the contexts in which we function; respecting property and taking care of equipment, the classroom, the school, and the larger community; and recognizing the importance of taking care of the environment as well as influencing others to take care of the environment. Also discuss how leaving equipment around for others to trip over is a safety issue.

▶ Develop a personal responsibility project in which the goal is to have the group put the equipment away every time after it is used. The measurable objective would be, "Each individual will put away the used equipment 100% of the time for 3 consecutive weeks." Have the group choose a reinforcer that they receive if they achieve their objective. Walk around the weight room while the participants are working out, reinforcing each person when they put equipment away and using a one-liner such as "Is that barbell back where it should be?" when equipment has not been put away.

▶ If only one or two individuals are leaving the equipment out, sit down with each one and facilitate a self-evaluation project in which they write a goal and a measurable objective for putting away equipment. Each day they evaluate themselves and chart their behavior. At the end of the project, they will evaluate whether they achieved their objective and if so, reinforce themselves with the chosen reinforcer.

▶ Have a reflection time after the session is over and ask if the participants showed respect for the weight room by cleaning it up when they were done. Ask them why it is important to take care of the environment, including examples of how their neighborhood would look if everyone left all their possessions out in their yard. Take some pictures of neighborhoods that have junk in the yards and share them with the participants. Have them make suggestions for how to clean up the yards. Then have a group project to clean the grounds of the recreation center. Make sure their cleanup efforts are recognized by others.

CASE 3
Molly, an Overly Aggressive Soccer Player

▶ Using Hellison's personal and social responsibility model, discuss the levels with Molly. Remind her that in level 1, individuals learn to control their own behavior and respect the rights and feelings of others. They also learn to recognize differences of opinion, to negotiate, and to resolve conflicts peacefully. Discuss ways that

Molly can respect others' feelings about issues. When Molly does get into a fight, have both participants communicate their feelings about the other's behaviors in an attempt to reach a mutual understanding.

▶ Help the players define sportsmanship and establish team rules for good sportsmanship.

▶ Reinforce players for good sportsmanship at practice and in games.

▶ Establish a Good Sportsmanship Award for the player who demonstrates honorable sporting behavior during the game. Give the award after each game.

▶ Discuss what respect means and define respectful behaviors, including respect for the game, coach, players, officials, teammates, and opponents. Have the players and their parents sign the list of respectful behaviors.

▶ Establish a Respect Award for the player who demonstrates the most respectful behavior. Give the award each game.

▶ Be sure Molly understands the league's policy on fighting, poor sportsmanship, and lack of respect. Go over the consequences for these behaviors and implement them as needed.

▶ As a coach, be a good role model and demonstrate good sportsmanship and respect.

▶ Teach Molly conflict management methods and encourage her to use them. Start with the 4-step approach.

▶ Teach Molly and the team how to use the talking bench.

Checklist 7.1 Promoting Personal Responsibility

Rate yourself in regard to the following statements.

	Consistently	Inconsistently	Never
Adult talk:			
I am aware of how my verbal and nonverbal language affects the individuals in my program.	☐	☐	☐
I send positive messages to individuals, seeking to enhance their sense of self-esteem.	☐	☐	☐
Participant talk:			
I do not allow individuals to blame others for their problems.	☐	☐	☐
I teach individuals how to rephrase their comments to reflect personal responsibility.	☐	☐	☐
Adult actions:			
I determine what responsibility means to me in a situation.	☐	☐	☐
I determine why such responsibility is important.	☐	☐	☐
I give individuals a list of the responsible behaviors I expect from them.	☐	☐	☐
I have individuals make a checklist of behaviors they are willing to take responsibility for, thereby encouraging them to evaluate themselves.	☐	☐	☐
I work with individuals to establish consequences for behaving responsibly and irresponsibly.	☐	☐	☐
I apply the consequences consistently.	☐	☐	☐
I encourage individuals to see the connection between feelings and behavior.	☐	☐	☐
I design activities that nurture personal responsibility.	☐	☐	☐
I give individuals choices of activities and levels of difficulty within each activity.	☐	☐	☐
I support individuals and encourage them to support each other in their choices.	☐	☐	☐
I assign personal responsibility projects.	☐	☐	☐
Participant actions:			
I give individuals opportunities to demonstrate responsible behavior.	☐	☐	☐
I design activities that promote social responsibility.	☐	☐	☐
I use cooperative games.	☐	☐	☐
I teach conflict management skills.	☐	☐	☐
I show individuals how to deal with peer pressure.	☐	☐	☐

Checklist 7.2 Strategies for Using Hellison's Levels

Rate yourself in regard to the following statements.

	Consistently	Inconsistently	Never
Awareness talks:			
I hold awareness talks as needed to increase awareness of the levels.	☐	☐	☐
I explain the levels.	☐	☐	☐
I reinforce the levels by posting them, verbally reminding individuals of them, and signaling them with the same number of fingers.	☐	☐	☐
I periodically conduct sharing sessions so that individuals can teach each other through discussion.	☐	☐	☐
Levels in action:			
I create chances for individuals to experience one or more levels during physical activity.	☐	☐	☐

I use direct questioning to encourage individuals to experience the levels.	☐	☐	☐
I implement service projects.	☐	☐	☐

Reflection time:

I include time for individuals to reflect on the levels.	☐	☐	☐
I facilitate discussion.	☐	☐	☐
I encourage individuals to write in a journal and give them feedback on what they have written.	☐	☐	☐
I encourage individuals to complete a personal responsibility project goal sheet (see figure 7.1).	☐	☐	☐
I encourage individuals to state the levels they feel they are working on and give reasons for their evaluation.	☐	☐	☐
I ask questions to get individuals to reflect on their behavior relative to the levels.	☐	☐	☐
I have the group participate in reflection by asking questions that they respond to as a group.	☐	☐	☐
I encourage individuals to write in a journal about their actions. I review the journal and give feedback.	☐	☐	☐
I encourage individuals to complete a reflection checklist (see figure 7.4), which I review and comment on.	☐	☐	☐

Individual and group decision making:

I provide opportunities for individuals to practice decision making.	☐	☐	☐
I encourage individuals or the group to develop fitness routines and perform them at their own pace.	☐	☐	☐
I encourage individuals to be peer tutors to give them experience teaching and evaluating others.	☐	☐	☐
I incorporate self-paced challenges that encourage individuals to work at their own rates and levels.	☐	☐	☐
I encourage individuals to negotiate and make choices at each of the levels.	☐	☐	☐

Group meetings:

I hold group meetings to allow individuals to express their views; raise issues; suggest solutions; lobby for their own interests; and share their opinions, feelings, and ideas about the physical activity program.	☐	☐	☐
I facilitate these meetings by asking specific yet open-ended questions.	☐	☐	☐
I encourage individuals to evaluate the program and offer input on a variety of topics, including making rules, telling how things are going, discussing problems that have occurred, and coming up with possible solutions to the problems.	☐	☐	☐
I establish rules of the meeting and share these with the group before the meeting and as needed.	☐	☐	☐

Counseling time:

I reserve time for interactions with individuals and groups to convey strengths and areas for improvement.	☐	☐	☐
I show a genuine interest in each individual in my program.	☐	☐	☐
I find out how each individual or group is doing, evaluate levels of responsibility, ask the individuals how their choices are working for them, ask them what they could do differently next time, and encourage them to develop a plan for change.	☐	☐	☐
I work closely with individuals and groups as they interact with the levels in mind so that they can incorporate these values into their lives.	☐	☐	☐
I establish respectful relationships with the individuals in my program.	☐	☐	☐

Checklist 7.3   Using Character Education

Rate yourself in regard to the following statements.

	Consistently	Inconsistently	Never
I strive to create a positive environment in which individuals will understand the benefit of physical activity and be intrinsically motivated to participate.	☐	☐	☐
I strive to create a sense of community in my physical activity environment.	☐	☐	☐
I provide specific activities to build character and enhance intrinsic motivation to participate in physical activity.	☐	☐	☐
I strive to be a good role model and demonstrate team building and good sportsmanship.	☐	☐	☐
I create a ritual at the beginning of each session to develop a welcoming atmosphere.	☐	☐	☐
I provide team-building activities throughout the session.	☐	☐	☐

Checklist 7.4   Using Self-Evaluation

Rate yourself in regard to the following statements.

	Consistently	Inconsistently	Never
I teach individuals to evaluate their own behavior by comparing it to a set of criteria.	☐	☐	☐
I reinforce individuals or encourage them to reinforce themselves when they meet the criteria.	☐	☐	☐
I describe and demonstrate behaviors that I want the individuals to perform, such as good sportsmanship.	☐	☐	☐
I ask individuals to reflect and tell what behaviors they did that demonstrated the concept.	☐	☐	☐
I encourage self-evaluation in groups. I facilitate the development of goals and encourage the groups to evaluate whether they have met each goal. I reinforce those groups who achieved the goals.	☐	☐	☐

Checklist 7.5   Using Conflict Management

Rate yourself in regard to the following statements.

	Consistently	Inconsistently	Never
I teach individuals the benefits of learning how to manage conflict rather than avoid it.	☐	☐	☐
I teach the 4-step approach to conflict management.	☐	☐	☐
I teach the communication skills necessary to manage conflict such as controlling emotions, expressing feelings, listening to others, mirroring, and compromising.	☐	☐	☐
I teach individuals the rules for conflict management: agree to the topic, discuss related issues, select a neutral place, listen respectfully, keep an open mind, no name calling, and understand that it is okay to agree to disagree.	☐	☐	☐
I guide individuals through the process of conflict management by asking the individuals what they did to stop the conflict, suggesting words that they could use, sending them back to use the words, talking to both parties to facilitate a solution, and reminding them of the rules.	☐	☐	☐
I teach individuals in my program to use the talking bench.	☐	☐	☐

Checklist 7.6 Using Positive Coaching

Rate yourself in regard to the following statements.

	Consistently	Inconsistently	Never
I create a positive environment where players want to be, a place where they feel safe, connected, accepted, worthy, and competent.	☐	☐	☐
I teach character-building values.	☐	☐	☐
I teach the behaviors that demonstrate good sportsmanship, point out and praise acts of good sportsmanship both on my team and on the opposing team, and encourage the development of positive relationships with teammates and opposing team members.	☐	☐	☐
I communicate the importance of good sportsmanship to the parents and encourage them to reinforce this and be good role models at home.	☐	☐	☐
I communicate the importance of good sportsmanship to the fans through letters, announcements at games, and recognizing fans who demonstrate good sportsmanship.	☐	☐	☐
I establish team rules and customs to create team spirit.	☐	☐	☐
I develop clear guidelines for dealing with unsportsmanlike behaviors.	☐	☐	☐
I teach respect for the game, coach, players, officials, teammates, and opponents.	☐	☐	☐
I teach mental toughness by teaching players to persevere, play hard throughout the game, and never give up.	☐	☐	☐
I instill a positive attitude in players by teaching them to approach problems as challenges, frustrations as learning experiences, and losing as an opportunity to improve.	☐	☐	☐
I strive to build the self-esteem of players by learning their names, treating them with respect, valuing their opinions and feelings, and really listening to them.	☐	☐	☐
I teach my players to value their mistakes and use them as motivators to improve.	☐	☐	☐
I teach my players to set personal goals that are challenging but attainable.	☐	☐	☐
I am specific when praising players' achievements so that they know exactly what they did well.	☐	☐	☐
I am honest and sincere.	☐	☐	☐
I recognize players' achievements in many ways, including verbally, in writing, with certificates and awards, and through phone calls.	☐	☐	☐
I find and recognize strength of character in my players.	☐	☐	☐
When players make a mistake, I talk with them in private to find out why they made the choice they made, ask them what they should have done instead, and give guidance only when needed.	☐	☐	☐
I teach responsibility by giving players opportunities to take responsibility for their own progress as well as their choices and actions.	☐	☐	☐
I use team goals—not the scoreboard—as an opportunity to evaluate the team.	☐	☐	☐
I deemphasize winning by defining winning as achieving personal and team goals, learning, connecting with others, making friends, having fun, and exhibiting good character.	☐	☐	☐
I do not mention the score of the game, just the accomplishments of individuals and the team.	☐	☐	☐
I treat my players the same after a win as I do after a loss.	☐	☐	☐
I am honest and never sacrifice integrity for a win.	☐	☐	☐
I always teach and encourage fair play.	☐	☐	☐
I teach my players that victory without sportsmanship, dignity, and honor is hollow.	☐	☐	☐

CHAPTER

8

Biophysical Approach

***W**hen traditional approaches have proven to be ineffective, collaborate with others to incorporate other approaches. We must find effective ways to enhance the performance and learning of children and youth.*

Frank's youth soccer coach is frustrated with Frank's behavior in practice games. For at least the past 2 seasons and especially the past 4 months, he has been inattentive, impulsive, and even aggressive. His behavior and attention-deficit/hyperactivity disorder have made it difficult for him to learn and it has taken away from the other players' learning. Frank's coach has created a highly structured learning environment and tried several methods to reduce these behaviors, including contracts and token economies. In addition, Frank is in private counseling with his parents and group counseling in school. Unfortunately, the counseling does not seem to be helping him behave and perform better in his youth sport program or in his classes at school.

Frank's parents want him to participate on the team with his friends but have accepted that if his behavior does not improve, he will be dropped from the team. They are considering other approaches, such as relaxation training, medication, and even diet management.

When traditional behavior management methods such as those previously discussed in this book are unable to remove or reduce a problem, consider adding other methods, including biophysical methods. The biophysical approaches we'll discuss in this chapter are based on the premise that behavior is not merely environmental, but is often related to biological variables such as genetic abnormalities, neurological impairments, chemical imbalances, and diet. Many times these behaviors are related. We'll examine approaches used in physical activity settings to redirect disruptive behaviors, particularly behaviors related to stress, medical conditions or medications, and nutritional deficiencies. But we can only give you an overview, so if you have not been trained in using these methods effectively, consider attending a workshop related to a specific method. Perhaps you can ask your school district, sport, or recreation program administrator to provide such a workshop.

In addition, you must learn to recognize when a problem is too big for you to solve alone. Don't hesitate to reach out to other professionals, such as a psychologist, dietitian, physician, or special educator, to get the help you need. One professional you may want to work with when it comes to the biophysical approach is the adapted physical educator. In the Trenches illustrates the role and responsibilities of an adapted physical educator.

RELAXATION TRAINING

We can define stress as an anxiety-inducing inability to effectively respond to environmental demands. In other words, when the equation between what is expected of individuals and what the individuals feel they can produce is out of balance, they feel stressed.

Stress can affect performance. Some factors that cause stress and anxiety are the death of a close family member, divorce or separation of parents, an unsafe living environment, personal injury or illness, health problems of a family member, grades, changes in their bodies, being yelled at, and changing schools (Gipson, Lowe, and McKenzie, 1994).

One approach that may help reduce stress is relaxation training. Life's intense pace can lead to potentially stressful situations. This stress may be positive and improve performance or negative and disrupt performance. Regardless, few individuals are aware of mounting tension or overstimulation and still fewer know how to deliberately calm down and relax at the appropriate time. Learning how to relax under stressful circumstances is a vital life skill. If individuals can be taught to calm down when they are getting upset, the incident may not escalate to an emotional outburst (Cipani, 1998). After they have learned the method they should periodically practice it when they are not upset to ensure they are able to relax during a stressful event.

A certain amount of tension is necessary for action and productivity, but excess tension hinders successful living, obstructing peak performance. Most often tension is mental in origin but manifests itself physically. For example, the cardiorespiratory, muscular, and neurological systems are affected by psychological stress (Pangrazi, 2004). For over 20 years we have known that stressful life events can increase the risk of disorders ranging from common health

IN THE TRENCHES

When Traditional Teaching Methods Fail
Lisa Silliman-French, Coordinator of the Adapted Physical Education Program and Programs for Students with Visual Impairments, Denton Independent School District, Denton, Texas

Many biophysical methods are only used in collaboration with other professionals. My role as an adapted physical education coordinator is to find possible resources such as psychologists or school nutritionists to assist the adapted or general physical educator. Seldom do I directly interact with physicians, though the school psychologist may provide information about an intervention such as medication or nutrition that may affect the performance of a student. I then share this information with the student's adapted or general physical educator.

Related to prescribed medication, my school district has developed disability fact sheets that include information about common medications students with specific disabilities may be using. We give the appropriate disability fact sheets to teachers who have students with specific disabilities that include behavior problems, as well as any additional infor-

mation such as instructional and activity modifications that will increase the possibility of safe and successful participation of all students.

Another area I work with teachers on is the behavioral intervention plan. Both the adapted and general physical educator must follow this plan, but in many schools they are not involved in its development. General physical educators in particular might not even receive the plan or have it explained to them. However, they need this information for effective programming, and in some situations regular follow-up meetings are needed to assist the physical educator, the student, and maybe the other students in class.

Similar information is of the utmost importance to not only physical educators, but coaches and recreation specialists as well. We all want individuals to become responsible and function at their maximum potential physically, emotionally, and socially.

---

complaints, such as hypertension, backaches, chest pain, indigestion, insomnia, dizziness, and headaches, to heart disease.

Benefits of Relaxation Training

Relaxation is a learned skill and can calm young people. They cannot be nervous or tense when their muscles are relaxed. Simply put, the training helps young people deal with stress in a socially acceptable manner.

Many people think of relaxation training as a method used primarily to provide better concentration and relieve anxiety. We know, for example, that it is essential for athletes to learn to regulate their response to the pressure of competition, and in turn, avoid any detrimental effects on performance. The same is true for the individuals in your physical activity setting.

Relaxation training allows young people to become more aware of their bodies, thereby gaining a sense of control over basic physiological functions such as breathing and heart rate. Beyond the physical, relaxation training helps individuals control anxiety, thereby decreasing the negative effects stress has on performance, including the following (Karlin and Breit, 2003):

- Muscular tension, which causes decreased muscular coordination (could be related to an attention deficit disorder or developmental coordination disorder)
- Narrowed and internal focus of attention when a broad focus is needed
- Labored respiration from asthma or emotional stress
- Increased metabolic rate, which wastes energy resources

• Central nervous dysfunction such as certain types of cerebral palsy that involve physiological stress with involuntary movements

Applying relaxation training in physical activity settings may reduce both disruptive behavior and injuries. Indeed, young people who are more relaxed are more focused, calm, and cooperative. You can apply this method to physical activity settings in numerous ways and significantly influence individuals' daily lives at the same time. For more in-depth information on relaxation training, see Greenberg (2002) and Weinberg and Gould (2003). Different types of relaxation exercises are appropriate for young people. First, however, consider the guidelines provided in figure 8.1.

Relaxation Exercises for Children

Young children usually adapt quickly to relaxation training. Older children and teenagers may feel silly and self-conscious and reject relaxation activities. Because of this you must be patient and allow time for the transition to more positive attitudes about these exercises (Edwards and Hof-

meier, 1991). Figure 8.2 presents some exercises for children that you could incorporate into a relaxation program.

Relaxation Exercises for Older Individuals

Offer the following exercises in sequence to older individuals. They can lie on their back in a quiet environment. Emphasize slow and rhythmic breathing, never holding their breath while performing the exercises (Pankau, 1980; Pica, 1997). Also have them tighten and relax the muscles of the body in the following order, having them tighten muscles for 5 to 10 seconds, then relax for 15 seconds before moving on to the next group.

1. Eyes, nose, and mouth
2. Neck
3. Chest and shoulders
4. Upper and middle back
5. Upper arms, lower arms, and hands
6. Stomach
7. Hips
8. Upper legs and knees
9. Feet and toes

GENERAL GUIDELINES FOR RELAXATION EXERCISES

1. Say, "Loosen tight clothes; lie in a comfortable position, with your feet slightly apart (approximately 6 inches) and flat on the floor, knees apart, and head resting in a comfortable position." Make sure the temperature is comfortable and lights are lowered with adequate space for each individual to do the relaxation exercises without distractions from others.

2. Voice control is important (Davis, 1991).
   A. Begin activities in a normal conversational tone, and slowly lower both the volume and tone of your voice as the individuals relax.
   B. Control the pace of your voice. Begin each technique in a normal or slightly slower speed. As the individuals begin to relax, gradually slow down the pace.

3. Encourage any distracting thoughts or sounds to "flow into the brain" and then tune them out.

4. Say, "Begin with your eyes open, but when I signal you (after 10 seconds), allow your eyes to slowly close to count of 5."

5. Continue, "Breathe through your nose, placing one hand on your chest and one hand on your stomach to feel the rise and fall of your breathing."

6. If necessary, use reinforcers to teach relaxation. The reinforcers could range from tangible to social reinforcers. Generally, praise is sufficient.

7. Get written consent for students with high blood pressure to participate in relaxation training exercises that involve tightening muscles, because isometric exercises may increase blood pressure. With these individuals, do only the more specific relaxation exercises that follow the starting activities.

8. Look for tension as evidenced by wrinkles in the forehead, sweating, fast heartbeat, crossed legs, grinding teeth, and flushed face. If possible, it may be beneficial to have the individuals wear a heart rate monitor or practice in front of a mirror.

9. Have individuals monitor their progress in writing. See worksheet 5 in appendix A for a sample performance record sheet. If you are interested in how well the individuals feel they have performed, instead of using Xs, ask them to tell you how well they believed they relaxed by rating themselves on a scale of 1 to 5. The higher the number, the more relaxed they felt.

Figure 8.1 Relaxation training has many positive effects on young people.

1. **Knees to chest.** Say, "While lying on your back, gently pull both your knees to your chest. Now pull your head up, then gently rock back and forth from your shoulders to your buttocks, pretending to be a rocking chair."

2. **Hands and arms.** Say, "Pretend there is a wet sponge in your left hand and try to squeeze the water from it as hard as you can. Drop the arm and relax. Do these two or three times and then repeat with the right hand."

3. **Arms and shoulders.** Say, "While lying on your back, pretend you are a lazy cat and stretch your arms straight up to the ceiling. Next raise them high above your head along the floor. Stretch even higher. Then drop your arms back to your sides." Repeat the exercise.

4. **Shoulders and neck.** Say, "Pretend you are a turtle sitting on a rock by a quiet pond, relaxing in the warm sun. An alligator passes by, so you pull your shoulders up to your ears and push your head into the shell house. The alligator passes, so you can come out and feel the sunshine again." Repeat two or three times.

5. **Jaw.** Say, "Pretend you are chewing a large bubble-gum jawbreaker. It is very hard to chew. You must use your neck muscles because the gum is so hard. Now relax." Repeat three or four times.

(continued)

Figure 8.2 Relaxation exercises for children.

6. **Hips.** "Make large circles with your hips as if using a hula hoop, and then slowly make the circles smaller. Next slowly raise your arms overhead and then back to your sides." Repeat three or four times.

7. **Legs and feet.** Say, "Pretend you are walking across a swamp in your bare feet with the mud squishing between your toes. Many times you have to push hard with your legs. Now step out of the swamp and relax your feet and toes." Repeat.

8. **Face and nose.** Say, "Pretend a large insect lands on your nose. Try to get the insect off your nose without using your hands. Try to wrinkle up your nose as many times as possible. Now relax." Repeat.

9. **Stomach.** Say, "Pretend a baby elephant is walking through the grass and stumbles right where you are resting on the ground. Get ready, make your stomach hard—tighten up! The elephant regains his balance and begins to move away. Oh no, he is coming back—get ready to tighten up!" Repeat.

Figure 8.2 *(continued)*

Music

Music offers wonderful possibilities for relaxation. It has even been suggested that some areas in the brain are only activated by music. In addition, music may engage the entire brain to improve behavior and moods (Blakemore, 2004). You may wish to introduce music into the relaxation program after individuals adequately perform the relaxation activities sitting or lying down in a comfortable position with their eyes closed. Instrumental music with strong and simple melody lines, whether classical or contemporary, works well because students find it easier to relax when they are not distracted by words. Only use music you have already heard to ensure it is suitable. Reif (1993) has identified music pieces that have a calming effect, including Debussy's *Clair de Lune* and Beethoven's *Für Elise.*

In addition, you can purchase music from the Sensory Comfort Company (www.sensorycomfort.com) that may reduce tension and stress. For instance, here are examples of modulation music:

- Mozart may enhance attention and learning.
- Baroque music may enhance attention and learning.
- Calming music may aid bedtime relaxation.

Visual Imagery

If desired, you can incorporate visual imagery with progressive relaxation training or use it separately. Some benefits of visual imagery are reduced stress, anxiety, and depression; greater ability to focus; and improved self-confidence. This method is widely used with athletes in sporting events because it may enhance sport performance (Weinberg and Gould, 2003). As with relaxation training, have individuals lie down in a comfortable position with their eyes closed. When they are comfortable, suggest one visual image at a time, allowing them ample time to create their own mental pictures. Make sure that each image is appropriate for the individuals' maturity and developmental levels. To get started, tell individuals to pretend to be one of the following:

1. A leaf floating down to the ground
2. An ice cube on the pavement, slowly melting as the sun comes up and gets hotter
3. A winged animal soaring above the earth
4. A rag doll, slowly falling to the floor
5. A slowly melting ice-cream cone on a hot summer day
6. A piece of spaghetti before and after being cooked

Additional visualization activities are presented in figure 8.3.

VISUALIZATION ACTIVITIES

Submarine on the go. Ask individuals to imagine they are in a miniature submarine that can travel through the blood vessels in the heart. Have them take refreshing oxygen to each part of the body, thinking about how feelings are expressed by each body part—for example, the arms move gracefully, the eyes open widely with excitement, and the face smiles with happiness.

Clock freeze. Have individuals watch a large clock with a second hand. Ask them to "freeze" the body until the second hand moves from a certain time to another. Then have them relax. Vary the lengths of tension and relaxation.

Activity freeze. Have individuals perform a physical activity, such as bouncing a ball, doing jumping jacks, or walking. Tell them to freeze at random and stand like a statue for 4 to 5 seconds.

Feather float. Drop a feather and have individuals pretend they are also a feather. Encourage them to see how slowly they can float like a feather to the floor.

Simon says. Have individuals perform slow movements when Simon says.

Skunk walk. Have individuals crawl slowly along the floor. Say, "If you want to be the skunk's friend, you cannot get too close to him, and you don't want to scare him, so move very, very slowly."

Mirror. Have individuals mirror each of your slow, deliberate movements. Vary the speed slightly.

Figure 8.3 Visual imagery can be part of progressive relaxation training.

MEDICATION

You must try to find out what medications individuals are taking, because medications will either negatively or positively affect motor performance and behavior. Ways to collect information include sending home a short survey for parents to fill out and talking directly with parents as well as with the school nurse, special education and resource teachers, and physicians.

This information is confidential. The Health Insurance Portability and Accountability Act (HIPAA) of 1996 protects the confidentially of all individuals with disabilities regarding their medical information. This act has four major objectives (Stevens, 2005). One is to guarantee the security and privacy of health information. Similarly, in the school setting the Individuals with Disabilities Education Act (IDEA) requires states to have detailed policies and procedures to ensure the confidentiality of any personally identifiable information collected, used, or maintained about a student with disabilities. All physical activity professionals must be cautious about indiscriminately speaking or providing information in written form about an individual's medical condition or disability to anyone, particularly to their paraprofessionals or volunteers. The key, though, is always the health and safety of the individuals!

Exercise and Medication

Many experts consider physical activity to be an alternative to drug treatment for reducing or eliminating certain behaviors. Regular exercise reduces adrenalin and other hormones, which the body produces naturally under stress. The exercise does not have to be strenuous or competitive; it has been reported that a daily 10-minute jog can reduce stress (Phillips, Kiernan, and King, 2003). Other investigators have also reported the positive relationship between physical activity and protection against the symptoms of depression and anxiety (Goodwin, 2003). While these findings support physical activity, some suggest that there is a need for more research with an emphasis on precise methodology (Phillips, Kiernan, and King, 2003).

Medication for Inappropriate Behavior

Many individuals with disabilities take prescribed medication to manage inappropriate behavior.

Psychopharmacological medications are among the most efficient and widely available means to modify behavior caused by deficiencies in the central nervous system. This type of medication produces biochemical, physiological, or psychological changes. While these changes can help modify behavior, they can also cause many adverse side effects. The incidence and severity of side effects vary depending on the medication, dosage, and individual. In addition, drugs alone will not enhance self-esteem or the ability to cope with problems.

You must know if an individual is receiving psychopharmacological medications and how the medication could affect the individual's social and motor performance. Table 8.1 offers brief explanations of the more traditional types of medications, dividing them into four major types. As the name implies, antidepressants are the most commonly used medication for treating depression. They affect the part of the brain that controls messages between nerve cells. The major tranquilizers reduce emotional arousal. They suppress the brain centers that control abnormal emotions and behavior. Then we have listed minor tranquilizers, sedatives, and hypnotics. These medications affect the limbic system of the brain, which controls emotions. Their use generally results in decreased arousal and motor activity. Stimulants include amphetamines and related compounds such as caffeine; these excite the central nervous system both physiologically and behaviorally.

Medication, Disabilities, and Behavior

Numerous disabilities are associated with inappropriate behavior, including emotional disturbance, attention-deficit/hyperactivity disorder (ADHD), traumatic brain injury, autism, and prenatal exposure to alcohol or drugs. In many cases, individuals with these types of disabilities may be on medication to help manage their behavior. It is estimated that 15 to 20% of students in special education programs receive one or more behavior-modifying medications (Forness, Kavale, Sweeney, and Crenshaw, 1999).

We are not recommending that you act as a physician. However, physical activity professionals can play an important supportive role to the physician and other medical personnel. You need to discuss medications in depth with a physician and consult with administrators regarding

Table 8.1 Uses and Potential Adverse Effects of Commonly Used Medication

Trade name	Generic name	Common uses	Potential adverse effects
ANTIDEPRESSANTS			
Elavil, Triavil	Amitriptyline	Depression	Blurred vision, confusion, dizziness, fatigue, fainting, hallucinations, headaches, seizures
Norpramin	Desipramine	Depression	Blurred vision, fatigue, fainting, headaches, unsteady gait
Sinequan	Doxepin	Depression, associated anxiety	Blurred vision, dizziness, fainting, hallucinations, headaches, irregular heartbeat, seizures, tremors
Imavate, Presamine, Tofranil	Imipramine	Depression	Blurred vision, dizziness, fatigue, fainting, hallucinations, hypoactivity, incoordination, seizures, tremors
Prozac	Fluoxetine hydrochloride	Depression	Anxiety, headaches, drowsiness, dizziness, muscle pain, weight loss
Zoloft	Sertraline hydrochloride	Depression, obsessive disorders	Headaches, tremors, dizziness, twitching, confusion, balance problems, postural hypotension, rashes, increased sweating
Wellbutrin	Bupropion hydrochloride	Depression	Seizures, arrhythmia, headaches, anxiety, confusion, tremors, rashes
Luvox	Fluvoxamine maleate	Obsessive-compulsive disorders	Seizures, impaired judgment, impaired thinking and motor skills, headaches
Paxil	Paroxetine	Obsessive-compulsive disorders, panic disorders	Headaches, sweating, nausea, dizziness
Effexor	Venlafaxine	Depression	Anxiety, nervousness, insomnia, headaches, sweating, nausea, anorexia, dizziness, tremors, blurred vision
Serzone	Nefazodone hydrochloride	Depression	Nausea, dizziness, blurred vision, confusion
Remeron	Mirtazapine	Depression	Headache, seizures, sweating, nausea, dizziness
MAJOR TRANQUILIZERS			
Thorazine	Chlorpromazine	Agitation, psychotic disorders, hyperactivity aggression	Confusion, fainting, hallucinations, mood changes, rapid heartbeat, tremors, unsteady gait, weight gain, blurred vision
Haldol	Haloperidol	Anxiety, agitation	Blurred vision, drowsiness, fainting, hallucinations, tremors, weight gain, sweating leading to overheating
Mellaril, Novoridazine, Thioril	Thioridazine	Anxiety, agitation	Drowsiness, fainting, muscle spasms, tremors, unsteady gait, weight gain
Navane	Thiothixene	Anxiety, agitation, psychotic disorders	Dizziness, drowsiness, fainting, less or unusual perspiration, muscle spasms, rapid heartbeat, tremors
Buspar	Buspirone hydrochloride	Anxiety, stress	Dizziness, nausea, headache, nervousness, lightheadedness, excitement

(continued)

Table 8.1 *(continued)*

Trade name	Generic name	Common uses	Potential adverse effects
MINOR TRANQUILIZERS, SEDATIVES, AND HYPNOTICS			
Novodipam, Rival, Valium, Vivol	Diazepam	Nervousness or tension	Confusion, dizziness, drowsiness, hallucinations, incoordination, tremors
Bamate, Equanil, Miltown	Meprobamate	Anxiety, nervousness or tension	Confusion, dizziness, fatigue, fainting, headaches, joint and muscle pain, seizures, unsteady gait
Gardenal, Solfoton	Phenobarbital	Anxiety, nervousness or tension	Confusion, dizziness, drowsiness, joint and muscle pain
STIMULANTS			
Benzedrine	Amphetamine	Hyperactivity in children	Blurred vision, chest pains, dizziness, headaches, irregular heartbeat, less or unusual perspiration, mood changes, rapid heartbeat, weight loss
Dexampex, Dexedrine, Ferndex	Dextro-amphetamine	Hyperactivity in children	Blurred vision, chest pains, dizziness, headaches, irregular heartbeat, less or unusual perspiration, mood changes, rapid heartbeat, unsteady gait
Ritalin	Methylpheni-date	Hyperactivity in children	Blurred vision, chest pains, dizziness, fatigue, headaches, mood changes, rapid heartbeat, weight loss
Cylert	Pemoline	Attention-deficit/hyperactivity disorder (ADHD)	Seizures, hallucinations, abnormal oculo-motor function, mild depression, dizziness, increased irritability, headaches, drowsiness

Adapted from K.D. Daniel, 1986, "Pharmacological treatment of psychiatric and neurodevelopmental disorders in children and adolescents (Part I)," *Clinical Pediatrics* 25: 65-71.

policies for prescribed medication. In addition, keep in mind that medications should be the last resort and are generally used in combination with other methods such as the behavior management methods discussed in chapters 3, 5, 6, and 7. Ultimately, the purpose of medication should be to make other interventions more effective.

Medical Survey

Ideally the physical activity professional reviews any available files to determine if there are any medical reasons indicating that an individual needs a modified program or needs to be supervised a little more closely. To shorten the process, though, just before the beginning of each school year, session, or program, send home a short survey regarding any medical conditions that individuals may have that could negatively influence safe and successful participation in your program. On the same form, ask about any prescribed medication the individual may be taking that could also be detrimental to behav-

ior, performance, or learning. Include space so that if individuals are taking medication, they or their parents can give you information about reactions and side effects that you should look for. Some parents or guardians will provide this information because they know you want to protect their child. But a few may not respond to this request because they are worried that you may single their child out during the program. Telephone such parents to reassure them that you will maintain the child's privacy and personally invite them to work with you to more effectively help them or their child grow and learn. If you still cannot get the information you need, at least document for legal purposes that you requested the information.

Other Sources of Medical Information

Many other professionals, particularly in the school environment, can help you obtain the medical information you need to meet each individual's needs. Begin by talking to the school nurse. The Council of Exceptional Children has designed a form on student medications for the school nurse to fill out. The purpose of this form is to help nurses provide such information to the teachers, who need to know when this information should be shared with recreational leaders and coaches who do not have access to a school nurse. As with the medical survey, if the parents or guardians do not want this information released, document that you made the effort. If individuals have a disability, contact their special education or resource teacher. As one of the individuals' teachers, you may review the individual's file. Then refer to table 8.1 to determine potential adverse effects for different medications. If you have any questions, contact the parents or guardians for written permission to speak to the child's physician about any concerns. Of course parental permission and confidentiality must be maintained. This process takes a little time, but, like the old saying goes, "Better to be safe than sorry." In fact, physicians want to collaborate with physical activity professionals when patients have medical conditions for which physical activity may play a positive or negative role in treatment (Jansma and French, 1994). It's up to us, however, to take the first step and open the lines of communication with local physicians.

NUTRITION

Diet and nutrition are important factors in behavior and learning. Many schools throughout the United States have initiated free breakfast and lunch programs not only to feed students but also to improve student's diets, increase school performance, and reduce behavior problems.

Diet Management

Food choices and quality affect the brain, which affects how an individual feels, thinks, and behaves. For some, diet may be associated with or may exacerbate such conditions as poor impulse control and tendencies toward violence and hyperactivity (Fishbein and Pease, 1994). Whether or not they display hyperactive tendencies, some individuals have unusual reactions to certain foods, including sugar and caffeine; nutritive elements such as zinc, calcium, magnesium, selenium, chromium, iron, or potassium; and foods such as milk, chocolate, cola, corn, eggs, peanuts,

citrus fruits, tomatoes, wheat and small grains, and food dyes and other additives.

While research results are limited and contradictory, many parents have reported positive changes from modifying their children's diets. While few parents strictly enforce a special diet, they will look for approaches that may work to reduce inappropriate behavior, for example, by reducing certain types of foods, such as those high in sugar. Parents have told us that based on their child's hyperactive or irritable behavior, they know when their child has had a sugar product on the way home from school. If you believe that this may be the case with an individual, encourage parents and child to monitor breakfast and lunch to avoid the negative effect the wrong foods can have on the child's behavior. In some environments, eating even birthday cake is discouraged because of possible behavior disruptions, reduced concentration, and hyperactivity (Shmerling, 2001). If food does influence a child's behavior, it usually does so in the first 30 to 90 minutes after eating (Fontenelle, 1992).

While you may not be surprised that food allergies and sensitivities can cause or exacerbate hyperactivity, irritability, impulsivity, and aggression, food allergies can affect some individuals in ways you may not expect. For example, some with ADHD who are allergic to certain foods or have asthma may actually increase inappropriate behaviors when they eat the food they're allergic to. What's more, some individuals are so sensitive to certain foods that even a minor slip in a restricted diet can lead to the undesirable behavior (Feingold, 1975). Others believe that while some individuals' behavior may improve through diet, miraculous improvement should not be expected (Jacobson, 2000). As you can see, solving the mystery of nutritional problems can be difficult. At the very least it takes knowledge, persistence, and a willingness to work with the parents.

Inadequate Nutrition

Some researchers have suggested that malnutrition may impair brain function to the extent that rewards and sanctions are not effective (Kanarek, 1994). If you think inadequate nutrition may be a possible reason for inappropriate behavior and poor performance, you can request that the parents and the individual conduct a meal–behavior evaluation using a special form, such as worksheet 6 in appendix A. This could help everyone working with the individual determine if a correlation between diet and behavior exists. If the data reveals a correlation, encourage the parents and individual to adjust the individual's diet. You may need to have a dietitian or an allergist help you analyze the data. Keep in mind, too, that some individuals may eat an adequate diet but their bodies may not absorb certain nutrients. Only a trained professional such as a physician or dietitian can determine if this is the case.

DISABILITIES THAT MAY AFFECT BEHAVIOR

In the following sections, we'll describe the most common disabilities that present behavioral challenges in physical activity settings. We provide information about common medications and effective methods for managing behavior associated with each disability. When studying this information, we encourage you to review the individual's records and talk to the parents to better understand the child's challenges and needs. Most if not all will be on an individualized education program (IEP), which contains valuable information about the child's needs and states how the school must serve those special needs. As one of the child's teachers, ask and expect to participate in periodic reviews of the IEP: As a physical educator, you bring a unique perspective to the review process. Coaches or recreation specialists can ask the participant or the participant's parents when appropriate for background information about the disability.

Attention-Deficit/Hyperactivity Disorder (ADHD)

Attention-deficit/hyperactivity disorder (ADHD) is often associated with behavior problems (Lavay, 2005). It is estimated that 3 to 7% of the school-aged population have this condition (APA, 2000). ADHD is far more common in boys than girls at a 3-to-1 ratio.

• Many experts believe that general behavior modification methods that are structured, consistent, and proactive should be used to manage the behavior of individuals with these disorders; this was one of the first teaching approaches to enable some individuals with ADHD to develop self-control in physical activity environments (Harvey, Fagan, and Kassis, 2003). Specifically, Trocki-Ables, French, and O'Connor (2001) reported that verbal

praise and tokens were effective in increasing the performance of boys with ADHD.

• In some cases, individual or group counseling and several other psychodynamic approaches have been applied (see chapter 7).

• Physical activity has been recommended as a possible intervention. Two specific forms of suggested exercise are taekwondo (Taekwondo tutor, 2003) and running (Higdon, 1999).

• Relaxation training can be an effective approach for helping individuals with learning disabilities and ADHD, thereby facilitating performance of motor tasks by helping individuals focus on the task (Brandon, Eason, and Smith, 1986).

• Medication has also been recommended in certain cases. However, medication is never used without other behavior management methods. Three major medications widely used to reduce hyperactivity and improve ability to focus are Ritalin, Dexedrine, and Cylert.

Most important is that parents and physical activity professionals work together. Everyone must be on the same page when it comes to implementing an effective behavior plan. Behavior plans can range from an informal, verbal understanding between the parents and the physical activity professional to a formal, written behavioral intervention plan for students who have been classified with a disability. Behavioral intervention plans are explained in more depth in the latter part of this chapter.

Autism

Autism is a developmental disability significantly affecting social interaction and verbal and nonverbal communication. Some other characteristics of autism include incessantly engaging in repetitive activities, resistance to changes in routine, and an inability to appropriately respond to perceptual stimuli (e.g., sounds, touch). The incidence of autism is estimated at 5 to 15 per 10,000 live births and it is four times more common in males than females (Sherrill, 2004). While the cause of autism is unknown, structural deficiencies, which may be contributing factors, have been discovered in the brains of individuals with autistic tendencies. It is believed that taking vitamins in large amounts might reduce characteristics or symptoms of autism (Edelson, 1999). Exercise on a regular basis, whether it is moderate or strenuous, has been reported to decrease stereotypic behaviors, hyperactivity, aggression, self-injury, and destructiveness (O'Connor, French, and Henderson, 2000). The exercise must be provided on a regular basis if it is to reduce depression, anger, disruptive behavior, and stereotypic behavior. It seems that physical activity, with its healthy benefits and low cost, should be one of the first approaches to reducing behavior problems, particularly compared to prescribed medications, which are more expensive and may have harmful side effects.

Following are methods to promote the learning of individuals with autism:

- Exercise at moderate intensity and make activities enjoyable and noncompetitive. Incorporate behavior management methods into a task-analysis approach to instruction (Collier and Reid, 2003; Houston-Wilson and Lieberman, 2003; Reid, O'Connor, and Lloyd, 2003).

- Allow time for the individuals to become familiar with the physical and social environment.

- Promote eye contact to develop this important social skill.

- Use clear and understandable language.

- Be aware of sensory preferences of information.

- Be aware that individuals may focus on just one cue within the environment, which might not be the important cue.

- Use prompts (visual, auditory) that could help lead to a correct response.

- Adapt tasks to build success.

- When appropriate give choices, which could reduce behavior problems.

- Use relaxation training to reduce stress and anxiety in individuals with autism. Provide the program on a one-to-one basis and adapt it to the individual; it could last about 20 minutes. Refer to the section on relaxation training earlier in this chapter.

Behavioral Disorders

Individuals with behavioral disorders are among the most challenging to teach in a physical activity environment. These individuals exhibit one or more of the following characteristics over a long period of time:

(a) an inability to learn that cannot be explained by intellectual, sensory, or health factors, (b) an inability to build or maintain satisfactory interpersonal relationships with peers and teachers, (c) inappropriate types of behavior or feelings under normal circumstances, (d) a general pervasive mood of unhappiness or depression, or (e) a tendency to develop physical symptoms or fears associated with personal or school problems. (Individuals with Disabilities 1997, 12422)

These individuals represent the fourth largest group of students receiving some type of special education in public schools.

While not everyone with this disability exhibits all of these characteristics, in general they are hyperactive, easily distracted, and impulsive. Some may steal, abuse alcohol or drugs, lie, or be withdrawn. It is no wonder physical activity professionals often become anxious and frustrated in their efforts to deal with these behaviors. Most of these individuals are challenging and difficult to teach.

Following are ways to promote performance and learning by individuals with behavioral disorders:

- If the cause is biophysical, such as neurological dysfunction, a physician may prescribe medication. To become more familiar with the most commonly prescribed medications, see table 8.1 (page 151). Refer to this table when examining student records so that you can ask more specific questions when investigating student problems.

- Another biophysical approach that has been suggested to reduce inappropriate behavior is regular physical activity. Physical activity in general has been shown to positively influence self-concept and anxiety (Biddle and Mutrie, 2001).

- Physical activity professionals must move beyond reliance on corrective and social control methods. Corrective methods are just one facet of a broad intervention agenda to treat individuals with behavioral disorders. The physical activity professional must consider what the payoff is for the individual who is engaging in inappropriate behavior, or what the individual gets out of engaging in the behavior (see methods in chapters 2 and 3).

- Some may lack the skills to perform expected tasks or may exhibit behaviors that help them avoid or escape those tasks. Spend time teaching them the basic skills.

- Common reactions exhibited by the individuals and illustrated teaching strategies, many of which involve the behavioral and psychodynamic approaches, are provided in table 8.2.

Table 8.2 Teaching Strategies for Reactions of Individuals With Behavioral Disorders

Common reactions	Teaching strategies
Aggression	If needed, incorporate a physical restraint, then token economy or a contract (see chapter 5).
Easily frustrated	Help individuals hurdle a difficult task by providing assistance or remove individuals from the situation for a few minutes.
Seeking attention	Inappropriate behavior should not be reinforced by attention such as coaxing. Good behavior can be rewarded through leadership roles (see chapter 5).
Extroverted or introverted behaviors	Physical activities should fulfill the student's psychomotor needs and counteract negative behavior.
	Aggressiveness, anger, and tantrums need to be handled with care; reasoning with the individual in this state will be fruitless.
	Foster attention to healthy relationships with activities that lead to interaction.
	One-to-one, small group, and larger group activities should be offered in progression.
Distractibility	Provide a structured setting and control all environmental stimuli.
	Emphasize relevant stimuli and reduce or eliminate distractive ones.
	Provide clear signals to initiate and end activities.
Difficulty relating to others	Use dual and group activities for older individuals and developmental play experiences for younger individuals.
	Use signal interference by providing nonverbal cues such as eye contact, hand gestures, and frowning.
Difficulty accepting change, criticism	Strive to create an appreciation of individual differences and a capacity to accept limitations without withdrawing from individuals.
	Consider cooperatively structured activities.
Heightened emotional stress	A systematic program of physical education activities will stimulate more physiological reactions and permit accepted channels of outbursts.
	Use proximity control by standing near the individuals during activities (see chapters 2 and 3).
Inability to direct self	Use a teacher-directed structured environment. Students need to fully comprehend rules, boundaries, and rest areas before the activity begins. Students often need their own spot where they sit for all opening and closing activities.
Poor self-concept	Offer systematic programs of physical education that provide success. The experience of success influences the person's appearance, body image, and feeling of self-worth.
	Individuals should be addressed by their first names.
Easily threatened	In the beginning, individuals should be engaged in nonthreatening and noncompetitive activities that involve conflicting situations.
	Consider the use of humor to defuse tense situations.
Challenging authority	Apply firm and consistent discipline combined with concern.
	Remain calm and, if needed, use physical restraint.
	Consider planned ignoring of mild inappropriate behavior while reinforcing appropriate behavior.
Short attention span	Offer a variety of activities within each session.
	Explain new tasks using short, simple phrases.
Misperceiving the reactions and intentions of others, including authority figures	Be honest and directly address concerns in a way that they easily understand.
Lack of understanding of and disregard for personal safety and rules	A structured environment with strict limits is important. Work with the individuals on a one-to-one basis.

From P. Jansma and R. French, 1994, *Physical education: Physical activity, sport, and recreation* (Englewood Cliffs, NJ: Prentice Hall).

Traumatic Brain Injury

Traumatic brain injury refers to a permanent injury caused by an external physical force leading to a concussion, contusion, or hemorrhage. Many physical problems are associated with this injury, including sensory and motor impairment, seizure disorders, and poor gait coordination. In numerous instances, psychosocial and behavioral deficiencies are present right after injury but change in nature over time (Asarnow, Satz, Light, and Lewis, 1991). The most prominent problems are anxiety, aggression, overestimation of abilities, depression, irritability, noncompliance, and psychomotor restlessness (Driver, Harmon, and Block, 2003). Anxiety can be accentuated if the individual exhibits problems executing physical and motor skills that could easily be performed before the injury. Each year over 1 million individuals in the United States are hospitalized for head injuries (Sherrill, 2004). Males are twice as likely as females to suffer a traumatic brain injury, with the highest incidence among young men 15 to 23 years of age (Porretta, 2000). Vehicle accidents, assaults, and falls are the most common causes of such injuries.

Most people with traumatic brain injuries recover without the aid of drugs. Others, however, must have drug therapy to manage depression, impulsive aggression, and moodiness. This is not surprising since the brain injury often affects the mechanism that controls emotions and behavior. Different types of antidepressants and stimulants interact on the specific systems. Counseling (see chapter 7) and behavioral approaches (see chapter 5) such as token economies may also help rehabilitate individuals with a traumatic brain disorder (Rose, 1988).

Physical activity professionals need to follow these guidelines for individuals with traumatic brain injuries:

- Determine, as much as possible, the extent of the injury and what the individual's present needs are.
- Provide consistent routines, and if there will be changes let the individual know ahead of time.
- Keep in contact with the individual's parents.
- Consider getting support from a counselor or psychologist.
- Modify teaching or coaching styles or methods, length of practices, and expectations as necessary.

- Physical activity has repeatedly been shown to positively influence not only physical fitness and motor skill improvement but also self-concept; affective experiences; and anxiety, depression, and stress. Physical activity professionals should therefore be an integral component of education and rehabilitation programs of individuals with traumatic brain injury (Driver, Harmon, and Block, 2003).

It is crucial to make sure the behavior is not neurological before attempting to use behavioral interventions, because these methods will not be effective and could increase anxiety and frustration if the behavior is neurological.

BEHAVIOR INTERVENTION PLAN

Many students who are disabled, particularly those who have ADHD, autism, or are behavior disordered, are on an IEP as well as an accompanying Behavior Intervention Plan (BIP). This plan contains strategies to address specific behaviors that significantly interfere with an individual's performance and learning or that of others. The BIP is developed by the individual's IEP team, who develop a written document to ensure appropriate programming for each student with a disability. The document describes the current trend of performance, identifying goals and objectives for the future, educational services, and personnel who can help with the stated goals and objectives. The members of the IEP team are the parents or guardians, district representatives, school psychologist, special educator, and teachers. A specific instance requires the IEP team to develop and implement a BIP, and that is when an individual has committed an illegal drug or weapons offense.

The basis of the BIP is a functional behavioral assessment that includes an observation and descriptive data from the teachers, parents, and other school staff; a review of common events that lead up to and follow the inappropriate behavior; and a review of the effectiveness of reinforcers and punishers used in the past. Forms are used for the functional behavioral assessment and the BIP (see figure 8.4).

Physical educators and school-based coaches must understand what a BIP is, how it is developed, and how it is implemented. You may have individuals in your classes or program that are on a BIP. In these cases, you should follow the BIP and even provide input into the intervention

BEHAVIORAL INTERVENTION PLAN

Student _____ Teacher _____ Date _____

Grade level _____ School _____

I. Goals and objectives in behavioral terms

Goal 1	Goal 2
Objective 1	Objective 1
Objective 2	Objective 2
Objective 3	Objective 3

II. Rules stated positively

A.	D.
B.	E.
C.	F.

III. Positive consequences of complying to rules

A.	D.
B.	E.
C.	F.

IV. Cues to set behavioral limits (proactive; generally nonverbal) _____

_____

_____

V. Punishers for not complying to rules

A.	D.
B.	E.
C.	F.

VI. Backup plan with the use of campus and off-campus resources _____

_____

_____

Figure 8.4 Goals and objectives are just some of the information you find in the behavioral intervention plan.

and evaluation of its effectiveness. In some cases the implementation should extend into the community such as in youth sport and physical recreation programs to provide a more comprehensive implementation, which expands the plan to the recreation specialist.

SUMMARY

Numerous biophysical methods can help you positively influence behavior. Decide what you can best incorporate into your physical activity setting. If nothing else, use relaxation training not only to help individuals with behavior problems but also to help all individuals cope with our fast-paced, anxiety-prone society.

Medication and nutritional approaches are usually initiated when traditional methods fail. In the medication approach, you may be asked to monitor the individual's behavior to note motor and behavioral changes. You may also be asked to help design the physical activity component that usually accompanies the nutritional approach, tailoring it to the individual's needs.

You and the other professionals working with individuals who exhibit inappropriate behaviors should consider medications only as a last resort. Moreover, medications need to be used in combination with other interventions, most notably the behavioral approach discussed in chapters 4, 5, and 6. Use medications only as a supplement to help make other interventions more effective.

WHAT DO YOU THINK?

1. What are the advantages and disadvantages of using biophysical methods from your point of view as a physical activity professional?

2. Develop a behavior intervention plan (BIP) for a young person you have worked with or are working with at this time (see figure 8.4).

3. Develop and practice the relaxation training program for an individual or a group. Write the program down and take notes as you implement the program in 3 to 5 sessions.

4. Numerous individuals take prescribed medication to manage their behavior. In a physical activity environment, (a) why is it important to determine who is taking this type of medication, and (b) what is your plan of action to work with them? In your response to question b, consider any resources you can use and what type of focus you need to develop.

5. Diet is not only important for optimal growth and development but may affect behavior as well. Do you think diet and its influence on behavior should be a consideration in the role of a physical activity professional? Explain.

6. Develop a plan for promoting responsible behavior for an individual with a disability who is in your physical activity program.

CASE STUDIES

For each of the three case studies in chapter 1 on page 13, select methods described in this chapter and discuss in detail how you would implement each of the methods to manage the behavior. After you have developed your own methods, read the following suggestions, which are only some of the many creative ways you might apply the information covered in this chapter.

CASE 1
Hector, a Disruptive 3rd Grader

▶ Teach basic relaxation exercises to the entire class, but have Hector practice them at home as well. In class when he feels upset or frustrated,

allow him to leave the activity area and practice his relaxation exercises, then return.

▶ Encourage Hector's parents to consider diet management, which will be monitored by the school staff during the school day.

▶ If all else fails, suggest that Hector's parents investigate medication. Request that the parents inform you and other involved school staff if he is placed on medication and what type so you can monitor his behavior and provide him with a safe environment. While Hector is on medication work with his other teachers to create a simple graph to chart his daily behavior.

(continued)

Case Studies   *(continued)*

CASE 2
Ashante, an Instructor in Charge of Weight-Room Cleanup

▸ Biophysical methods seem inappropriate for improving clients' behavior at the community recreation center. Other techniques discussed in chapters 2 through 7 are certainly more useful, so note the case studies at the end of those chapters for illustrative solutions to this problem.

▸ Ashante may want to consider using some of the relaxation techniques for herself before she begins her quest to clean up the weight room. The relaxation exercises for young people as well as visual imagery exercises could be effective for reducing frustration and may allow Ashante to more effectively focus on developing and implementing the plan of action.

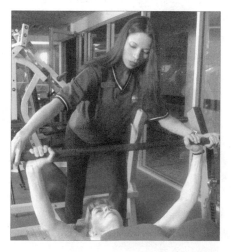

CASE 3
Molly, an Overly Aggressive Soccer Player

▸ The inappropriate behavior of one person, Molly, is not only negatively affecting the coach but the complete environment. The other players are upset, the fans are attempting to influence the coach's behavior, and even the officials are involved in controlling the game. Molly's behavior must be stopped. It is hoped that effective use of the methods presented in chapters 2 through 7 would reduce or eliminate Molly's inappropriate behavior. However, it may be time to consider using some biophysical approaches singularly or in combination with methods addressed earlier.

▸ For practices and games Molly can use visual imagery incorporating positive approaches to deal with specific situations that set her off.

▸ Determine when Molly is beginning to lose control and remove her from the practice or game to perform relaxation exercises. When she seems to calm down she will earn the privilege to return to the game.

▸ If these methods fail, consider removal from the team until other methods can be determined with the assistance of professionals such as a physician and nutritionist with support from a behavior-modification specialist to allow her to become an effective member of the team.

Developing Your Own Behavior Management Plan

*W*hen teachers apply various discipline techniques, they hope not only that misbehavior will cease but that students will further internalize self-discipline and display it in the classroom and elsewhere.

Charles, 2002, p. 3

Now that we've given you a broad overview of behavior management methods, you may be thinking, "How do I put it all together?" We certainly don't believe that any one method or plan is the only way to go. Many different variables affect the success of a plan in a given setting. Some variables that can affect the plan include group size, age, maturity levels, background, discipline used at home and at school, personality, parental support, and so on.

Other important variables are your knowledge, experience, and personality. Knowing how to be proactive and prevent problem behaviors (chapters 2 and 3), reinforce appropriate behaviors (chapter 5), and reduce inappropriate behaviors (chapter 6) is the first step. Experience with these methods will help you know what does and doesn't work in certain situations and with certain individuals. And your personality will play a large role in determining what methods you are comfortable using. For example, if you are controlling by nature, you may not want to share power, so it would probably be difficult for you to allow individuals to evaluate their own behaviors and develop a plan to change them.

We have developed a 10-step approach that will guide the development of your behavior management plan (see figure 9.1). We'll discuss the steps to follow and suggest factors to consider in developing a plan to meet the needs of you and your students or participants. These ideas are an eclectic compilation of a number of educational experts (Charles, 2002; Hunter, 2000; Kelly and Melograno, 2003; Schempp, 2003).

We will ask you to reflect on your own values and beliefs as you develop your philosophy of teaching, coaching, or leadership and your philosophy of behavior management. This will guide your development of a personalized behavior management plan. We have based the questions we pose in this chapter on our own philosophies and experiences to guide you through the process. The sample answers are just that—samples—one way to look at an issue. They are not intended to be *the* definitive answers. Writing down your answers to these questions may help clarify your thoughts. This reflective process will help you at any stage of your career, whether you are in your 1st, 5th, or 17th year as a physical activity professional. Indeed, writing may help you reflect on your experiences and assess your ideas and practices so that you may see more clearly what areas you want to improve.

As you go through the 10 steps, think about your own physical activity setting. When developing your behavior management plan, use checklist 9.1 (page 174) to check off each of the steps as you complete them. But simply being able to answer "Yes, I am consistent" to each statement will not make your program effective. View the checklist as a tool for reviewing and assimilating the information covered in this book as you strive to tailor the methods to meet your needs.

THE 10-STEP APPROACH

Step 1:
  Develop your philosophy as a physical activity professional.

Step 2:
  Examine your strengths and weaknesses as a physical activity professional.

Step 3:
  Develop goals for your setting.

Step 4:
  Develop your philosophy of behavior management.

Step 5:
  Examine your strengths and weaknesses as a behavior manager.

Step 6:
  Based on your philosophy, establish behavior management goals for your setting.

Step 7:
  Write measurable behaviors for each method you have outlined to reach your goals.

Step 8:
  Implement the measurable behaviors and collect data to determine whether they have been achieved.

Step 9:
  Revise or replace methods that were ineffective.

Step 10:
  Be reflective.

Figure 9.1 A 10-step approach to developing your behavior management plan.

STEP 1
Develop Your Philosophy As a Physical Activity Professional

Whether you are teaching students in a physical education class, coaching a team, or leading recreation groups at the local community center, you must think about the values and beliefs you hold about your position in order to develop your philosophy. Let's look at a few questions that will help guide you through this process, followed by sample answers.

Why did you become a teacher, coach, or recreation specialist?

- I wanted to be a teacher so that I could facilitate learning in my students.
- I wanted to be a coach so that I could help build character in today's young people.
- I wanted to be a recreation specialist so that I could create healthy physical activity options for children in after-school programs at the community center.

What excites you about your work?

- I am excited about seeing the look in students' eyes when they learn a new skill.
- I am excited to help my players learn the game of soccer.
- I am excited about helping participants build character and seeing them develop as conscious human beings.

What are your values and beliefs?

- I believe that all children have a right to learn.
- I believe participants need to be actively involved in the learning process to benefit from their physical activity experience.
- I believe that participants must have opportunities to reach their potential physically, cognitively, socially, and personally.

What do you believe your role is?

- My role is to create a safe, nurturing environment conducive to physical, social, and emotional learning.
- My role is to love and accept each individual for who they are right now, not who I might want them to be.

- My role is to create opportunities for individuals to be actively involved in the learning process.
- My role is to create opportunities that challenge participants and motivate them to reach their potential.

What character skills do you want individuals to learn?

- I would like my students to respect others.
- I would like my players to learn that teamwork is essential.
- I would like my participants to learn that helping others improve is just as important as improving their own skills.
- I would like individuals to know that honesty is always the best policy.

What is the individual's role in the learning process?

- The individual's role is to take advantage of the opportunities presented and to take an active role in the learning process.
- The individual's role is to grow physically, socially, and emotionally.
- The individual's role is to internalize self-discipline.
- The individual's role is to be willing to build character and to see its benefits for the individual, the group, and society.

Does your role go beyond the established physical activity setting?

- Yes, I feel that education is a holistic system in which individuals learn to be responsible citizens who want to contribute positively to society.

If so, in what other areas do you play a role?

- As their teacher, I can be a good role model and provide opportunities for them to build character and learn responsible behaviors. Through teachable moments, I can provide them with knowledge and guidance.
- My role goes beyond the team, because I feel that coaching is a holistic system in which players learn to be responsible citizens who want to contribute positively to society.

What are your three biggest concerns about your work?

- I am concerned that my students will not be motivated to learn.

- I am concerned that my players will not respect me as their coach.
- I am concerned that the participants in my community after-school program will not want to participate in the activities that I have planned.

STEP 2
Examine Your Strengths and Weaknesses As a Physical Activity Professional

We all have strengths and we all have weaknesses in relation to the role we play as professionals. It is important to recognize our strengths so that we can build on them. It is also important to recognize our weaknesses so that we can plan strategies to work on changing them to make us more effective professionals.

What have you learned from the physical activity professionals you have known?

- Think about those teachers, coaches, and recreation specialists you have had in school, on teams, or in the community center. No doubt there were some that you admired and some you did not particularly like. You can learn from all of them.

What characteristics do you admire most?

- I admire physical activity professionals who listen, care, are genuine, are vulnerable, are intuitive, are fair, and have a sense of humor and a playful spirit.

What characteristics do you like least and would not want to model?

- I would not want to be overbearing, controlling, unreasonable, dishonest, unfair, and more concerned with winning or academics than with building character and improving skills.

What characteristics do you have that will make you a good physical activity professional?

- Realistic self-confidence
- Love and acceptance of young people as individuals
- Positive attitude toward life and young people

- Belief that all young people have the desire and the ability to learn
- Understanding of the behavior of young people
- Curiosity and a willingness to learn
- Sense of humor
- Respect for young people, others, the learning environment, the game, and so on
- Playful spirit

What characteristics do you have that you might want to change to become a better physical activity professional?

- Impatience
- Inflexibility
- Lack of assertiveness
- Lack of enthusiasm

How will you work on these characteristics to change them?

- Whenever I become impatient, I will remind myself that the individuals are learning at their own rate and are trying as hard as they can.
- Whenever I am forced to change my plans, I will brainstorm and write down three or four ways I can change my plan and still meet my objectives.

STEP 3
Develop Goals for Your Setting

List all your goals. Then look over your list and think about the goals and their importance to you. Rank the goals in order of importance and determine two goals you want to work on first. For each goal give at least three methods you will use to achieve it.

Sample teaching goals

- Goal 1: Students will be motivated to be physically active now and for a lifetime.
- Goal 2: Students will learn critical-thinking skills and self-responsibility.

Sample coaching goals

- Goal 1: Players will give 100% when they are practicing so that they can improve their performance and become better players.
- Goal 2: Players will respect the abilities of their teammates.

Sample recreation goals

- Goal 1: Participants will learn a variety of games so that they can recreate in their leisure time.
- Goal 2: Participants will build character through recreation.

Now that you know the values and beliefs that form your professional philosophy, have examined your qualities as a leader in the field, and have established goals, you are ready to examine your philosophy of behavior management.

STEP 4
Develop Your Philosophy of Behavior Management

Now that we have learned theories, concepts, and methods to manage behavior, we must develop our own individual philosophy of behavior management, which will serve as our framework for our behavior management plan. We begin by examining our values and beliefs. From those we develop our philosophy. Based on our philosophy, we establish our role in the process as well as the role of the students or participants.

What are your values and beliefs about behavior management?

- I value responsible people who respect others.
- I believe that individuals are willing and able to take responsibility for their behavior if the opportunities to do so are presented in a timely and appropriate manner.
- I believe that everyone deserves respect as an individual with different strengths. They have voices, ideas, and opinions that deserve to be heard. They have the capacity to make good decisions.
- I value connectedness.
- I believe everyone wants to be connected to others.

What is your philosophy of behavior management?

- My philosophy of behavior management is that learning can only take place when a positive environment is established in which individuals are encouraged to learn and progress in a supportive environment.

All persons must learn what responsibility means, what responsible behaviors are, and how to take responsibility for their behaviors. Everyone deserves respect for who they are right now, not who I might want them to be. All opinions have a right to be voiced and heard. Above all else we must strive to keep individuals connected to us and to others.

What role does the physical activity professional play in behavior management?

- Facilitate the development of rules, taking into consideration participant input (see chapter 3).
- Evaluate participants' efforts to follow the rules.
- Take control if disruptive behaviors occur by applying consequences.
- Teach what responsibility is, what responsible behaviors are, and provide opportunities for individuals to take responsibility for their own behavior, development, and well-being.
- Share power with the participants.
- Create opportunities for individuals to learn values and build character.

What role do the individuals play?

- Provide input into the physical activity rules.
- Evaluate their adherence to the rules.
- Learn to take responsibility for their behavior.
- Learn to show respect for others, the activity, and the physical activity professional.
- Learn character traits of team building, honesty, respect, cooperation, community, and so on (see chapter 7).

STEP 5
Examine Your Strengths and Weaknesses As a Behavior Manager

We all have strengths and weaknesses related to our ability to effectively manage behavior. Recognizing these allows us to build on our strengths and plan strategies to change our weaknesses to make us more effective managers of behavior.

What characteristics do you have that will make you a good behavior manager (see chapter 2)?

- I am consistent.
- I am fair.
- I am firm.
- I am respectful of the individual abilities of participants.

What characteristics do you have that you might want to change to make you a better behavior manager?

- I am controlling.
- I am afraid to share power with the participants.
- I have low self-esteem.

How will you work on these characteristics to change them?

- I will find opportunities to gradually shift power to the participants so that I can learn that they can handle it and will be more responsible because of it.
- I will relinquish control in situations that feel safe.
- I will emphasize my successes and look at my mistakes as efforts to improve.

STEP 6
Based on Your Philosophy, Establish Goals for Your Setting

For each goal give at least three methods you will use to achieve that particular goal. Include proactive methods to prevent behavior problems (chapter 3), reinforcement methods to increase appropriate behaviors (chapter 5), and methods to decrease inappropriate behaviors (chapter 6). Consider also the humanistic methods discussed in chapter 7 and biophysical methods discussed in chapter 8. When fitting these goals into your behavior management plan, draw from the approaches that best fit your personality and philosophy.

Goal 1: Create positive student–teacher, player–coach, or participant–recreation specialist relationships

    a. Get to know your participants.

    b. Observe, focus on strengths, and praise appropriate behaviors.

    c. Develop mutual respect.

Goal 2: Create a safe, nurturing environment conducive to learning.

    a. Establish rules (see chapter 3).

    b. Give participants a voice and allow them to provide input.

    c. Provide opportunities for leadership.

Goal 3: Create positive peer relationships.

    a. Use peer tutors.

    b. Teach conflict management skills and reinforce individuals for managing conflicts on their own (see chapter 7).

    c. Encourage participants to work together on projects.

Goal 4: Create an environment in which individuals are provided opportunities to take responsibility for their own behavior.

    a. Teach what responsibility is.

    b. Discuss what responsible behaviors are.

    c. Allow for input into group rules.

    d. Guide individuals' development of their own personal responsibility plan (see chapter 7).

    e. Allow the opportunity for self-evaluation (see chapter 7).

    f. Encourage individuals to take responsibility for their successes and failures.

Goal 5: Create an environment conducive to building self-concept for all individuals.

    a. Create opportunities for individuals to be successful. Reinforce their successes. If they make mistakes, reinforce the effort and encourage them to try again.

    b. Create opportunities for individuals to reinforce each other's efforts.

STEP 7
Write Measurable Behaviors for Each Method

In chapter 4 you learned how to write measurable behaviors. Practice writing these for each of the methods you listed for your goals in step 6. Measurable behaviors have the following components: audience, behavior, conditions, and criteria. For example, a measurable behavior might be, "The participant (audience) will pick up the equipment (behavior) on the playground (condition) at least 4 days a week (criteria)."

Let's look at our first behavior management goal and the methods to achieve that goal.

Goal 1: Create positive student–teacher, player–coach, or participant–recreation specialist relationships.

    a. Get to know your participants.

    b. Observe, focus on strengths, and praise appropriate behaviors.

    c. Develop mutual respect.

Consider ways you could measure these methods. Then write measurable behaviors for each method. For example, one way to get to know individuals is to learn their names. A measurable behavior to determine whether you know their names would be, "I will call all individuals by their correct name with 95% accuracy from week 2 through week 8." A measurable behavior for the second method might be, "I will focus on the strengths of the individuals and reinforce appro-

priate behaviors with verbal praise at a ratio of 5 positive statements to 1 corrective feedback for 4 consecutive weeks."

STEP 8
Implement Measurable Behaviors and Collect Data

Once you have written measurable behaviors for each of the methods you will use to achieve your goals, implement the measurable behaviors. It is easiest to keep track of your goals and behaviors by developing a measurable behavior chart. On this chart, make a box by each objective where you put the date that the objective is mastered. See figure 9.2 for a sample chart.

Make sure that each behavior has a time line in which to accomplish the behavior, such as, "I will address each player and say something positive during practice for 10 consecutive practices." After you addressed each player for 10 consecutive practices, you can put the date on the chart.

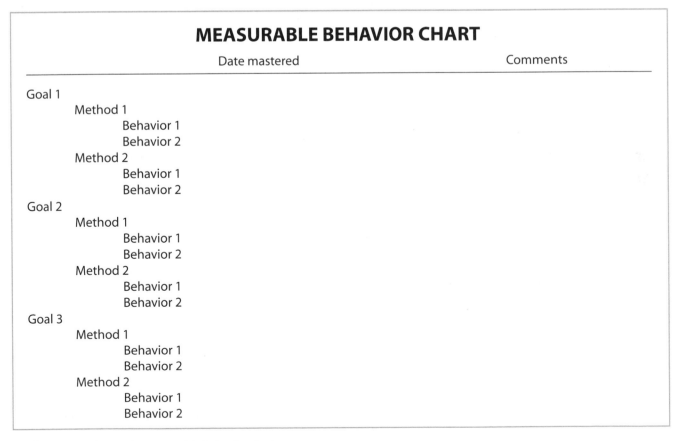

MEASURABLE BEHAVIOR CHART

Date mastered   Comments

Goal 1
    Method 1
        Behavior 1
        Behavior 2
    Method 2
        Behavior 1
        Behavior 2
Goal 2
    Method 1
        Behavior 1
        Behavior 2
    Method 2
        Behavior 1
        Behavior 2
Goal 3
    Method 1
        Behavior 1
        Behavior 2
    Method 2
        Behavior 1
        Behavior 2

Figure 9.2   A sample measurable behavior chart.

STEP 9
Revise or Replace Ineffective Methods

If you have written behaviors so that they are measurable, you ought to be able to determine whether you have achieved them or not. On your measurable behavior chart you can put a happy face and the date next to the behaviors that were achieved. For the behaviors that were not achieved, you need to try harder to achieve them, revise them, or replace them with other behaviors that might better help you achieve your goal.

STEP 10
Be Reflective

Once you have gone through the first 9 steps, you should have a rough draft of your behavior management plan. This will serve as a working document for you as you begin the next year of teaching, season of coaching, or session of working at the community center. We will now take you through a reflection process that will enable you to look at what you are doing, examine the methods you used to see if they are still working, and see sample comments physical activity professionals may make as they learn to develop and modify their own plan. Your plan is a work in progress and requires continuous reflection and evaluation.

Have You Examined Your Lessons, Practices, or Activities?

Learning increases and misbehavior decreases with well-planned lessons, practices, or activities. Lessons or practices and support activities should be stimulating, provide a sense of accomplishment, and be paced to maximize participant engagement in productive tasks. Incorporate individuals' interests, involve individuals in the learning process, teach more than facts, and take into consideration individual learning styles. Individualized instruction allows participants to work at their own pace on tasks that are appropriate for their skill level. Peer tutoring and instructional grouping can help you match instruction to ability when large participant–leader ratios limit the time available for individualizing instruction (see figure 9.3).

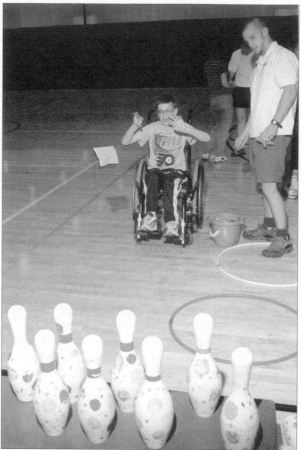

© Human Kinetics

Figure 9.3 Peer tutoring allows for more individualized instruction.

Following is a middle school physical educator reflecting on her lessons:

Analyzing my instructional strategies, I recognized that students did not seem interested in some of my lessons. For example, when I taught how to find the target heart rate, by the end of the period about half of the class was not paying attention. Perhaps the way I presented the information was not exciting. I think I covered too much information in our short lesson time, and some students did not have the math skills to determine their target heart rate. I needed to create more exciting ways to present the material, and I needed to individualize instruction as some students were not challenged and others were struggling. So I decided to make four changes. First, I planned to take at least two class periods to present the material. Second, I planned to develop some fun application exercises to get the students more involved, such as finding the resting heart rate of a friend in class and then figuring out what each other's target heart rate is. Third, I planned to take time to teach the prerequisite math skills or coordinate this with the math teacher so the students could do the problems presented in my class. Fourth, I planned to use more peer tutors, learning stations, and small group instruction.

Have You Considered Your Professional Style?

Examine your teaching, coaching, or leadership style. Are you democratic or authoritarian? Are you participant-centered or leader-centered? Are you extroverted or introverted? Are you enthusiastic or more subdued? Are you warm or do you like to keep some distance? Do you require plenty of structure or only a little?

For example, a high school football coach reflects on his coaching style:

Thinking back on my first 5 years of coaching, I would classify my coaching style as mostly autocratic. The last couple of years, though, I would say that I am leaning more toward a democratic style. I feel I am more player-centered now. I am extroverted and enthusiastic. I care about my players as individuals.

Have You Considered Your Setting?

As you design your behavior management plan, think about the individuals in your group. Consider ages, grade levels, and socioeconomic statuses. Consider the value placed on physical activity at home as well as the behavior management methods employed by the parents. Pay particular attention to learning styles, skills, interests, abilities, and personalities. Each person comes to you with different thoughts, feelings, attitudes, and experiences warranting your attention. It is important to match these characteristics with your behavior management plan. After looking at each individual, look at the group as a whole. The task is much easier when the group is relatively homogeneous than when there is a wide range of abilities, interests, and values. For the more heterogeneous group, you may need to develop different methods for individuals or subgroups. This is a challenging aspect of being a physical activity professional. Use the participant informa-

tion worksheet (worksheet 8 in appendix A) to guide you.

A coed basketball coach at an urban recreation center reflects on his setting:

The players on my team are 9 to 10 years old in the 4th grade. Their socioeconomic statuses range from upper lower class to lower middle class. In some homes, participation in sport is valued highly; in others, it is not valued at all. They come from homes in which parents employ behavior management methods that may or may not be effective. They have a wide range of abilities, interests, and talents. Because of the heterogeneous nature of the players on my team, I do not use the same methods with all of my players. For example, Jamie cries when I even give him a stern look; he needs me to show him I care about him. So when I need to discuss a problem behavior with him I do so gently. In contrast, Lara does not listen when I tell her to be quiet, to stop bouncing the ball, or to participate in an activity. She is belligerent when I reprimand her, and she often refuses to go to time-out when I tell her. With Jamie, I will talk with him and tell him what behavior is inappropriate and why. I'll ask him to stop the inappropriate behavior and tell him what behavior I would like him to perform. For example, I might say, "Jamie, when you bounce the ball the other players cannot hear my instructions. Please hold the ball." With Lara, I would take the ball and hold it myself while standing next to her (see figure 9.4).

Consider community and socioeconomic factors in your organization, such as the availability of resources and funds, organizational structure, and politics of the local school or advisory board. All of these factors affect the types of problems you might encounter in your physical activity setting as well as the resources available.

Some organizations may have a general behavior management plan that you must consider when developing your personal plan to ensure consistency in promoting responsible behavior. Physical activity professionals must communicate with each other on a regular basis, discussing problems with the established plan and revising the plan as needed.

A recreation specialist in a rural community center in the Midwest reflects on community factors:

The community in which my recreation center is located is interested in providing

Figure 9.4 Some players need the coach to hold the ball so that they will not bounce it while the coach is giving instructions.

leisure activities in an after-school program. However, no one really takes a leadership role in trying to increase community involvement in the center. The available resources and funds are minimal. We do have a behavior management plan that was developed about 8 years ago, but the center's staff has never really been trained in this plan. Staff members develop their own plans and not much communication goes on among the staff unless we encounter a particularly disruptive participant who misbehaves in several activities. In such a case we confer, trying to determine a consistent behavior management plan to use with the participant in question.

Do You Establish Positive Relationships With the Individuals?

Positive relationships between leaders and individuals are associated with positive attitudes toward

school, sport, or recreation activities; increased academic achievement or performance; and more positive behavior (Glover and Anderson, 2003). Participants want to know that you care about them as individuals. You can show you care in many ways, such as greeting them by name when you first see them, asking them a personal question like what they did over the weekend or how their visit was with Uncle George, and reinforcing them for good behavior, participation, or skill performance.

A 3rd-year elementary school physical education teacher reflects on her relationships with her students:

I realized that during the past 2 years I was so concerned with following the district's physical education curriculum and meeting standards that I did not take time to establish positive relationships with my students. I decided to set goals for myself each week to try to increase positive interactions with my students. So during week 1, I made it my goal to learn each student's name and speak to everyone at least once during class either by asking them a question about them or by recognizing something they did in class, such as saying, "Jo, you were great as a peer tutor today, thanks for your help." (See figure 9.5.)

Figure 9.5 Recognizing positive behaviors helps establish healthy student–teacher relationships.

Do You Facilitate the Development of Positive Peer Relationships?

Many behavior problems involve peer conflict. You can implement physical activities that enhance positive, supportive peer relationships. Acquaintance activities can help break the ice and reduce anxiety and inhibitions. Many instructional activities reinforce cooperation and reduce competition (see figure 9.6). Cooperative games (Fluegelman, 1976, 1981; Grineski, 1996) are fun and help develop a sense of camaraderie and cooperation. You can reinforce cooperative behaviors while individuals are participating in activities. Dissolve cliques by splitting them up and having them be leaders in other groups that are performing a cooperative group activity. Sometimes open dialogue or a group discussion is necessary to combat peer pressure and cliques.

A recreation specialist at an urban community recreation center reflects on facilitating peer relationships:

In analyzing my methods for developing positive peer relationships, I recognized that I had not used acquaintance activities and had not incorporated games designed to enhance cooperation. I had not been attentive to any cooperative behaviors the participants may have exhibited. So I found some acquaintance activities and some fun, cooperative games to play with them that also included trust and team-building activities. I am working to be more attentive to the cooperative behaviors that participants exhibit during activity sessions and I am making an earnest attempt to reinforce those who cooperate and demonstrate caring for others.

Do You Implement Methods That Improve Self-Concept?

Participants must perceive the physical activity setting as a positive, nurturing environment in which they feel safe and their needs are met. You can help create this environment by establishing safety rules, giving clear instructions, and encouraging individuals to try difficult skills. Instructional activities that are challenging but programmed so that each individual can be successful will enhance self-concept. Providing opportunities for individuals to develop positive relationships with their peers will increase motivation to learn and will enhance positive attitudes. Showing that you care and respect each person will also enhance self-concept.

Figure 9.6 Cooperative games help develop a sense of camaraderie.

A coach of a girl's softball team for 8- to 10-year-olds reflects on improving the self-concept of her players:

I feel I have been conscientious about establishing and enforcing safety rules, but I think I could be more emphatic about making sure all participants understand my instructions. Once I gave instructions that they were to wait in the dugout until their turn at bat. But Sam, Tracy, Jo, and J.J. were all standing by the first baseline, and Tracy got hit by a foul ball. I pledged to make sure all players are following instructions. I think that I have provided challenging skills during practices, but I recognized that I was not as supportive as I could have been of those who were having trouble with the fundamental skills. I just praised them and thought that would motivate them to do better next time. So I began working to find more creative ways to teach the players, such as giving them more individualized instruction personally or through a peer tutor. Once they learn the skill, I make sure to notice and reinforce their effort. I have begun using peer tutors to teach others how to do the skill. I also created opportunities for players to develop positive relationships with their peers by assigning group projects in which they work together, such as developing a Sports Fun Day to raise money for softball equipment for the team.

Have You Determined Methods for Managing Conflict?

Refer to chapter 7 for methods of teaching conflict management. When taught how to manage conflict, individuals develop self-control, empathy, and self-respect; learn how to interact more effectively with their peers; develop an understanding about interpersonal conflicts; and improve their communication skills. There are 4 steps to teaching these skills. The first is to identify and express feelings. The second step is to discuss feelings while the other person is listening, clarifying feelings until they are understood. The third step is to have both parties reach an agreement to find a peaceful solution. The last step is to discuss the need to compromise to arrive at a fair outcome.

A hockey coach reflects on managing conflict:

My methods for resolving conflict have improved. I find myself teaching my players to manage conflict on their own instead of coming to me to solve disputes. We use the 4 steps for managing conflict. I allow them to sit somewhere (the talking bench) and discuss the conflict, going through each step. They feel empowered and most of the time they are able to resolve conflicts without any input from me.

Have You Implemented Changes and Analyzed the Results?

You cannot simply talk about changes, you must make them. Then you must analyze the results as objectively as possible. For example, a high school physical education teacher realized,

When I learned all of the students' names and made a point to talk personally with each one at least once a day, I noticed a positive change in their attitudes toward me. They were friendlier to me when they came into the class and would actually go out of the way to come and talk with me in the lunchroom. In addition, they were more interested in the things we were learning in class and did better on the tests.

A middle school soccer coach reflects on implementing changes:

I made it a point to let the players take part in the fun acquaintance games at the beginning of practice each day. These games got the players more involved with each other, so they participated more during practice. I also incorporated a fun, cooperative game into practice every Friday. The players seemed to laugh a lot more, help each other more at practice, and encourage each other even after mistakes in games.

I have established a peer tutor system in which the individuals who know the skill are tutors for those who are still learning. This method has been beneficial for both the individuals being tutored, as they get more individual attention, and the tutors, as it boosts their self-esteem. This approach also reinforces the skill in a more interesting way for the tutor. Our team sport day to help children with disabilities involved in recreational soccer was a big success in getting teammates to work together. I could see many friendships developing among teammates as they planned the drills, skill stations, and games for the children with disabilities.

ONGOING EVALUATION

After following the 10 steps to develop a behavior management plan (see figure 9.1 and checklist 9.1), you will have a first draft. This plan, however, will need ongoing monitoring, evaluation, and revision. Take into account changes in yourself and the individuals in your program. Be patient; effective changes in behavior take time.

A physical education teacher at a large urban high school provides her reflection:

My school population is transient with students moving in and out at a high rate. In December, I recognized that I was having more trouble with attendance and participation than I had at the beginning of the school year. No wonder! Since September, I had been given 23 new students and had lost 15. The new students definitely seemed less interested in physical education than the ones I had lost. They were often late for class or absent altogether. They forgot their gym clothes, refused to participate fully, and failed to turn in assignments. Some of the students that knew my expectations began to follow suit. I knew I had to reexamine my behavior management plan, and fast! I looked at my class outline to make sure that I had spelled out class rules, routines, and procedures. Sure enough, I had clearly stated these as well as the number of points lost off the final grade for not complying. I recognized that this consequence was not effective with the new students, so I had to try another approach.

I decided to hold discussions with each of my classes. I asked probing questions to determine what the students did and did not like about the physical education program. I asked them to suggest changes that could make class more interesting. They offered some good suggestions, and we decided to modify class content to include the following: (a) a weight-training program, (b) short-line file sprints with a soccer ball instead of wind sprints, (c) more time to play games and less practice time spent on drills, (d) fitness tests to help each student develop an individualized fitness program, and (e) teams and contests to see which team could perform the most fitness activities.

I agreed to spend some time over Christmas vacation revising the curriculum to reflect their input. With the new curriculum the students had a vested interest in the program, and tardiness decreased by 50%, attendance increased by 30%, bringing clean gym clothes increased by 40%, participation in all class activities increased by 50%, and completion of assignments increased by 60%. The students even asked me if they could plan a fitness day for the local elementary school!

After a year of following the 10-step process, I knew that I had grown as a teacher. I could see this in the way my students responded to me inside and outside of the gym. By the end of May, many of the students who had given me so much grief last November and December when they transferred into my classes came to visit with me after school because they knew I cared about them. This rapport made behavior management considerably easier. The students knew that I said what I meant, meant what I said, and did what I said I was going to do—all in a very matter-of-fact, but warm, positive, and friendly manner. They knew I was there for them as a mentor if they needed it, and they knew I would work with them instead of against them to solve any problems we had.

Still, I have many ideas for getting off to a stronger start this coming fall. For example, I am going to assign a peer mentor to each new student to smooth the transition for everyone. Because the power of positive reinforcement worked so effectively last year, I am going to find more ways to accentuate the positive, like creating a Super Stars bulletin board featuring a student from each class who has improved performance or behavior the most each week. One of my main goals is to stay more alert to potential problems and intervene either before trouble starts or more quickly if it has already started instead of waiting until something bothers me so much I can't stand it. Finally, in order to give my students more one-on-one attention, I am going to involve community volunteers more in my classes. Hopefully, this will prevent attention-seeking misbehavior.

I must remember that change is a continual process that I need to reflect on and assess continually. I'm sure I'll keep modifying my approach as I learn and grow. After all, teaching is the only profession I know of in which I'll get a fresh start every year.

CONCLUSION
You Can Do It!

Promoting responsible behavior takes time and energy, but it is possible! Individuals want you to care enough to help them take responsibility for their behavior. The benefits you and they will reap are well worth the effort. You will feel more productive as a physical activity professional. You will spend more time teaching, coaching, or leading and less time managing behavior. Your participants will be more successful physically, socially, and emotionally. Their self-concept will be enhanced and they will have a more positive attitude.

To be an effective behavior manager, you must be flexible, prepared, organized, interested, confident in your role, and aware of your own strengths and weaknesses. You must be reflective, analyze situations, study the variables involved, and determine which methods will work best in different situations with different individuals. Most importantly, you must be able to objectively analyze your own style and be willing to change.

Behavior management is an ongoing process filled with ups and downs. There will be times when you will want to throw in the towel and apply for a desk job. Even when you are demoralized and think no one appreciates all that you are trying to do, don't give up! If you apply the information in this book, you will become more effective, and the ups will far outnumber the downs. More and more you will see the positive influence you are having on people's lives and will feel fulfilled. When an individual comes up to you and says, "Thanks for caring about me. I learned a lot from you," you will know that all the time and energy you put into your behavior management plan was worth it.

Checklist 9.1   The 10-Step Approach

When developing your behavioral management plan, check off each step as you complete it.

_____ 1. I have examined my values and beliefs and have developed my philosophy of teaching, coaching, or leading recreation groups.

_____ 2. I have examined my strengths and weaknesses as a physical activity professional and have developed strategies to change my weaknesses.

_____ 3. I have developed teaching, coaching, or recreation goals.

_____ 4. I have examined my values and beliefs and have developed my philosophy of behavior management.

_____ 5. I have examined my strengths and weaknesses as a behavior manager and have developed strategies to change my weaknesses.

_____ 6. Based on my philosophy, I have established behavior management goals for my situation.

_____ 7. I have written measurable behaviors for each method I outlined to reach my goals.

_____ 8. I have implemented the measurable behaviors and collected data to determine whether they were achieved or not.

_____ 9. I have revised or replaced the methods that were not effective.

_____ 10. I have been reflective. I have implemented the changes that I determined needed to be made.

Worksheets for
Collecting Information

Worksheet 1
Frequency Recording Chart

Name _____

Initial date of observation _____   Dates of observation _____

Dates

_____ _____ _____ _____ _____ _____ _____ _____ _____ _____ _____ _____

12	12	12	12	12	12	12	12	12	12	12	12
11	11	11	11	11	11	11	11	11	11	11	11
10	10	10	10	10	10	10	10	10	10	10	10
9	9	9	9	9	9	9	9	9	9	9	9
8	8	8	8	8	8	8	8	8	8	8	8
7	7	7	7	7	7	7	7	7	7	7	7
6	6	6	6	6	6	6	6	6	6	6	6
5	5	5	5	5	5	5	5	5	5	5	5
4	4	4	4	4	4	4	4	4	4	4	4
3	3	3	3	3	3	3	3	3	3	3	3
2	2	2	2	2	2	2	2	2	2	2	2
1	1	1	1	1	1	1	1	1	1	1	1
0	0	0	0	0	0	0	0	0	0	0	0

Cross out a number each time the behavior occurs.

Circle the total number of times the behavior actually occurs for that particular date.

Connect the circles to form a graph.

From *Positive Behavior Management in Physical Activity Settings, Second Edition,* by Barry W. Lavay, Ron French, and Hester L. Henderson, 2006, Champaign, IL: Human Kinetics. Adapted from Walker, Shea, and Bauer (2004).

Worksheet 2
Physical Activity Reinforcer Preference List

Name _____ Class or Group _____

If you were to be rewarded, what physical activities would you like most? From the following list circle your top three rewards:

1. Basketball
2. Cross-country running
3. Flag football
4. Floor hockey
5. Frisbee
6. Jump rope
7. Ladder walking (forming human ladders)
8. Poi balls (from performing art show)
9. Soccer
10. Softball
11. Sport option (a variety of equipment is brought out and you can participate in any activity you like)
12. Volleyball
13. Water relays (requires movement of water and a water-balloon toss)
14. Other:_____

From *Positive Behavior Management in Physical Activity Settings, Second Edition*, by Barry W. Lavay, Ron French, and Hester L. Henderson, 2006, Champaign, IL: Human Kinetics. Reprinted with permission from the 1997 *Journal of Physical Education, Recreation & Dance*, a publication of the American Alliance for Health, Physical Education, Recreation and Dance, 1900 Association Dr., Reston, VA 20191.

Worksheet 3
Point Exchange Card

Weekly physical education point chart

Name: _____ Class period: _____ Date: _____

Class rule	M	T	W	Th	F	Total
Proper dress						
Following teacher directions						
Performing all warm-up exercises						
Completing skill performance worksheet						
Cooperating with classmates during activities						
Weekly point total						

How to Use the Point Card

Class rules have been previously discussed and are further explained on the class rules chart posted on the bulletin board.

1. Check each box for following each of the class rules.
2. Each mark is worth 1 point.
3. Students who receive 18 points or more earn the privilege of participating in the Friday sport option voted on by the class.
4. Students who earn 17 points or fewer will participate in the physical education lesson of the day, and hopefully you will work to earn the class sport option the following week!

I will periodically check point cards. You and your partner are responsible for correctly and honestly filling out your point card.

From *Positive Behavior Management in Physical Activity Settings, Second Edition,* by Barry W. Lavay, Ron French, and Hester L. Henderson, 2006, Champaign, IL: Human Kinetics.

Worksheet 4
Behavior Management Trifold Poster Board

Be Creative Have Fun!

Attach file folders to keep track of stickers, reward coupons, (elementary), or fitness tickets (middle school / high school) that students can choose from.

File folders can carry some of the cue cards used while teaching.

File folders can hold certificates, surprises, or special construction medals for when you catch the students "being good."

In this section post the name and picture of the "Student of the Week" or those students who help others.

This is your portable management system

Calendar

Develop a calendar to identify units taught, theme-based activities, and/or special events (e.g., off-campus activities, guest speakers). This also can contain future planning for students' self-responsibility toward next day/week goals.

Strive to be the BEST!

Rules

In this area state your class rules and routines that guide and reinforce teacher-student / student-teacher responsibilities.

You can post student responsibility behaviors here.

Teamwork

Students can create and adopt teamwork slogans like "Panther Pride" or "With Each Step We Build Our Future."

Display a large visual for student responsibility levels. Have teacher and students design levels of student responsibility.

For example:

Slam Dunk
- Cooperates and helps others
- Engages in activities consistently
- Is a team player

3 Point Shot
- Cooperates with others
- Engages in activities some of the time

Air Ball
- Does not cooperate with others
- Does not engage in activities
- Plays alone

From *Positive Behavior Management in Physical Activity Settings, Second Edition,* by Barry W. Lavay, Ron French, and Hester L. Henderson, 2006, Champaign, IL: Human Kinetics. Barbara Lawrence, Los Angeles Unified School District; Lavay et al. (2003).

Worksheet 5
Relaxation Training Log Sheet

Name _____

Today's date _____ Due date _____

Directions: Lying on your back, perform relaxation activities for the following body parts. Be sure to breathe correctly. Over the next 2 weeks spend 15 to 20 minutes daily practicing these exercises, marking Xs in the correct boxes to show that you performed the exercise for that day.

Body part	M	T	W	Th	F	M	T	W	Th	F
1. Knees to chest										
2. Hands and arms										
3. Arms and shoulders										
4. Shoulders and neck										
5. Jaw										
6. Hips										
7. Legs and feet										
8. Face and nose										
9. Stomach										

From *Positive Behavior Management in Physical Activity Settings, Second Edition,* by Barry W. Lavay, Ron French, and Hester L. Henderson, 2006, Champaign, IL: Human Kinetics.

Worksheet 6
Nutritional Evaluation Form

Directions: Use this form daily to determine if a correlation exists between diet and behavior.

Date and time behavior occurred	Behavior	Food consumed at meal or snack

From *Positive Behavior Management in Physical Activity Settings, Second Edition,* by Barry W. Lavay, Ron French, and Hester L. Henderson, 2006, Champaign, IL: Human Kinetics.

Worksheet 7
Participant Information Worksheet

Use this worksheet to examine your unique situation as you design your behavior management plan. The answers to the following questions will help you develop behavior management methods for your group.

What is the age level or grade level of the individuals? _____

_____

What are the socioeconomic statuses of the parents? _____

_____

What value do the parents place on participation in physical activity? _____

_____

What behavior management methods are employed in the home? _____

_____

How are the individuals unique in the following areas?

Learning styles

Skill levels

Interests

Abilities

Personalities

Thoughts, feelings, and attitudes

Experiences

Is the group homogeneous? _____

Is the group heterogeneous? _____

From *Positive Behavior Management in Physical Activity Settings, Second Edition,* by Barry W. Lavay, Ron French, and Hester L. Henderson, 2006, Champaign, IL: Human Kinetics.

B

Behavior Management Web Sites

The following is a list of Web sites we have found useful. Most of the Web sites can be used directly or modified for physical activity professionals.

Bonnie's Fitware Inc.

www.pesoftware.com

This Web site provides information on physical activity, including software products, presentations, online learning, book support, newsletters, and resources. In the resource section, there are articles on topics of interest to physical activity professionals, such as the importance of not using exercise as punishment.

Center for Effective Discipline

www.stophitting.com

This Web site provides information disseminated through the Center for Effective Discipline. It includes articles, position papers, and answers for parents about discipline at home and at school, with the common goal of abolishing corporal punishment.

Center for the 4th and 5th Rs

www.cortland.edu/c4n5rs

The Center for the 4th and 5th Rs serves as a regional, state, and national resource in character education. Character education is essential to building a moral society and developing schools that are civil and caring communities. The Center publishes articles on character education, sponsors an annual summer institute in character education, publishes a newsletter, and is building a network of schools committed to teaching respect, responsibility, and other core ethical values as the basis of good character. The Web site provides information about the Center as well as online newsletters, books and publications, national reports, articles, assessments, and resources.

Character Counts!

www.charactercounts.org

This Web site provides information on Character Counts!, a nonprofit, nonpartisan, nonsectarian character education organization whose goal is to teach the Six Pillars of Character: trustworthiness, respect, responsibility, fairness, caring, and citizenship. It has a coalition that includes thousands of schools, communities, and nonprofit organizations, and it offers training seminars, teaching tools, materials, character awards, and discussion forums.

Classroom Management, Managing Student Conduct, and Effective Praise Guidelines

www.adprima.com/managing.htm

The ADPRIMA Web site provides ideas for general classroom management. Many of the ideas are designed to assist beginning teachers.

Committee for Children

www.cfchildren.org

This Web site provides information about social and emotional learning in the form of articles, current news, events, and training. It describes a variety of programs, including a violence-prevention curriculum, a bullying-prevention program, and a personal-safety curriculum. It also offers information about research on social and emotional issues, support for educators, and resources for parents and advocates.

Conflict Resolution Information Source

http://crinfo.org

This Web site offers a free, keyword-coded cata-log of over 20,000 Web, print, organizational, and other conflict resolution resources. Many powerful browsing and searching tools are available to help you find information that addresses your specific needs. There is an education section that offers information about conflict programs and teaching materials such as curricula, games, exercises, and other resources for teaching peace and conflict topics in primary and secondary schools.

Dr. Becky Bailey's Loving Guidance

http://beckybailey.com

This Web site provides information about conscious discipline, a comprehensive classroom manage-ment program and a social–emotional curriculum. It is based on current brain research, child-develop-ment information, and developmentally appropri-ate practices. Conscious discipline is designed to change the lives of adults first, who then change the lives of children. The most frequent comment heard in response to the conscious discipline pro-gram is that it is life-changing. Conscious discipline teaches relationship skills that help adults in all interactions, including at home with family, at work with colleagues, and at school with children. The Web site provides workshop information, products, success stories, discipline tips, and more.

Dr. Mac's Amazing Behavior Management Advice Site

www.behavioradvisor.com

This Web site offers literally thousands of tips on promoting responsible behavior and provides step-by-step directions for implementing interven-tions. It also has a bulletin board where you can post your disciplinary concerns and receive sug-gestions from teachers around the world. This is an informative, fun, and user-friendly Web site.

Education World

www.educationworld.com/a_curr/curr155.shtml

This Web site provides information related to physical activity, environment, health, and behavior management. A sample topic is teach-ing children to make moral decisions.

The Fine Art of Discipline

http://curry.edschool.virginia.edu/go/edis771/98webquests/professional/plisamconnell/Web_Quest-Professional.htm

This Web site offers strategies for developing a schoolwide discipline policy. It includes definitions of frequently used terms, a discipline inventory that teachers can take to assess their own classroom dis-cipline beliefs, and an overview of the most widely used behavior management approaches.

Library in the Sky

www.nwrel.org/sky

The Library in the Sky is a database of interesting and useful educational Web sites. You can find the information you want by using the search or user tabs or by looking under departments (including physical education) or materials. You can locate useful sites by doing a search, such as "teacher lesson plans and classroom management."

Love and Logic

www.loveandlogic.com

This Web site is maintained by the Love and Logic Institute. It offers information on the institute as well as seminars, articles, and FAQs. The institute provides training materials that teach its unique approach to raising children. This approach puts teachers and parents in control, teaches children to be responsible, and prepares them for the real world. Also offered are an extensive line of prod-ucts based on the Love and Logic philosophy, including books, audiocassettes, compact discs, videotapes, and training programs.

National Education Association (NEA)

www.nea.org/tips/manage/index.html

The National Education Association (NEA) provides teachers with information on manag-ing classes. The focus is on striking a balance between freedom and discipline, which makes the difference between a well-run class and a class in chaos. Some of the topics are preven-tion, behavior control, staying ahead, attendance, and inclusion.

Ohio Commission on Dispute Resolution and Conflict Management

http://disputeresolution.ohio.gov

This Web site provides information on the Ohio Commission on Dispute Resolution and Conflict Management, which was established in 1989 to provide constructive, nonviolent forums, processes, and methods for resolving disputes. It provides information on how to create a comprehensive conflict management program. There are articles on conflict resolution in higher education and information about conflict management training in schools.

Out on a Limb: A Guide to Getting Along

www.urbanext.uiuc.edu/conflict

This is an interactive conflict management Web site for children, published by Urban Programs Resource Network. This Web site is designed to help teach young people how to better manage the conflicts and challenges they face on a daily basis. The activities on the Web site are designed primarily for children in the 3rd grade, but can be used to entertain and educate children in the 2nd and 4th grades as well. The video is also available in Spanish.

PE Central

www.PEcentral.org (go to the Creating a Positive Learning Climate link)

This site includes classroom management information, lesson ideas, tips for beginning teachers, PE rules, FAQs, articles, books, and links to Web sites. Physical educators can submit classroom management lesson ideas. Also included is a list of rules submitted by different physical educators.

Positive Discipline

http://positivediscipline.com

This Web site provides information on the positive discipline program. This program teaches important social and life skills in a manner that is respectful to both adults and young people. Its goal is to raise young people to be responsible, respectful, and resourceful members of their community. It is based on the theory that children who have a sense of connection with their community and whose input is regarded as meaningful are less likely to engage in disruptive behavior. The link for teachers includes a feature question, a feature article, information on workshops, and books that are good resources. The link for parents includes a feature question, a feature article, parent success stories, and information on parenting classes.

ProTeacher

www.proteacher.com/030000.shtml

This Web site provides teachers with numerous methods for promoting positive behavior. Topics include fights, rewards, classroom routines, and conduct.

Schoolwide Behavior Management Programs

http://maxweber.hunter.cuny.edu

This Web site discusses how to develop a schoolwide behavior management system that promotes positive behavior and diminishes inappropriate student actions. Examples of schoolwide programs are linked to this site.

Schoolwide and Classroom Discipline

www.nwrel.org/scpd/sirs/5/cu9.html

This Web site contains an article that documents the history and current research status of classroom discipline in schools. It discusses effective and ineffective behavior management practices and includes an extensive list of references.

You Can Handle Them All

www.disciplinehelp.com

This Web site provides methods for redirecting inappropriate behavior. It identifies 117 inappropriate behaviors that range from angry to whiner.

References

Allen, J. I. (1980). Jogging can modify disruptive behaviors. *Teaching Exceptional Children, 13,* 66-70.

American Psychiatric Association (APA). (2000). *Diagnostic and statistical manual of mental disorders* (4th ed.). Washington, D.C.: Author.

Asarnow, R. F., Satz, P., Light, R., & Lewis, R. (1991). Behavior problems and adaptive functioning in children with mild and severe closed head injury. *Journal of Pediatric Psychology, 16,* 543-555.

Barnett, D. J. (1998). A coach's letter to parents. *Youth Sports Coach: The Official Newsletter of the National Youth Sports Coaches Association*, December.

Bartlett, L. D., Weisenstein, G.R., & Etscheidt, S. (2002). *Successful inclusion for educational leaders.* Columbus, OH: Merrill-Prentice Hall.

Biddle, S. J., & Mutrie, N. (2001). *Psychology of physical activity: Determinants, well-being, and interventions.* London: Routledge.

Blakemore, C. L. (2004). Brain research strategies for physical educators. *Journal of Physical Education, Recreation and Dance, 75*(1), 31-41.

Blue, F. R. (1979). Aerobic running as a treatment for moderate depression. *Perceptual and Motor Skills 48*(1), 228.

Bolton, R. (1979). *People skills: How to assert yourself, listen to others, and resolve conflicts.* New York: Simon and Schuster.

Boyce, B. A. (2003). *Improving your teaching skills: A guide for student teachers and practitioners.* New York: McGraw-Hill.

Brandon, J. E., Eason, R. L., & Smith, T. L. (1986). Behavioral relaxation training and motor performance of learning disabled children with hyperactive behaviors. *Adapted Physical Activity Quarterly, 3,* 67-79.

Cain, C. S. (2004). Behavior management strategies. Retrieved March 11, 2005, from www.universalclass.com.

Charles, C. M. (2002). *Building classroom discipline* (7th ed.). Boston: Allyn and Bacon.

Cipani, E. (1998). *Classroom management for all teachers: Eleven effective plans.* Columbus, OH: Merrill.

Clifford, C., & Feezell, R. M. (1997). *Coaching for character.* Champaign, IL: Human Kinetics.

Coaches Council. (2001). *The Coaches code of conduct position paper.* Reston, VA: NASPE.

Collier, D., & Hebert, F. (2004). Undergraduate physical education teacher preparation: What practitioners tell us. *Physical Educator, 61*(2), 102-112.

Collier, D., & Reid, G. (2003). The autism spectrum disorders: Preventing and coping with difficult behaviors, Part IV. *Palaestra, 19*(3), 36-45.

Cook, B. G., Tankersley, M., Cook, L., & Landrum, T. L. (2000). Teachers' attitudes toward their included students with disabilities. *Exceptional Children, 67*(1), 115-135.

Cooper, J. O., Heron, T. E., & Heward, W. L. (1987). *Applied behavior analysis.* Columbus, OH: Merrill.

Curwin, R. L., & Mendler, A. N. (1988). Packaged discipline programs: Let the buyer beware. *Educational Leadership, 83,* 68-71.

Cusimano, B. E., Darst, P. W., & van der Mars, H. (1993). Improving your instruction through evaluation. *Strategies, 7*(2), 26-29.

Datillo, J., & Murphy, W. D. (1987). *Behavior modification in therapeutic recreation.* State College, PA: Venture.

Davis, R. (1991). Teaching stress management in an elementary classroom. *Journal of Physical Education, Recreation and Dance, 62*(2), 65-66, 70.

Dawson-Rodriques, K., Lavay, B., Butt, K., & Lacourse, M. (1997). Methods to reduce transition time in physical education. *Journal of Physical Education, Recreation and Dance, 68*(9), 30-33.

Donahue, B. (2001). The effective use of positive statements with athletes. Retrieved March 11, 2005, from www.coacheseducation.com.

Doyne, E. J., Chambless, D. L., & Bentley, L. E. (1983). Aerobic exercise as a treatment for depression in women. *Behavior Therapy, 14,* 434-440.

Driver, S., Harmon, M., & Block, M. (2003). Devising a safe and successful physical education program for children with a brain injury. *Journal of Physical Education, Recreation and Dance, 74*(7), 41-50.

Edelson, S. (1999). Autism: Overview of autism. Retrieved March 11, 2005, from www.brainnet.org/autism.htm.

Edwards, V. D., & Hofmeier, J. (1991). A stress management program for elementary and special populations children. *Journal of Physical Education, Recreation and Dance, 62*(2), 61-64.

Feingold, B. F. (1975). *Why your child is hyperactive.* New York: Random House.

Fishbein, D. H., & Pease, S. E. (1994). Diet, nutrition, and aggression. *The Psychology of Aggression, 213*(4), 117-141.

Fluegelman, A. (1976). *The new games book.* San Fransisco: New Games Foundation.

Fluegelman, A. (1981). *More new games.* San Fransisco: New Games Foundation.

Fontenelle, D. H. (1992). *Are you listening?* Bryon, CA: Front Row Experience.

Forness, S. R., Kavale, K. A., Sweeney, D. P., & Crenshaw, T. M. (1999). The future of research and practice in behavioral disorders: Psychopharmacology and its school implications. *Behavioral Disorders, 24*(4), 305-318.

Fox News Channel. (2004, June 01). Girl stabbed to death in Japanese school. Retrieved June 17, 2004, from www.foxnews.com/printer_friendly_story/0,3566,121404,00.html.

French, R. W., & Henderson, H. L. (1993). *Creative approaches to managing student behavior in physical education.* Park City, UT: Family Development Resources.

French, R., & Lavay, B. (Eds.) (1990). *Behavior management techniques for physical educators and recreators.* Kearney, NE: Educational System Associates.

French, R., Lavay, B., & Henderson, H. (1985). Take a lap. *Physical Educator, 42,* 180-185.

French, R., & Silliman-French, L. (2000). Accommodating students with behavior problems. In M. Block (Ed.), *Including students with disabilities in general physical education* (2nd ed.) (pp. 307-336). Baltimore: Paul Brookes.

Fronske, H., & Birch, N. (1995). Overcoming roadblocks to communication. *Strategies, 8*(8), 22-25.

Gipson, M., Lowe, S., & McKenzie, T. (1994). Sport psychology: Improving performance. In E. McGown (Ed.), *Science of coaching volleyball* (pp. 23-33). Champaign, IL: Human Kinetics.

Glover, D. R., & Anderson, L. A. (2003). *Character education.* Champaign, IL: Human Kinetics.

Goodwin, R. D. (2003). Association between physical activity and mental disorders among adults in the United States. *Preventive Medicine, 36*(6), 698-703.

Gordon, T. (1994). *T.E.T: Physical educator effectiveness training.* New York: David McKay.

Graham, G. (2001). *Teaching children physical education: Becoming a master teacher* (2nd ed.). Champaign, IL: Human Kinetics.

Graham, G., Holt/Hale, S. A., & Parker, M. (2004). *Children moving: A reflective approach to teaching physical education* (6th ed.). Boston: McGraw-Hill.

Greenberg, J. S. (2002). *Comprehensive stress management.* Boston: McGraw Hill.

Grineski, S. (1996). *Cooperative learning in physical education.* Champaign, IL: Human Kinetics.

Hall, W. (2004, April 27). Girls more often turning to violence. *Denton Record-Chronicle,* p. 1A.

Harrison, J. M., Blakemore, C. L., Buck, M. M., & Pellecttu, T. L. (1996). *Instructional strategies for secondary school physical education* (3rd ed.). Madison, WI: Brown and Benchmark.

Hartzell, G. N., & Petrie, T. A. (1992). The principal and discipline: Working with school structures, teachers, and students. *Clearing House, 65*(6), 376-381.

Harvey, W., Fagan, T., & Kassis, J. (2003). Enabling students with ADHD to use self-control in physical activities. *Palaestra, 19*(3), 32-35.

Helion, J.G. (1996). If we build it, they will come: Creating an emotionally safe physical education environment. *Journal of Physical Education, Recreation and Dance, 67*(6), 40-44.

Hellison, D. (2003). *Teaching responsibility through physical activity* (2nd ed.). Champaign, IL: Human Kinetics.

Hellison, D. R., & Templin, T. J. (1991). *A reflective approach to teaching physical education.* Champaign, IL: Human Kinetics.

Henderson, H. L., & French, R. (1990). How to use verbal reprimands in a positive manner. *Physical Educator, 47*(4), 193-196.

Hichwa, J. (1998). *Right fielders are people too: An inclusive approach to teaching middle school physical education.* Champaign, IL: Human Kinetics.

Higdon, H. (1999, July). Getting their attention. *Runner's World,* 87-89.

Hill, G., & Brodin, K. L. (2004). Physical education teachers' perceptions of the adequacy of university coursework in preparation for teaching. *Physical Educator, 61*(2), 75-87.

Himberg, C. (2000, January). CASPER demands: No more exercise as punishment! *Teaching Elementary Physical Education, 11*(1), 17-18.

Himberg, C., Hutchinson, G. E., & Roussell, J. M. (2003). *Teaching secondary physical education: Preparing adolescents to be active for life.* Champaign, IL: Human Kinetics.

Horrocks, R. N. (1978). Resolving conflict in the classroom. *Journal of Physical Education and Recreation, 48*(9), 20-21.

Houston-Wilson, C., & Lieberman, L. F. (2003). Strategies for teaching students with autism in physical education. *Journal of Physical Education, Recreation and Dance, 74*(6), 40-44.

Hunter, E. M. (2000). *Methods of positive coaching for youth recreation soccer.* Service-Learning Scholars Program. Salt Lake City: University of Utah.

Imbrogno, A. R. (2000). Corporal punishment in America's public schools and the U.N. convention on the rights of a participant: A case for nonratification. *Journal of Law and Education, 29*(2), 125-147.

Individuals with Disabilities Education Act (IDEA) Amendments of 1997. (1997). U.S. Department of Education. Washington, D.C.: GPO.

Ingersoll, R. G. (1895). *Some reasons why: A lecture.* New York: C.P. Farrell.

Jacobson, M. (2000, July/August). ADHD and diet: How food affects mood. *Mothering, 101,* 39-42.

Jansma, P., & French, R. (1994). *Special physical education*. Englewood Cliffs, NJ: Prentice Hall.

Johnson, H. A. (1986). *Classroom management and school discipline problems: Implications for training teachers of black youth*. National Conference on Preparation and Survival of Black Public School Teachers. Norfolk, VA.

Kahan, D. (2003). Religious boundaries in public school physical activity settings. *Journal of Physical Education, Recreation, and Dance, 74*(3), 28-31.

Kanarek, R. B. (1994). *Nutrition and violent behavior: Understanding and preventing violence*. (Vol. 2). Washington, D.C.: National Academics Press. www.naturalproductsinsider.com/articles/041study8.html.

Karlin, K., & Breit, N. (2003, November). *The role of relaxation training in adapted physical education*. 32nd National Conference on Physical Activity for Exceptional Individuals. San Diego, CA.

Kelly, L. (1995). *Adapted physical education national standards*. Champaign, IL: Human Kinetics.

Kelly, L. E., & Melograno, V. J. (2003). *Developing the physical education curriculum: An achievement-based approach*. Champaign, IL: Human Kinetics.

Kleinman, I. (2003). *Too dangerous to teach* (2nd ed.). St. Victoria, BC: Trafford.

Kounin, J. (1970). *Discipline and group management in classrooms*. New York: Holt, Rinehart and Winston.

LaMaster, K. (2003). Using technology to super size your teaching materials. *Strategies, 17*(1), 11-12.

Lavay, B. (2005). Specific learning disabilities. In J. P. Winnick (Ed.), *Adapted physical education and sport* (4th ed.) (pp. 189-204). Champaign, IL: Human Kinetics.

Lavay, B., French, R., Henderson, H., Silliman-French, L., Alexander, S., & Lawrence, B. (2003, November). *Behavior management methods that empower students rather than control their behavior*. 32nd National Physical Activity Conference for Exceptional Individuals. San Diego, CA.

Lavay, B., & Steinhaus, G. (1997). *The College Park School: Providing effective physical education to students with severe emotional disturbance*. 26th National Physical Activity Conference for Exceptional Individuals. Las Vegas, NV.

Lieberman, L. J., & Houston-Wilson, C. (2002). *Strategies for inclusion: A handbook for physical educators*. Champaign, IL: Human Kinetics.

Lincoln, M. (2002). *Conflict resolution communication*. Lanham, MD: Scarecrow Press.

Loovis, E. M. (2005). Behavior management. In J. P. Winnick (Ed.), *Adapted physical education and sport* (4th ed.) (pp. 155-172). Champaign, IL: Human Kinetics.

Markos, N. J., & Boyce, A. B. (1999). What is your class management IQ? *Strategies, 12*(6), 20-23.

Mayer, R. J. (1995). *Conflict management: The courage to confront*. Columbus, OH: Battelle Press.

Mitchell, M., & Hewitt, P. (2002). Not dressing is disobedience, not just a nuisance. *Journal of Physical Education, Recreation and Dance, 73*(6), 28-31.

Moone, T. (1997). Teaching students with respect. *Teaching Elementary Physical Education, 8*(5), 16-18.

Nakamura, R. M. (1996). *The power of positive coaching*. Sudbury, MA: Jones and Bartlett.

National Association for Sport and Physical Education (NASPE). (2001, July). *The Coaches code of conduct*. Reston, VA: AAHPERD.

National Association for Sport and Physical Education (NASPE). (2004). *Moving into the future: National standards for physical education* (2nd ed.). Reston, VA: Author.

National Association for Sport and Physical Education (NASPE) and American Alliance for Health, Physical Education, Recreation and Dance (AAHPERD). (2001). *Guideline for advanced physical education programming reports*. Reston, VA: Author.

National Center for Education Statistics. (2003). Indicators of school crime and safety. Institute of Education Sciences, U.S. Department of Education. Retrieved March 11, 2005, from http://nces.ed.gov/pubs2003/schoolcrime.

National Recreation and Park Association (NRPA). (2004). *Standards and criteria for baccalaureate programs in recreation, park resources, and leisure services: A program of specialized accreditation*. Ashburn, VA: Author.

National Recreation and Park Association (NRPA) and the American Association for Leisure and Recreation (AALR) Council on Accreditation. (2004). Standards and evaluative criteria for baccalaureate programs in recreation, park resources and leisure services. Retrieved December 10, 2004, from www.nrpa.org.

O'Connor, J., French, R., & Henderson, H. (2000). Use of physical activity to improve behavior of young children with autism: Two for one. *Palaestra, 16*(3), 22-29.

Odyssey of the Mind newsletter. (1995, Fall). p. 5.

Ohio Commission on Dispute Resolution and Conflict Management. (2001). Retrieved March 11, 2005, from http://disputeresolution.ohio.gov.

Ommundsen, Y. (2002). Can sports and physical activity promote young people's psychosocial health? *Norwegian Medical Association Journal, 120*(29), 3573-3577.

Pangrazi, R. P. (2004). *Dynamic physical education for elementary school children* (14th ed.). San Francisco: Pearson, Benjamin, Cummings.

Pangrazi, R. P., & Darst, P. W. (1997). *Dynamic physical education for secondary school students* (3rd ed.). Boston: Allyn and Bacon.

Pankau, M. (1980). Teach your athletes how to relax. *Coaching Review, 3*(14), 30-32.

Parker, M., & Hellison, D. (2001). Teaching responsibility in physical education: Standards, outcomes, and beyond. *Journal of Physical Education, Recreation and Dance, 72*(9), 25-27.

Patrick, C. A., Ward, P., & Crouch, D. W. (1998). Effects of holding students accountable for social behaviors during volleyball games in elementary physical education. *Journal of Teaching in Physical Education, 17,* 143-156.

Petray-Rowcliffe, C. K., Williams, E. W., Lavay, B. W., & Hakim-Butt, K. L. (2002). Ongoing, systematic self-assessment of preservice physical education teachers' behaviors. *Journal of Physical Education, Recreation and Dance, 73*(7), 49-55.

Phillips, W. T., Kiernan, M., & King, A. C. (2003). Physical activity as a nonpharmacological treatment for depression: A review. *Complementary Health Practice Review, 8*(2), 139-152.

Pica, R. (1997). Relax. *Teaching Elementary Physical Education, 8,* 10-11.

Porretta, D. L. (2000). Cerebral palsy, stroke, and traumatic brain injury. In J. P. Winnick (Ed.), *Adapted physical education and sport* (3rd ed.) (pp. 181-198). Champaign, IL: Human Kinetics.

Premack, D. (1959).Toward empirical behavioral laws: I. Positive reinforcement. *Psychological Review, 66,* 219-233.

Reid, G., O'Connor, J., & Lloyd, M. (2003). The autism spectrum disorders: Physical activity instruction. *Palaestra, 14*(2), 20-26, 47.

Reif, S. A. (1993). *How to reach and teach ADD/ADHD children.* West Nyack, NY: The Center for Research in Education.

Rink, J. E. (2002). *Teaching physical education for learning* (4th ed.). Boston: McGraw Hill.

Rose, M. J. (1988). The place of drugs in the management of behavior disorders after traumatic brain injury. *Journal of Head Rehabilitation, 3*(3), 7-13.

Ross, C. E., & Hayes, D. (1988). Exercise and psychological well-being in the community. *American Journal of Epidemiology, 127,* 762-771.

Safe and Drug-Free Schools and Communities Act. (2001). Title IV, Part A, Subpart 1 as amended by the No Child Left Behind Act (PL 107-110). U.S. Department of Education. Washington, D.C.: GPO.

Sainato, D. M., Strain, P. S., Lefebvre, D., & Rapp, N. (1990). Effects of self-evaluation on the independent work skills of preschool children. *Exceptional Children, 56*(6), 540-549.

Salend, S. J., Whittaker, C. R., & Reeder, E. (1993). Group evaluation: A collaborative, peer-mediated behavior management system. *Exceptional Children, 59*(3), 203-209.

Sanders, A. N. (1989). Class management skills. *Strategies, 2*(3), 14-18.

San Diego County Office of Education. (2003). *Adapted education exemplars: Based on California standards for the teaching profession.* Beginning Teacher Support and Assessment. San Diego: Author.

Sands, W. A., Henderson, H. L., & Kilgore, J. (1999). The anger trap. *Technique, 19*(6), 6-10.

Sariscsany, M. J. (1991). Motivating physical education students through music. *Physical Educator, 48*(2), 93-94.

Schempp, P. G. (2003). *Teaching sport and physical activity: Insights into the road to excellence.* Champaign, IL: Human Kinetics.

Secor, S. (2001). Teaching children about conflict resolution. The Conflict Resolution Information Source. Retrieved March 11, 2005, from www.crinfo.org.

Sherrill, C. (2004). *Adapted physical activity, recreation, and sport: Crossdisciplinary and lifespan* (6th ed.). Boston: McGraw-Hill.

Shmerling, R. (2001, June 4). Harvard commentary: The influence of sugar on childhood behavior. Retrieved September 23, 2004, from www.intelihealth.com.

Siedentop, D., & Tannehill, D. (2000). *Developing teaching skills in physical education* (4th ed.). Mountainview, CA: Mayfield.

Smith, R. E., & Smoll, F. L. (1990). Athletic performance anxiety. In H. Leitenberg (Ed.), *Handbook of social and evaluation anxiety* (pp. 417-454). New York: Plenum Press.

Sprink, R. S. (1996). Is positive reinforcement the same as bribery? *CEC Today, 3*(3), 14.

Stevens, T. (2005). HIPAA solutions. Retrieved February 26, 2005, from www.hipaaplus.com/abouthippa.htm.

Stiehl, J. (1993). Becoming responsible: Theoretical and practical considerations. *Journal of Physical Education, Recreation and Dance, 64*(5), 38-40, 57-59, 70-71.

Summerford, C. (1996). Locker room boot camp. *Journal of Physical Education, Recreation and Dance, 67*(6), 4-5.

Taekwondo tutor. (2003). Retrieved May 15, 2003, from http://tkdtutor.com/05Instructors/AttentionDeficit Disorder.htm.

Tileston, D. W. (2000). *10 best teaching practices: How brain research, learning styles, and standards define teaching competencies.* Thousand Oaks, CA: Corwin Press.

Trocki-Ables, P., French, R., & O'Connor, J. (2001). Use of primary and secondary reinforcers after performance of a 1-mile walk/run by boys with attention-deficit/hyperactivity disorder. *Perceptual and Motor Skills, 93,* 461-464.

U.S. Department of Education. (2000). Office for Civil Rights, Elementary and Secondary School Civil Rights Compliance Report. Compiled by the National Coalition to Abolish Corporal Punishment in Schools: Columbus, OH: www.stophitting.com.

U.S. Department of Education, Office of Elementary and Secondary Education. (2002). *No Child Left Behind: A desktop reference.* Washington, D.C.: GPO.

U.S. Department of Health and Human Services. (1997). *Guidelines for schools and community programs to promote lifelong physical activity among young people.* Atlanta, GA: CDC.

Vogler, E. W., & French, R. (1983). The effects of a group contingency strategy on behaviorally disordered students in physical education. *Research Quarterly for Exercise and Sport, 54,* 273-277.

Vollmer, T. R. (2002, Winter). Punishment happens: Some comments on Lerman and Vorndran's review. *Journal of Applied Behavioral Analysis, 35,* 469-473.

Walker, J. E., Shea, T. M., & Bauer, A. M. (2004). *Behavior management: A practical approach for educators* (8th ed.). New York: Prentice Hall.

Watson, D., & Lounsbery, M. F. (2000). D.A.P.S.I.S.: Strategies for phoning home. *Strategies, 13*(6), 16-18.

Weinberg, R. S., & Gould, D. (2003). *Foundations of sport exercise psychology* (3rd ed.). Champaign, IL: Human Kinetics.

White, A. G., & Bailey, J. S. (1990). Reducing disruptive behaviors of elementary physical education students with sit and watch. *Journal of Applied Behavior Analysis, 23,* 353-359.

Williams, E. W. (1995). Learn students names in a flash. *Strategies, 8*(5), 25-29.

Williams, M. A. (1975). Natural rates of teacher approval and disapproval in the classroom. *Journal of Applied Behavior Analysis, 8,* 367-372.

Williams, P. A., Alley, R. D., & Henson, K. J. (1999). *Managing secondary classrooms.* Boston: Allyn and Bacon.

Wuest, D., & Lombardo, B. (1994). *Curriculum and instruction: The secondary school physical education experience.* St. Louis: Mosby.

Zeira, A., Astor, R. A., & Benbenishty, R. (2004). School violence in Israel: Perceptions of homeroom teachers. *School Psychology International, 25*(2), 149-166.

Index

Note: The italicized *f* and *t* following page numbers refers to figures and tables, respectively.

About the Authors

Barry W. Lavay, PhD (left), is a professor and the adapted physical education program coordinator in the department of kinesiology at California State University at Long Beach. He has 30 years of experience as a university professor and teacher in physical education teacher education. He has given more than 75 scholarly presentations at the international, national, regional, and state levels. He has written or coauthored numerous articles, textbooks, chapters, and curriculum guides, many on the topic of behavior management. His continued scholarship, research, and writing regarding behavior management have kept him up to date on the theories and practices in the field. He is the recipient of the 2001 AAHPERD Adapted Physical Activity Council Professional Recognition Award. Dr. Lavay received his doctorate in physical education from the University of New Mexico in 1983.

Ron French, EdD, CAPE (right), is a professor in the department of kinesiology at Texas Woman's University in Denton. Since 1981 he has taught a graduate course on behavior management in

physical education and sport. A former public school physical educator, he has presented at over 65 workshops, conferences, and conventions and written or coauthored more than 48 articles and two manuals on the topic of behavior management. In 1971 Dr. French received his doctorate in special education and special physical education from the University of California at Los Angeles.

Hester L. Henderson, PhD (center), is an associate professor and the special physical education program director in the department of exercise and sport science at the University of Utah. She was an elementary school teacher for eight years and has been a university professor since 1983. She has taught a course in behavior management in the physical education teacher education program for 22 years. She has authored or coauthored two other books and 37 journal articles on the topic. Dr. Henderson has made 86 scholarly presentations at the international, national, regional, state, and local levels. Dr. Henderson received her doctoral degree in special education from Utah State University (Logan) in 1978.